I0085969

WAITING FOR DIGNITY

WAITING FOR DIGNITY

LEGITIMACY AND AUTHORITY IN AFGHANISTAN

FLORIAN WEIGAND

Columbia University Press   *New York*

Columbia University Press
Publishers Since 1893
New York   Chichester, West Sussex
cup.columbia.edu

Copyright © 2022 Florian Weigand
All rights reserved

Library of Congress Cataloging-in-Publication Data
Names: Weigand, Florian, author.
Title: Waiting for dignity: legitimacy and authority in Afghanistan /
Florian Weigand.
Description: New York, NY: Columbia University Press, 2022. |
Includes bibliographical references and index.
Identifiers: LCCN 2021059512 (print) | LCCN 2021059513 (ebook) |
ISBN 9780231200486 (hardback) | ISBN 9780231200493 (trade
paperback) | ISBN 9780231553643 (ebook)
Subjects: LCSH: Legitimacy of governments—Afghanistan. |
Government accountability—Afghanistan. | Democratization—
Afghanistan. | Postwar reconstruction—Afghanistan. | Taliban. |
Afghanistan—Politics and government—2001-
Classification: LCC JQ1765.A7 W45 2022 (print) | LCC JQ1765.A7
(ebook) | DDC 320.9581—dc23/eng/20220308
LC record available at https://lccn.loc.gov/2021059512
LC ebook record available at https://lccn.loc.gov/2021059513

Cover design: Milenda Nan Ok Lee
Cover photo: Jim Huylebroek

CONTENTS

Acknowledgments   *vii*

Introduction   1

1 Conflict-Torn Spaces and Legitimacy   20

2 The State   51

3 Strongmen and Warlords   140

4 The Taliban   182

5 Community Authorities   235

6 Waiting for Dignity   272

Notes   295
Bibliography   329
Index   349

ACKNOWLEDGMENTS

This book is the result of a long journey enabled and shaped by many people. Most importantly, I want to thank each person in Afghanistan who took the time to talk to me and, through sharing their views, influenced my way of thinking and allowed me to learn. Ultimately, this book belongs to the people I interviewed and is meant to reflect their views and opinions.

Mary Kaldor at the London School of Economics and Political Science (LSE) was a key supporter of this research project, providing invaluable advice and input through long discussions and enabling my fieldwork in Afghanistan. This book was made possible by Eric Schwartz and Lowell Frye at Columbia University Press, who guided me with incredible patience and helpful advice through the publication process. Toby Dodge, Koen Vlassenroot, and two anonymous reviewers provided extremely valuable and constructive comments on the way. Ashley Jackson has been a brilliant partner in crime, both at the Centre for the Study of Armed Groups and while traveling through rural Afghan provinces. Jim Huylebroek, who together with Assad Nissar always made me feel like I still had a home in Kabul, took the outstanding cover photo that encapsulates the theme of the book so much better than all my written words.

My sincere thanks also go to a number of other people who commented and provided feedback. Jörg Friedrichs played a particularly important role—his thoughtful comments helped me structure my conceptual and theoretical ideas. Max Gallien, Stuart Gordon, David Keen, Abe Simons, Rajesh Venugopal, Sam Vincent, and Anna Wolkenhauer provided critical feedback, taking a great deal of time to discuss my drafts and ideas with me. Maitreyee Avachat, Kate Epstein, Ben Kolstad, Karen Stocz, Elizabeth Storer, and Helen Walker made this book much more readable.

In Afghanistan, my research would have been impossible without the help of the Peace Training and Research Organization (PTRO), in particular Maiwand Rahimi and Mirwais Wardak. I will never forget my time traveling the country with Maiwand for the interviews and his great skill of distracting me with jokes and banter while driving. Many other people at PTRO, including those in the provincial offices, were essential for conducting my research. Abdul Khalik, I have not forgotten about the canaries you want from Europe. Numerous other people supported my research, including Sayed Abdulwali, Saifallah Bigzad, Awrangzib Hakimi, Haroon Hakimi, Niaz Mohammad Hussaini, Qutbuddin Kohi, Rohullah Muradi, Somal Nazari, Ezzatullah Raji, Ahmad Rafi Rasouli, Safrah, Iqbal Sapand, Hamed Sarferazi, Aziz Ahmad Tassal, and Nasrat Ullah.

Many more individuals advanced my general thinking and understanding of Afghanistan through helpful conversations over the years. Many thanks especially to Ershad Ahmadi, Sakuntala Akmeemana, Rahmatullah Amiri, Ibraheem Bahiss, Mustafa Basij-Rasikh, Jasmine Bhatia, Mark Bowden, John Mohammed Butt, William Carter, Kate Clark, Mélissa Cornet,

Mike Fane, Erica Gaston, Stefanie Glinski, Thomas Gutersohn, Ed Hadley, Tobias Haque, Felisa Hervey, Haseeb Humayoon, Anne Jasim-Falher, Juliane "Lenny" Linke, Romain Malejacq, David Mansfield, Franz Marty, Mujib Mashal, Nishank Motwani, Orzala Nemat, Stéphane Nicolas, Mustafa Nouri, Sune Engel Rasmussen, Nigel Roberts, Thomas Ruttig, Bilal Sarwary, Dominik Schmid, Lyla Schwartz, Graeme Smith, Ermina Strutinschi, Marika Theros, Eliza Urwin, Andrew Watkins, Ayesha Wolasmal, Ellinor Zeino, and many more.

Writing this book took me back to the time of our house in Kabul's Qala-e-Fatullah neighborhood with many wonderful people, including Romy Blickle, Tina Blohm, Flore de Taisne, Mukhtar and Waris Haidari, Yuni Handayani, Thomas Harrison-Prentice, Kiana Hayeri, Cindy Issac, Sweta Kannan, Cornelia Krautgasser, Maira Küppers, Rachel Morrow, Andrew Quilty, Holly Robinson, Florian Schmidbauer, Neda Taiyebi, Luc Verna, and Humayun Zadran. I also want to thank the superb crowd at the United Nations Assistance Mission in Afghanistan, especially Hamidullah Amini, Danae Bougas, Sophie Broenimann, Steve Brooking, Stephanie Case, Fernando Cavalcante, Kathrin Daepp, Alan Fellows, Aliasuddin Ghousy, Chase Hannon, Ingrid Hayden, Shafi Khan, Lucy Perkins, Lisa Reefke, Romana Schweiger, Rohan Titus, Pauliina Törmä, Charity Watson, and Abdul Bashir Zahoory—and everyone who enabled life at Alpha, particularly the Gurkhas and the cafeteria team. There are many, many more, who contributed in various ways to my time in Afghanistan. I would like to thank each one of you.

In London, I would like to thank the people who work or used to work at the LSE and the Conflict and Civil Society Research Unit, providing me with a fantastic environment for my research, in particular Audrey Alejandro, Ali Ali, Ruben

Andersson, Pritish Behuria, Matthew Benson, Vesna Bojičić-Dželilović, David Brenner, Luke Cooper, Amy Crinnion, Alex de Waal, Ruth Fitzharris, Wendy Foulds, Susan Hoult, Rachel Ibreck, Ellie Knott, Mary Martin, Gustav Meibauer, Azaria Morgan, Jose Olivas-Osuna, Iavor Rangelov, Johannes Rieken, Anouk Rigterink, Mareike Schomerus, Sabine Selchow, Dominika Spyratou, Geoffrey Swenson, Paul Thornbury, Massoumeh Torfeh, and Rim Turkmani. The students at LSE, especially in my DV434 classes on human security, with their sharp analyses, critical thoughts, and exciting research ideas, contributed greatly to my thinking at the time of writing. Finally, I would like to thank the community of people at the LSE Rock Climbing Society, Ye Olde White Horse, and George IV, who made sure that I took necessary breaks from writing. I also gratefully acknowledge the support of the Economic and Social Research Council.[1]

This book project was a long and special time of my life, and I would like to thank my friends and family who were part of this journey and the people I met on the way. I am especially grateful to Shalaka Thakur, who had to read this book in its numerous versions and made it better each time, and Sabine and Robert Weigand, for accepting that I chose Afghanistan for my research, for their encouragement on the way, and for always supporting me.

WAITING FOR DIGNITY

INTRODUCTION

"Our main concern is not the implementation of Islamic laws . . . but the absence of justice and the corruption of the government," a Taliban commander summarized the motivation for his fight, leaning back on the *toshaks* spread out on the floor. "I am not alone," he added, "twenty-five to forty commanders are waiting for my orders, along with at least six thousand men. If our demands are not addressed, we may take decisive action against the government."[1] In 2014, many years before the Taliban regained control in Afghanistan and when much of the world still believed in the success of the international project in the country, the commander and I were drinking tea in the heart of the Afghan state, in the center of a major city.

The commander's threat was not hollow. In the following years, the influence of the state in Afghanistan slowly declined, while the Taliban extended their control. Following a half-hearted attempt to negotiate peace, President Biden announced the withdrawal of all U.S. troops from Afghanistan in April 2021 after nearly twenty years of war, which had killed an estimated 170,000 people and had cost the United States alone more than $2 trillion.[2]

Taliban fighters reached the presidential palace in Kabul on August 15, 2021, taking control of the state they had been fighting. On the final stretch, the Taliban advanced fast. The country's provincial capitals had fallen to the Taliban within ten days, often being handed over peacefully by the security forces. In Kabul, the white Taliban flags reemerged as fast as they had disappeared almost exactly twenty years before.

On September 20, 2001, when the dust of the collapsed World Trade Center had not fully settled, George W. Bush had announced the beginning of a "war on terror." His attention was focused on Afghanistan, governed by the Taliban movement since 1996, which he suspected to be sheltering Osama Bin Laden. Bush explained:

> In Afghanistan, we see al-Qaida's vision for the world. Afghanistan's people have been brutalized—many are starving and many have fled. Women are not allowed to attend school. You can be jailed for owning a television. Religion can be practiced only as their leaders dictate. A man can be jailed in Afghanistan if his beard is not long enough. The United States respects the people of Afghanistan—after all, we are currently its largest source of humanitarian aid—but we condemn the Taliban regime. It is not only repressing its own people, it is threatening people everywhere by sponsoring and sheltering and supplying terrorists. By aiding and abetting murder, the Taliban regime is committing murder.[3]

On October 7, 2001, American and British forces began to bomb the Taliban's positions in Afghanistan. On November 14, 2001, Kabul, the capital, fell. After a few weeks, the war appeared to be over, and Afghanistan seemed to be "liberated" from the Taliban. Life quickly returned to the streets of Kabul. Men could shave their beards, and women could walk the streets without headscarves. Meanwhile, the victorious parties met in the

German city of Bonn in December of the same year to strike a deal on Afghanistan's future. They developed a plan for building a new Afghan state, a Weberian monopoly of the legitimate use of force, to govern on the basis of human rights as well as democratic, traditional, and Islamic principles. They promised a state the people of Afghanistan and the international community would see as legitimate.

However, the political order that grew over the following years stood in sharp contrast to the expectations of 2001. Not only did the Taliban reemerge, but multiple authorities competed for influence in a fragmented country where human rights violations occurred daily. The Afghan state fought the Taliban. The state and the Taliban alike tried to crush the so-called Islamic State Khorasan Province. Strongmen and warlords that maintained personal armed forces exploited people and established their own thiefdoms and areas of influence within the country. At the same time, elders and councils were often the most important authorities at the community level.

The Afghan state and the international community failed to construct a monopoly of force in the country. But did they also fail to build legitimacy and lose the battle for public support to other authorities? If so, why? Crucially, did the growing influence and ultimate capture of the state by the Taliban rest on coercion only, or did people consider them to be more legitimate than the state? And what role does their interpretation of Islam, which the international community decries, play in this legitimacy? Do people appreciate the role strongmen and warlords played? Or do people, after all, only trust traditional community-based authorities? And what do people's views on legitimacy mean for the future of Afghanistan?

Understanding people's perceptions and views on legitimacy is crucial for international interventions in conflict zones that aim to build peace or a state with public support. George W.

Bush claimed that Taliban repression of Afghans added a motive to the U.S. invasion and emphasized that he respects the people of Afghanistan. But living up to this basic claim of respect requires a dialogue with the people of Afghanistan. It requires asking them what their expectations are and how they want to be governed while accepting debate, competing viewpoints, and conflicting options. Many years after Bush left office, the voices of the people in Afghanistan have been rarely heard in either the policy world or academia. The assessment of the situation in Afghanistan and of which authorities are "good" and "bad," legitimate or illegitimate, is usually an external one, based on criteria of what people in the West want.

Even the dominant conceptual understanding of legitimacy, building on Weber's work and his distinction among rational-legality, tradition, and charisma as sources of legitimacy, was developed in the context of state formation in Europe in the early twentieth century. It is questionable as to what extent it helps us to understand the dynamics of legitimacy in a conflict zone today. A vast amount of the literature on legitimacy has evolved from Weber's foundation, looking at the nuances of legitimacy in bureaucratic and rational-legal systems that are prominent in states with a high level of monopolization of force. However, to date, there is no conceptual understanding of legitimacy in conflict-torn spaces with minimal monopolization of force where there are two or even more competing authorities.

This book redirects the focus of attention from external assumptions on legitimacy to the people in Afghanistan. It investigates whom they consider legitimate or illegitimate and for what reasons, shedding light on what strategies of "building legitimacy" work. It proposes that what matters is *interactive dignity*, which requires authorities to treat people equally as citizens on a day-to-day basis. The book rests on a conceptual understanding of legitimacy that I adjusted to the dynamics of conflict zones and almost five hundred interviews conducted in Afghanistan between 2014 and 2019. Interviewees included ordinary people as well as the various authorities at the time, such as insurgents, warlords, and government officials, considering as many different perceptions and worldviews as possible. On that basis, I pieced together a bigger picture, incorporating the various views I was exposed to.

This book adds to an improved conceptual and analytical understanding of legitimacy in political science and sociology. In addition, it contributes to the empirical understanding of Afghanistan and its political order. It outlines the sources of legitimacy of various authorities in Afghanistan, which are usually studied by different disciplines, helping us to understand why, for instance, some people supported the Taliban while others preferred the Afghan state. While offering a unique perspective on the dynamics in Afghanistan from 2001 to 2021, the findings also hold important lessons for the country's future. Finally, combining the conceptual suggestions and the empirical material and comparing people's views on different authorities, the analysis of the Afghan context allows us to draw more theoretical conclusions on the mechanisms of legitimacy in conflict-torn spaces. These findings can help us understand the failures in Afghanistan and, perhaps, other conflict-torn spaces and contribute to a move away from peacebuilding and state-building efforts that rest on ideological assumptions of what ought to be built to policies grounded in an understanding of affected people's perceptions.

Chapter 1 sets the scene conceptually and analytically. Here, I explain why Afghanistan's political order can be seen as an arena of competition and coordination for multiple authorities. I suggest three analytical ideal types as sources of authority that can help to explain obedience to social control: *coercion*, which achieves obedience through force, violence, and threats;[4] *instrumental legitimacy*, which "buys" obedience by responding to needs; and the traditional, more *substantive understanding of legitimacy*, which is underpinned by shared values and a belief in rightfulness. In addition, I propose investigating what *aspects of authority* matter and whether people's expectations and perceptions relate to authorities' *actions*, *history*, or the *idea* the authority stands for.

In chapters 2–5, I apply the framework and analyze different authorities in Afghanistan, which were identified as being particularly important through the interviews. Each chapter is grounded in an exploration of the history of the respective authority, illustrating how its structures and institutions have evolved. There is also a discussion of what the literature suggests about its legitimacy. Building on the interviews I conducted, I then compare the authority's self-perception with the public perception of its legitimacy. The research shows that any authority in Afghanistan can construct some legitimacy. In different communities, different authorities are considered to be more or less legitimate.

Chapter 2 is the first empirical chapter. I look at the formal Afghan state that was established in 2001 and existed until the Taliban takeover in 2021, which—despite consisting of neo-patrimonial networks and having apparent weaknesses—remained a key authority in many parts of the country at the time of the interviews, at least in the urban and more populated parts of the country. Here, people had to navigate police checkpoints and deal with the state bureaucracy to access services or settle conflicts. Drawing on my interviews, the chapter illustrates that most people were not only dissatisfied with the state but also made precise distinctions between the legitimacy of different state authorities. For instance, many people believed that the army was driven by idealism and a desire to serve the country, accepting low salaries and high risks. But they saw the police as corrupt and extractive, a source of insecurity rather than security.

Chapter 3 investigates the legitimacy of warlords and strongmen. With Western funding, many of these men gained influence in Afghanistan, first as Mujahedin fighters against the Soviet occupation and later, after 9/11, against the Taliban. They remained powerful in the following years, often becoming part of or closely linked to the state. In some provinces, strongmen had even monopolized force to a large extent, while in other provinces, multiple strongmen competed for influence. Chapter 4 shows that while the interviewed strongmen claimed that they worked for the people and had their support, they did not seem to have widespread legitimacy. In fact, most people I talked to in Afghanistan considered warlords to be violent and extractive.

Chapter 4 considers the Taliban and their growing influence in Afghanistan before they gained control of the state. The interviews demonstrate that many people did not assess the legitimacy of the Taliban or whether they should join the movement on the basis of its history or ideology. Some people joined the Taliban as a way of opposing the state, and others who joined had suffered abuses by the state or its international allies. People in bigger cities tended to perceive the Taliban as a threat to their security, but views in rural areas varied. Some saw the Taliban as extractive and oppressive actors, while others viewed them as legitimate authorities with conflict resolution that was faster and fairer than what state authorities offered.

The final empirical chapter, chapter 5, examines community authorities. It shows that, particularly in the context of conflict resolution, councils and elders played a key role at the time of the research. But, despite being viewed as "traditional"

authorities, they did not get their legitimacy primarily from tradition. Rather, people preferred community authorities to state
institutions because they were close and easy to access and, ultimately, because they considered their procedures to be fairer and
less corrupt than the state's. Hence, new community authorities
evolved, even in cities.

The picture that emerges out of the empirical chapters and
the answer to the question of why people consider an authority
to be legitimate is what I refer to as *interactive dignity*. The proposed theory counters the view that the Afghan state was viewed
as legitimate because of its democratic ideals or the services it
provided. It contests the notion that the Taliban are perceived
as legitimate because of their interpretation of Islam, and it
questions the extent to which community authorities are considered to be legitimate for traditional reasons. The findings
challenge the view that underpinned many policy interventions
in Afghanistan, assuming that legitimacy can be constructed
through democratic elections, the simple delivery of public services, or by empowering "traditional" institutions.

People's main concern is not what ideology an authority represents or how it gained power and whether it was according to
democratic or traditional procedures. What matters are authorities' actions—but in a more complex sense than "service delivery"
implies. The findings suggest that, in the absence of Weberian
rational-legal structures ensuring accountability at the macrolevel, the *day-to-day interaction* between authorities and people
is particularly important. A basic requirement for authorities
to construct instrumental legitimacy is to be *accessible* and have
predictable procedures. The characteristics of the interaction and
attitudes reflected by it are key to constructing more substantive and, hence, lasting legitimacy. People are concerned with the
process of service delivery, not just the output.

The values that underpin people's expectations with regard to interaction are usually not based on a certain ideology, whether it be democracy, religion, or tradition. People simply want to and are waiting to be treated with *dignity*, as equal citizens. They expect authorities to interact with them in a fair manner and treat them with respect. They also expect authorities to serve the people, not themselves or a foreign agenda, and they often categorize authorities on the basis of their personal experiences of interacting with them. The legitimacy of an authority in Afghanistan often rests on a perception that the other available authorities are even more corrupt rather than a full-fledged belief in the authority itself.

To gain legitimacy in conflict-torn spaces, authorities need to focus on interactions with people rather than purely on results and outputs. By respecting people's dignity and treating them accordingly, authorities can construct substantive legitimacy that goes beyond addressing the needs of the people.

METHODOLOGY

The exploratory mission of this book, aiming at developing new ideas about the reasons why people consider authority—whether that of the state or otherwise—to be (il)legitimate, was underpinned by certain ontological assumptions and epistemological conclusions in line with strands of constructivism and critical realism. I was not trying to reveal "truth" but wanted to understand perceptions and their construction. The empirical research allowed me to disentangle different realities and examine how different groups of people perceive authorities and their legitimacy. I looked for patterns with regard to the mechanisms of why people consider any authority to be legitimate—or not.

My approach mirrored a hermeneutic circle, a constant back and forth in which my empirical findings shaped my conceptual framework, which I then used to analyze my empirical findings, a methodology that some describe as "abductive."[5] Hence, both the existing literature and my empirical research informed my conceptual understanding of legitimacy and its sources.

I mainly investigated people's perceptions through several rounds of interviews. In 2014/2015, I conducted 271 interviews in four provinces of Afghanistan in the course of around one and a half years of research in the country. The population studied in this phase included the authorities along with the ordinary people who were affected by them locally and, therefore, responsible for bestowing them with legitimacy. Looking at both allowed me to compare the self-perception of the authorities and their claim of legitimacy with how members of the public perceived them and to see the extent to which these matched up. In 2019, together with a team of researchers, I conducted an additional 227 interviews in Herat and Faryab provinces. Most of these interviewees were ordinary people living in Taliban-controlled areas, in addition to Taliban judges. The interviews aimed at gaining a better understanding of the views of people living under their authority, especially with regard to the Taliban's justice system.[6]

Perceptions, Not Facts—Ontological Assumptions and Epistemological Conclusions

To investigate legitimacy empirically, I explore how people perceive authorities and how these authorities perceive themselves. Hence, while I deductively develop a definition of legitimacy as a starting point for my research, I do not "measure" legitimacy on the basis of "objective" standards but suggest that how people perceive an authority defines the extent and type of legitimacy they ascribe to it.

My focus on perceptions is the consequence of certain ontological assumptions about the world, resulting in a particular way of approaching knowledge. Of course, I assume that reality exists. However, the way we, as human beings, perceive this reality is socially constructed. Hence, I situated myself between social constructivism and critical realism. In agreement with social constructivists like Berger and Luckmann,[7] I consider social constructions important. I think that while our perception is socially constructed, not all layers of reality are. In line with critical realists such as Bhaskar, I believe that cautious generalizations can be made, as structural factors can affect perceptions, determining, for instance, what "truth" prevails in a society.[8] Nonetheless, I do not share the confidence of critical realists that we can uncover reality, and I do not agree with their structuralist view that a focus on the actor is always out of place.

Thus, there is no generally true way of understanding reality, but everybody may, to some extent, have their own reality. Every person is socialized in a specific way, depending on geography, culture, family, friends, and, of course, the language we use to describe phenomena. This "baggage" shapes our views on what reality is and how it works. Hence, people's perceptions also differ. Meanwhile, each individual perception, grounded in a distinct biography, is real. In this book, I bring multiple individual perceptions and individual realities together to gain a more comprehensive understanding of authorities' legitimacy in Afghanistan, how people perceive authorities, why they do so, and the factors that influence these perceptions. In particular, this book aims at giving "ordinary people" in Afghanistan a voice,[9] especially as much of the recent analysis and commentary on the country has been written by outsiders. Green illustrates how even Afghanistan's history has been defined by scholars from abroad, emphasizing the importance of considering "voices from below."[10]

Nonetheless, my own worldview and perspective play a role, as it inevitably does when analyzing social phenomena.[11] Adopting Gadamer's position, Reiter rightly calls it "naïve" to try to prevent this.[12] I drafted the interview questions, interacted with the interviewees, and interpreted their responses. Who I am and what I think certainly affected my research design, the responses I received in interviews, and the conclusions drawn. I went to Afghanistan as a researcher, an outsider, who had grown up and was socialized in Europe—a "foreign intervener" myself.[13] So, even though this book aims to give a voice to the people of Afghanistan, it also reflects my own personality.

Case Study Approach

As the research project could not cover the entire population of Afghanistan, I selected different geographic case studies for my interviews, applying a light form of what Gerring calls "diverse" strategy.[14] Because case studies allow in-depth studies of a particular research question, they are particularly useful for exploratory analyses and concept development.

Building on my epistemological assumptions and my aim of generating new ideas instead of testing existing hypotheses, I did not try to construct a representative sample in a positivist sense. However, as I set out to generate meaningful new hypotheses on why perceptions of authority and specifically legitimacy may differ, I decided on a comparative research design. As Andersen notes, legitimacy can have different meanings in different communities.[15] Hence, I sought variation in terms of political order and existing authorities as well as in terms of potentially relevant group characteristics of people (needs, values), which may depend on geography, for instance, because of cultural traits in the case studies. Having this variation allows me to draw conclusions on the explanatory importance of different factors, which may underpin the perception of authority and its legitimacy.

Implementing this strategy as well as, crucially, access considerations, I focused on four out of thirty-four provinces of Afghanistan (see figure o.i) for my research in 2014: Herat (west), Balkh (north), Nangarhar (east), and Kabul (central). Many characteristics of the people researched and the political order, including ethnic composition and history (of governance), in these provinces were likely to differ due to their location in relation to neighboring countries, among other reasons. Within each province, I selected at least three districts, including an urban district, a rural district that is close to the city, and a district that is far away from the provincial capital. Districts in which different groups vie over control were particularly relevant for the research, considering my interest in views on competing authorities.[16] In 2019, we conducted additional research in Taliban-controlled areas, selecting Herat (west) and Faryab (north-west) provinces to add to our understanding of the Taliban as an authority, which mainly draws on research from the south and southeast of Afghanistan.[17] Returning to Herat after five years also allowed me to analyze changes over time.

BADAKHSHAN
Wakhan
TAKHAR
KUNDUZ
BALKH
JOWZJAN
FARYAB
SAMANGAN
BAGHLAN
SAR-E PUL
NURISTAN
PANJSHIR
KUNAR
PARWAN
LAGHMAN
KAPISA
KABUL
NANGARHAR
BADGHIS
BAMYAN
WARDAK
LOGAR
PAKTIYA
KHOST
HERAT
GHOR
DAYKUNDI
GHAZNI
PAKTIKA
FARAH
URUZGAN
ZABUL
NIMROZ
HELMAND
KANDAHAR
Gulran
Kushk
Kohsan
Ghoryan
Adraskan
Shindand
Anar Darah
Obeh
Karukh
Farsi
Qadis
Jowand
Murghab
Qaisar
Kohistan
Chaghcharan
Tulak
Shahrak
Du Lainah
Saghar
Taywarah
Pasaband
Kohistanat
Balkhab
Yakawlang
Bamyan
Sayghan
Kahmard
Panjab
Waras
Nawur
Gizab
Pur Chaman
Bala Buluk
Gulistan
Farah
Bakwa
Washer
Nad 'Ali
Marjah
Khash Rod
Chakhansur
Zaranj
Reg-e Khan Neshin
Garm Ser
Chahar Burjak
Dishu
Registan
Shorabak
Spin Boldak
Arghistan
Ma'ruf
Maywand
Qalat
Shinkai
Shah Wali Kot
Nesh
Gomal
Wur Mamay
Terwo
Jaghuri
Baghran
Now Zad
Dowlatabad
Warsaj
Khash Rud

Methods of Data Collection

To investigate people's perceptions and the mechanisms that underpin them, I mainly relied on interviews, which can contribute to a better understanding of complex contexts. The interviews were in-depth and triggered by open-ended questions. As legitimacy is an abstract social phenomenon that has different meanings in different languages and that different people understand differently, I did not bring up the term "legitimacy" in the interviews. Instead, I used two thematic examples of exercising social control to investigate perceptions that can be related to how I conceptualize legitimacy: "security provision" and "conflict resolution."

As people have to obey social control in these contexts, people's perceptions of such relationships, their expectations, and their (re)actions help us to explore their understandings of authority and legitimacy. The conceptual relevance of this approach will be discussed in more detail in chapter 1, but both security provision and conflict resolution are particularly relevant in conflict-torn spaces and are therefore examples of social control people can easily relate to. At the same time, political scientists and sociologists commonly assume that the provision of security and justice are core factors for legitimizing authority. The two themes are particularly useful in gaining an understanding of the relationship between coercion and legitimacy. While most actors in the security sector have the ability to exercise force, the literature on policing in Western countries indicates that successful security provision results from voluntary obedience, hence, legitimacy—not from coercion. Conversely, many actors providing conflict

---

FIGURE 0.1 Provinces and districts of Afghanistan
(adapted from University of Texas Library, 2014)

resolution may be limited in their abilities to exercise physical force but rely on legitimacy—or more indirect means of coercion, such as social pressure. Going beyond the thematic examples, I also asked the interviewees more general questions about the various authorities, the roles they play, their views on them, and the reasons that underpin their opinions.

The book is based on 498 interviews—271 interviews conducted in 2014/2015 and 227 interviews from 2019. I conducted 100 interviews with authorities (20 percent), 373 interviews with members of the public (75 percent), and 25 interviews with key informants (5 percent).[18] The interviews from 2014/2015 fall into three groups.[19] First, there is the *public*, the citizens, subjects, or the "ordinary people" who are affected by the authorities, obey their social control, and can bestow legitimacy. This was the starting point of my research, as only the public can actually confer legitimacy. Most of my interviews, 173 in 2014/2015, were with members of this group. I sought a balance with regard to age, sex, income, social position, and district of residence. However, women and people living in Taliban-controlled areas were underrepresented.

The second group of interviewees was the *authorities* at the time, who were identified in the interviews with ordinary people. The main authorities that the interviewees brought up were state actors, Taliban, strongmen, and community authorities. As I will discuss in more detail in the next chapter, my objective was to investigate their self-perception, to understand their personal motives, on what basis they claim legitimacy, how they justify their authority, and their thoughts on their own local legitimacy. While it was not always clear what was propaganda and what was "honest" self-perception, the interviews show how authorities want to be perceived. In this way, they add to the overall understanding of legitimacy in Afghanistan. In contrast to the interviews with ordinary people, my primary aim in these interviews was not only to understand the structural factors that underpin differences and similarities in their perceptions but also to gain a more in-depth understanding of individual motives, reasoning, and claims. In total, I conducted seventy-three interviews with authorities in 2014/2015. These interviews were more extensive than with ordinary people, sometimes lasting up to more than three hours. The interviews were also less structured and often delved more into interviewees' personal biographies. In asking about interviewees' personal lives, I sought examples to understand how and why they became or joined a particular authority.

Finally, I interviewed twenty-five *civil society activists* as *key informants*. These actors have an interest in and a knowledge of Afghanistan's political dynamics that go beyond their individual experience of authority. The interviews were unstructured and provided me with the context, overarching narratives, and background information on the political dynamics in the different provinces and districts.

In 2019, together with Ashley Jackson and a team of researchers, I conducted additional research specifically in Taliban-controlled areas.[20] Two hundred and twenty-seven interviews were conducted on two separate trips in February and May 2019 in Faryab and Herat provinces.[21] The interviews aimed at understanding people's views on Taliban justice, and they fall into two groups. Two hundred interviewees were members of the *public*, who had been claimants or defendants in Taliban-court cases. Interviewing women from Taliban-controlled areas was particularly challenging, resulting in their perspective remaining underrepresented. However, thirty women who had been claimants in Taliban-court cases shared their views with us. Twenty-seven interviewees were *authorities*, including five Taliban judges and twenty-two elders.

In addition to interviews, ethnography shaped the findings of my research project. On an epistemological level, ethnography influenced my interest in people's systems of meaning and my inductive way of working. In addition, ethnography played a role in terms of the applied methods, despite being centered around interviews. Yanow suggests that interviews can be ethnographic if they aim at gaining "conceptual access to the unwritten, unspoken, common sense, every-day, tacit knowledge."[22] This project aimed at such conceptual access through interviews as well as observations. My writing reflects this. My observations are part of the narrative. While conducting my field research, I lived and worked without the hard security measures that most foreigners in Afghanistan experience at their employers' insistence, restricting their abilities to interact with people.[23] Hence, my assumptions and conclusions are not based on interview material alone, but they were also informed by observations, informal conversations, and, crucially, friendships in Afghanistan.

Data Analysis

I analyzed the data thematically, looking for patterns to identify shared narratives among the different groups according to the conceptual framework. In the interviews with members of the public, I especially focused on descriptions of their relationships with different authorities and the extent to which they perceived actors as coercive and/or legitimate. Therefore, I was particularly interested in expressions of support, acceptance, indifference, dissent, and resistance, looking at them as indicators of perceived legitimacy—or the lack of it. I categorized the beliefs and needs the interviewees voiced to explain their views and what aspect of authority their perceptions were about, distinguishing, for instance, among authorities' actions, histories, and ideologies. Carving out these narratives in terms of who is perceived as a coercive and/or legitimate authority as well as the reasons underpinning the perceptions allowed me to draw conclusions regarding the extent and type of legitimacy participants ascribe to a given authority. For this book, I then selected quotes that seemed to represent the narratives particularly well based on my analysis of all interviews while also engaging with the "outliers"—the views that appeared to contradict these narratives. Conversely, my approach to the interviews with authorities was less formalized. I looked for claims of legitimacy, explanations of their motives, and assumptions about their local legitimacy in the data.

In all the empirical chapters, I contextualize my primary research with a brief section on the authority's history, which allows us to gain a better understanding of how each authority and its official claims of legitimacy evolved. I further triangulate the findings by comparing them with other studies. In particular, I draw on the results of surveys of people's perceptions in Afghanistan—even though such data has to be treated carefully due to a prevailing urban bias.[24]

For those who want to dig deeper and go further than any survey, study or book possibly can, if you have the opportunity, I can only recommend having conversations with people across Afghanistan and to listen to their stories.

1

CONFLICT-TORN SPACES AND LEGITIMACY

The violent competition over power in Afghanistan between 2001 and 2021 illustrates the failure to establish a state with broad-based legitimacy. Indeed, scholars have diagnosed a legitimacy crisis in Afghanistan for many years.[1] Policy makers, both inside and outside of the country, have suggested ways of addressing the crisis, predicting that to do so will bring peace or stability. However, we have rarely probed the meaning of "legitimacy" or related the concept to the complexity of Afghanistan. Traditional definitions of the state and legitimacy based on Weber's work quickly reach their analytical limits in conflict zones.

The term "legitimacy," like many other social concepts, is frequently used but only rarely defined. The literature on legitimacy usually deals with specific actions—such as the legitimacy of the use of force in certain situations, like an international military intervention—or else it investigates the legitimacy of the state. Our understanding of state legitimacy was developed in the context of political orders that are characterized by a high degree of monopolization of force and institutionalized bureaucratic systems. Conflict-torn spaces are different. Conflict, by definition, diminishes the monopolization of force. In contrast to bureaucratic settings, conflict does not take place within the institutionalized structures of the state but outside of it. The formal state is part of the conflict, fighting other actors.

To enable an analysis of legitimacy in such a context, I suggest leaving the static understanding of the Weberian ideal-typical state behind and focusing on what is present rather than what is not. Even if the level of monopolization of force is low and the number of authorities is high, these authorities are part of one political order. I look at political order as a dynamic arena in which various authorities coexist, interact, compete, and coordinate. Authority entails social control, whether as a relationship of command and obedience or as the commanding entity. The formal state is only one of these authorities. In the case of Afghanistan, there were also insurgencies, most prominently the Taliban, together with strongmen and community authorities, as well as foreign actors.

But how can we conceptualize the legitimacy of an authority like an armed group or insurgency? In the absence of a Weberian monopoly of force, we have to widen our conceptual understanding of legitimacy, making it applicable to more dynamic political orders with various authorities. I propose to view legitimacy as one of two ideal-typical sources of authority. Authority can rest on coercion, which achieves obedience through force and threats, or it is underpinned by legitimacy, which I define as voluntary obedience. There are two ways of understanding and, accordingly, constructing legitimacy. Legitimacy can either be instrumental because the authority "buys" obedience by responding to needs, or it can be more substantive, involving shared values and a belief in rightfulness. The policy literature often focuses on instrumental legitimacy while traditional literature in the social sciences, including Max Weber's definition, focuses on substantive legitimacy.

But it is not only the needs and beliefs that underpin people's perception that matter. In a dynamic political order, different authorities may have different strengths and weaknesses that are important for their legitimacy. For instance, community authorities may be legitimate because of their history and how they gained authority, which people may consider right for traditional reasons, while the Taliban might be viewed as legitimate because of its actions, which some people may view as right for religious reasons. Hence, we have to go beyond viewing authority as one entity, and, instead, we have to investigate what aspects of authority matter. People's perception of legitimacy may be linked specifically to an authority's actions, its history, the idea it stands for, or other aspects. For a comprehensive analysis of legitimacy, we have to examine how the multiple possible aspects of authority, as well as people's needs and beliefs, relate to one another and what combinations enable authorities to construct legitimacy.

POLITICAL ORDER AND AUTHORITY

The dominant lens to describe political order, the context in which we analyze legitimacy, is state-centric. Most of the literature in political science relates to states. Even if we look at international politics or subnational governance, the nation-state is our referent object. Given that our world is organized in states that are separated by borders, such a focus broadly makes sense. But the state is not only one of the most fundamental concepts in political science; it is also one of the most contested. Like every other concept in social science, the state is not a categorization of stable objects but an abstraction of unstable social systems. As Kuhn intimates,[2] this instability requires a constant hermeneutic reinterpretation, which makes it difficult to agree on a common understanding of what a state is. However, even vastly different schools of thought tend to rely heavily on the concept of the state. Many definitions ascribe a certain generalized function to the state according to an underlying ideology.[3] For instance, Marxists often describe the state as an instrument for one class to dominate another.[4] In contrast, pluralists often define the state as a forum to find a compromise among different interests.[5] These definitions are fundamentally different from Weber's, which has come to dominate in the literature.

Weber's Understanding of the State

Weber emphasizes that the state "cannot be defined in terms of ends," as there is "scarcely any task it has not taken in hand." Rather, it must be defined "in terms of the specific means peculiar to it, namely the use of physical force." Thus, Weber famously defines the modern state as "a human community that (successfully) claims the monopoly of the legitimate use of physical force within a given territory."[6] Weber's work is analytically valuable as the ideal to "interpret historical and social occurrences in terms of the prevailing value orientation that give them their meaning without imposing the investigator's value judgment on them".[7] Thus, it allows a value-free (*wertfrei*) analysis. The state, as Weber defines it, is a pure "ideal type"—a term he means analytically, not normatively—a methodological utopia that "cannot be found empirically anywhere in reality."[8]

While it is analytically more valuable than functional definitions of the state, Weber's understanding is not well suited to capture today's conflict-torn spaces. Even though he does not claim that the ideal type of the modern state captures any empirical reality, conflict-torn spaces' distance from his ideal renders it particularly ill suited. Weber's understanding of the state rests on his analysis of polities in Europe. Historically, the formation of the European states is closely associated with war. Tilly illustrates how wars contributed to the monopolization of the legitimate use of physical force and the formation of nation-states in Western Europe, particularly the French state, from 1600 onward.[9] His work builds on Elias's observation of a trend away from monopoly-free competition toward the formation of monopolies of the legitimate use of force as well as economic means in Europe.[10]

Arguably, however, the European wars of the seventeenth and eighteenth centuries are different from contemporary forms of violent conflict, such that Kaldor calls them "new wars."[11] Contesters in violent conflicts today are more concerned with political control than military control; their conflicts often have a global dimension; and a plurality of groups partly control the force.[12] Even though some scholars question to what extent new wars are empirically new, the impact of ongoing globalization on violent conflicts is difficult to brush aside.[13] Contemporary violent conflicts fuel a war economy with global links. Thriving war economies are mutually beneficial enterprises for the involved parties, creating incentives to continue the war. This can be seen in Afghanistan, where drugs and arms were traded across the invisible lines that divided territories controlled by the state from those controlled by insurgents,[14] and where not only the state but also the Taliban benefitted from the foreign aid that was pumped into the country.

However, the Weberian ideal-typical definition of statehood is dominant and underpins the work of numerous scholars, such as that of North and Evans, Rueschemeyer, and Skocpol.[15] The theories of such proponents are therefore much more difficult to apply to a context such as Afghanistan. Indeed, the same can be said of many established categories similarly based on the idea of an ideal-typical state, such as formal vs. informal, local vs. provincial, and national vs. international. Such dichotomies do not adequately grasp conflict-torn spaces conceptually. For instance, the formal de jure state and other informal authorities can often not be distinguished clearly in Afghanistan, where patronage networks often were an important source of public services.[16]

As a consequence of the dominance of the Weberian understanding of statehood, territories with a low degree of monopolization of force are often considered to be "fragile" or "failed."[17] The concept of state fragility is a negative definition and puts very different forms of political order into one category, which its deviation from the Weberian ideal alone defines. It does not consider that, with the absence of a monopoly of force, spaces are not institution-free altogether but are rather governed by a different set of rules. For instance, Keen illustrates how violent conflicts can turn into a stable order even while their political and economic arrangements differ radically from typical nation-states.[18] Despite the war, some form of order seemed to be in place in Afghanistan. Barfield and Nojumi argue that "considering Afghanistan a failed or failing state because its government does not exert control over the whole country is misleading. Historically, the Afghan state's physical control of a specific territory has never been a valid reference in assessing its ability to govern."[19]

Bourdieu's Understanding of the State

A different and somewhat more suitable conceptualization of the state is offered by Bourdieu, who closely studied the dynamics of power. While his understanding of the state draws substantially on Weber, it is also embedded in his own work and links to other concepts developed by him, such as symbolic capital and fields. Bourdieu offered his probably most well-known definition of the state in a lecture in 1990:

> I made an addition to the famous definition of Max Weber, who defined the state [as the] 'monopoly of legitimate violence', which I corrected by adding 'monopoly of legitimate physical *and symbolic* violence,' inasmuch as the monopoly of symbolic violence is the condition for possession of the exercise of the monopoly of physical violence itself.[20]

For Bourdieu, symbolic violence entails the ability to exercise authority without physical force through institutions, laws, and classifications that naturalize power relations—a dimension of statehood that he thinks is not sufficiently considered by Weber.[21] Maintaining a monopoly of legitimate symbolic violence, the state is viewed as having the right to structure social order. According to Bourdieu, "Timetables, budget periods, calendars, our whole social life is structured by the state—and, by the same token, so is our thought."[22] Bourdieu assumes that states can also establish a monopoly of legitimate force only by being viewed as having the right to structure social order.

As in the case of Weber, Elias, and Tilly, Bourdieu's understanding of the state is grounded in the analysis of state formation in Europe. He argues that what he calls "dynastic states"—states that were identified with a person such as a prince or king and were prominent in Europe between 1330 and 1650—concentrated military, economic, as well as, going beyond Elias and Tilly, symbolic capital.[23] Thereby, the idea of symbolic capital encapsulates Bourdieu's understanding of legitimacy.[24] Bourdieu describes symbolic capital as a form of capital that is relational and recognized,[25] constituting what "any holder of capital holds as an extra."[26] This could, for instance, be the symbolic effect of economic capital, which ensures recognition. Bourdieu views this accumulation of the different kinds of capitals, including symbolic capital, to be specific to the state, making it a "power over powers."[27]

According to Bourdieu's analysis, the dynastic state later transformed into the modern state.[28] While previously power was concentrated in an individual, in the modern state it is "divided and shared between different persons with relations of competition between them,"[29] in what Bourdieu famously calls "field of power." The concept of the field is central to Bourdieu's work, according to which societies consist of various fields with distinct practices (e.g., economy, politics, art, universities).[30] According to Bourdieu, the linkages among the various fields constitute a "meta-field" or field of power—the modern state. This field of power describes an arena of competition for different fields and holders of different types of capital.[31] Hence, in a way, the state holds the monopoly of legitimate symbolic violence by being the "referee" in the struggle over it.[32]

This more lively though certainly also more complex understanding of the state as a field of power makes Bourdieu's definition more able to capture the competitive dynamics of conflict zones than Weber's ideal type, which appears rather static in comparison. However, as Bourdieu's view on the state is also grounded in the analysis of state formation and trends of monopolization in Europe, it similarly does not fully capture the essence of the state in a conflict zone like Afghanistan, where competition also happens outside of the state, where the state certainly is no "power over powers," and has a monopoly of neither physical nor symbolic violence. And while Bourdieu rightfully emphasizes the importance of legitimacy, he moves our attention away from physical violence, which remains a crucial aspect of power in conflict zones.

The State in Conflict-Torn Spaces

Having established that conflict-torn spaces are insufficiently captured by the definition of the state proposed by Weber and Bourdieu, I suggest an understanding that draws on elements of both by viewing political order as a constantly changing *arena of interaction for authorities* (figure 1.1). This conception follows Weber in the sense that it acknowledges the importance of force and coercion within a given territory. But it also, at least heuristically, adopts Bourdieu's more dynamic notion of competition within a field of power, considering the political order to be in a process of permanent transformation and ultimately giving more space to plural authorities, which are shaping and being

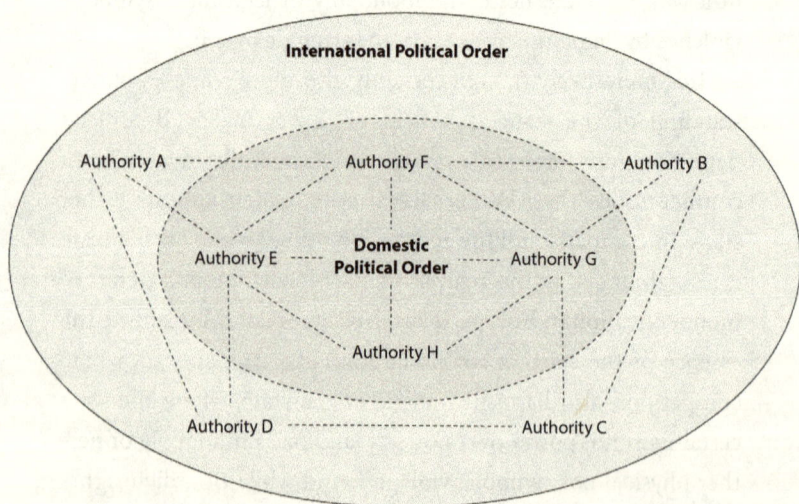

FIGURE 1.1 Political order

shaped by interactions on and across local, national and international levels.[33]

The idea of an arena of interaction draws on Bourdieu's work and his understanding of the state. Using Bourdieu's language, the wider political order of Afghanistan can be viewed as a metafield in which there was an ongoing competition among various of what Weber would call authorities.[34] These authorities have characteristics of fields, as there was a struggle between those who dominate and those who are dominated and the competition over success and influence. However, in contrast to Bourdieu's understanding of the state, in a conflict-torn space, the state is not actually a metafield. Lacking a monopoly of force, the state is only one of the *authorities* in the wider arena and is confronted with the authority of armed groups and other types of authority, such as traditional ones. Applying Bourdieu's metaphor, the state is not the referee but just one player.

Ultimately, there can be different levels of interaction. In Afghanistan, on the one hand, there was competition over the metafield among the different authorities that constituted Afghanistan's political order, such as the state and the Taliban as well as heavily involved international actors. On the other hand, there was competition within each authority, for instance, over success and dominance within the Taliban movement and over how to use the Taliban to influence the metafield and shape Afghanistan's wider political order.[35]

Political order is the playing field on which authorities, both in the form of individuals and groups or organizations, interact. This interaction can be forceful and competitive as well as coordinated or cooperative. Authorities may even engage in different forms of interaction at the same time. The arena of interaction is not egalitarian, but the state is not necessarily hierarchically above other authorities. The relationship among these authorities is dynamic and may be under constant transformation—for instance, with some elements of the authorities collaborating while fighting one another in public.

My focus on authority aligns with a growing trend moving beyond the Weberian state when conceptualizing and analyzing political order, particularly in the context of African countries.[36] These strands of literature respond to the insufficiency of the contemporary understanding of political order. As Agnew points out, "political authority is not restricted to states and . . . is thereby not necessarily exclusively territorial."[37] Hence, choosing authority as the unit of analysis allows flexibility in dealing with the globalized world order.[38] While adopting this understanding, the divide among levels of governance and the separation among global or international, domestic or national, and local is not relevant.

For this view on political order, I still consider Weber's work to be fundamental. The German term *Herrschaft*, which can also translate as "domination," suggests an analysis of governance beyond government. Weber defines the term as "the chance of a specific (or: of all) command(s) being obeyed by a specifiable group of people."[39] Building on this, I use the expression "authority" to describe social control as a relationship of both command and obedience and, accordingly, the (commanding) actor or entity whose social control a group of people obeys, thus having a structuring influence on their lives.[40] To define who is an authority and to distinguish among authorities, I suggest adopting an empirical view and building on the perceptions and labels the people who have to obey their social control use.

In the interviews that I conducted in Afghanistan, people most frequently referred to the state; insurgents, most prominently the Taliban at the time; community authorities, such as elders and councils; and individual strongmen as the major authorities within the country's political order. While foreign actors have played an important role in Afghanistan's political order, the authority of Western actors became increasingly indirect over the years until 2021, with many countries operating through other authorities, mainly the Afghan state, in the context of a reduced international presence. I structured this book according to the main authorities identified by the interviewees.[41]

LEGITIMACY: WHAT DO WE KNOW?

Conceptualizing Afghanistan's political order as an arena of interaction of multiple authorities, including but not exclusively focused on the state, acknowledges the complexity of conflict zones while maintaining conceptual clarity. It broadens the view and makes the investigation of the legitimacy of these authorities separately possible. But like the understanding of political order and the state, the definition of legitimacy is contested. Derived from the neo-Latin word *legitimus* (lawful, legal, legitimate), the word has been used in a wide range of contexts, and its definition has changed over time.[42] In medieval European thought, for instance, it described a person who—in contrast to a tyrant—ruled according to the law and the will of God.[43]

Two closely related *concepts of legitimacy* can be differentiated: normative and empirical legitimacy.[44] Philosophers and political theorists have long discussed the conditions whereby a political order or an authority can be considered to be legitimate. There is an ongoing debate as to the requirements that an authority must fulfill to achieve such *normative* legitimacy. For example, Arendt argues that "power springs up whenever people get together and act in concert, but it derives its legitimacy from the initial getting together rather than from any action that then may follow."[45] Explicitly or implicitly, normative definitions of legitimacy are often linked to the concepts of security and justice. For instance, according to Hobbes's idea of the social contract, people give up individual freedoms and transfer rights to authority in exchange for security. As long as the authority ensures the protection of the people, it is legitimate.

By contrast, I adopt an *empirical* view of legitimacy in line with my empirical understanding of authority. Hence, I investigate legitimacy from the point of view of the people governed and analyze why people in Afghanistan consider an authority to be legitimate, instead of making these judgments myself according to my normative standards. The empirical concept of legitimacy rests on Weber's understanding and his general strategy to make research as independent as possible from the researcher's own views and values.[46] Accordingly, investigating empirical legitimacy requires an analysis of the attitudes and beliefs of people.

Adopting an empirical understanding of legitimacy for an analysis requires first specifying the concept and knowing what to look for in an empirical setting. I suggest viewing legitimacy as a source of authority—as voluntary obedience to social control. Conceptually speaking, people have two options as to why they accept or even support an authority and obey it: either people *want to* or they *have to* obey. Voluntary obedience is based on *legitimacy*, whereas involuntary obedience is based on *coercion*. If authority rests on coercion, people are threatened or forced to obey in a violent or nonviolent way, including through the symbolic use of force. When applying this conceptual divide analytically to empirical research, there is a continuum between the two ideal types. For instance, instead of categorizing the army of a country as legitimate and an insurgency group as coercive, people might have more balanced views. A person may acknowledge that the army is coercive but, nonetheless, consider it to be *more legitimate* than insurgents. Perception dictates how coercive and/or legitimate an authority is. For instance, social pressure can force people to obey. Nonetheless, the perception of those who obey determines if this is coercion or legitimacy.

Conceptually, the suggested definition of authority implies an *ability to impact*. Legitimacy and coercion enable an authority to exercise social control. However, legitimacy and coercion may also exist without the ability to impact, and people may assess the legitimacy and coerciveness of an authority outside relationships in which they obey. For example, someone may consider the Afghan state to be legitimate even when living in a fully insurgency-controlled area and not having access to the Afghan state. Adopting Aristotle's distinction between actuality and potentiality, we can distinguish two forms of authority. For those who are not subject to an actor's social control, those that it is unable to impact, authority is only *potential*. But if legitimacy and coercion enable obedience, we can speak of *actual authority*. This is particularly important in conflict-torn spaces, where the relationship between authority and territory and the ability to impact are in flux.

Instrumental vs. Substantive Legitimacy

In developing the conceptual understanding of legitimacy, I suggest distinguishing between two different kinds of theoretical reasons for voluntary obedience, which reflect two fundamentally different ways of looking at legitimacy. I term the rational assessment of the usefulness of authority *instrumental legitimacy*, describing to what extent an authority responds to *needs*. People may voluntarily obey authority simply because it is beneficial or because they have no alternative. Based on the rationality and assessments of *usefulness*, instrumental legitimacy may align with rational-choice theory, the understanding of the human as a self-interested *homo oeconomicus*, and positivist research methods in general. Instrumental definitions of legitimacy also appear in the policy literature, for instance, with suggestions to enhance legitimacy through service delivery or improved performance. But Weber persuasively argues that obedience, which rests on material interests and rational calculations of advantages, is unstable.[47] It only lasts as long as people benefit or have the hope of benefitting again in the future. Hence, instrumental legitimacy is of a short-term nature.

Conversely, what I call *substantive legitimacy* is a more abstract normative judgment, a *belief in rightfulness*, which shared values underpin. Substantive definitions of legitimacy dominate the social science literature and go beyond the simple rational assessment of advantages and disadvantages as they are centered around beliefs. For instance, Weber argues that "the basis of every system of authority, and correspondingly of every kind of willingness to obey, is a belief."[48] Drawing on Bourdieu, substantive legitimacy can also be described as symbolic capital, capital that is recognized by people, reflecting "a belief . . . by virtue of which persons wielding authority are endowed with prestige."[49] If a person believes that an entity has the right to exercise social control, he or she may also accept personal disadvantages. Hence, according to Weber, long-term voluntary obedience requires belief in the legitimacy of an authority (*Legitimitäts-glauben*).[50] Considering substantive forms of legitimacy enables a more comprehensive analysis of a *homo sociologicus*, who is a member of society and is also guided by values and belief, opening up the space for a wider range of methods. Therefore, when empirically investigating legitimacy, we need to explore the reasons for people's views, the explanation of their opinions and actions, and whether they are based on beliefs and values, usefulness—or coercion.

The conceptual divide between *beliefs* and *needs* or *rightfulness* and *usefulness* that I am introducing to the debate on legitimacy builds on a long tradition of distinguishing the reasons that explain social action along similar lines. For instance, Weber developed four types of social action, including instrumental rationality (*Zweckrationalität*), based on utility, and value rationality (*Wertrationalität*).[51] Habermas, in his theory of communicative action, goes beyond Weber's focus on what drives an individual in society and also considers the relations between people.[52] He argues that actions are either oriented instrumentally to individual success or to agreement (*Verständigung*), a normative consensus.[53] However, in contrast to the more general literature on social action, the two suggested definitions of legitimacy focus more specifically on explaining obedience to social control. Instrumental and substantive legitimacy are two complementary, not mutually exclusive, reasons why people obey authority. Both needs and beliefs underpin people's expectations with regard to authority. How much instrumental and substantive legitimacy an authority has ultimately depends on the extent to which people's perception of an authority match their *needs-based* and *belief-based expectations*.

Legitimacy in Conflict-Torn Spaces

In conflict zones, where people's basic needs are not met, instrumental legitimacy is of particular importance. Goodhand described how the war economy in Afghanistan, for most people, was a "coping economy." While commanders and businessmen benefitted from the war and shadow economies, the majority of people in Afghanistan remained poor, trying "to cope and maintain asset bases through low-risk activities, or to survive through asset erosion."[54] Under such conditions, authorities could be able to construct instrumental legitimacy easily by providing goods, services, money, or employment.

But what underpins substantive legitimacy in a context like Afghanistan is less clear, given the competing sources of legitimacy that exist under conflict. There are various possible *sources of substantive legitimacy*, which can be categorized in different ways. Weber famously distinguishes among rational-legal, charismatic, and traditional legitimacy, describing different mechanisms or sources of substantive legitimacy that underpin the belief in the right to exercise social control.[55] Each of these ideal types describes a specific claim of the legitimacy of an authority (*Legitimitätsanspruch*) that responds to a certain belief in what constitutes a legitimate authority (*Legitimitätsglauben*). The idea of rational-legal legitimacy rests on the belief in formal rules and a functioning bureaucracy. Traditional legitimacy is based on customs and routines, legitimizing authority because it has not changed for a long period of time. A particularly complex form of legitimacy is charisma, which lies in the belief of people in the extraordinary (*außeralltägliche*) qualities of an individual, which makes him or her appear to be an envoy of God, a role model, or leader.[56] However, Weber explicitly specifies that the three ideal types of legitimate authority only capture "modern" contexts.[57] His typology is tailored to settings that are characterized by a monopoly of force, where political order and authority are one and the same and where authority is a coherent entity or system based on one idea of authority or principle of governance, such as rational-legality or tradition, that provides the authority with a claim of legitimacy that also determines the authority's practices.

Other theorists' conceptualization of substantive legitimacy tends to focus on the legitimacy of the state and legitimacy *within rational-legal contexts*. In contrast to Weber, this literature does not look at the reasons that underpin people's beliefs in legitimacy but focuses on different *aspects of authority* that affect legitimacy in political orders characterized by rational-legality. In a way, it specifies the rational-legal source of legitimacy (figure 1.2). For instance, Scharpf investigates legitimacy "under modern (Western) conditions" and describes *input* and *output* legitimacy as two dimensions of a democratic system, where output goes beyond simple service delivery and is linked to the input of the people through representative institutions that ensure accountability.[58] Algappa has a more detailed look at the "output" of the state and recommends distinguishing

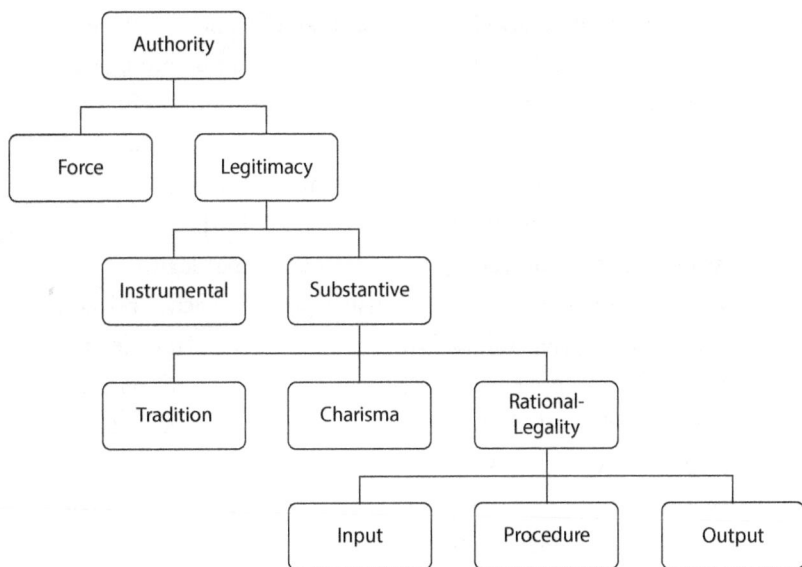

FIGURE 1.2 Rational-legal sources of substantive legitimacy

performance, the effective use of power, from procedural elements of legitimacy, which he defines as the conformity to rules.[59] Similarly, psychology literature, looking particularly at democratic policing, offers for consideration the *procedures* of how police officers interact with the public as an important aspect of authority that matters for the construction of legitimacy.[60] However, it remains unclear to what extent this literature applies to a conflict-torn space.

Discussions of the sources of substantive legitimacy in conflict-torn spaces have been scant. Derived from the literature on rational-legal contexts, what exists reflects the conceptual divide between output and performance on the one hand, and processes and input on the other. Denney and colleagues summarize: "Some see legitimacy as an output- or performance-based product, which emerges when political authorities deliver tangible outcomes to populations (such as services, economic opportunities or security). Others see it as a function of process, which can refer to how inclusive the government is throughout the process of policy making and resource distribution."[61] This narrow focus has three crucial limitations. First, the conceptual divide between input and output legitimacy is of limited value for the analysis of nonrational-legal contexts. In the absence of institutions that connect input and output, output legitimacy is barely instrumental, simply addressing people's needs and not being linked to their values. Other possibly more adaptable and hence fruitful approaches to legitimacy, such as Tyler's on procedures of in psychology literature, have not been considered much in the debate.[62] Second, there is not much empirical evidence on the role service delivery can play in the construction of legitimacy in conflict zones. A notable exception here is Sturge and coauthors' study, which suggests that service delivery only enhances the legitimacy of the state if people can participate in the decision-making process.[63] Third, the debate is centered around the legitimacy of the state and does not consider the legitimacy of other authorities that exist in political orders with a low level of monopolization of force. Denney and colleagues accordingly call for a "multidimensional understanding" of legitimacy.[64]

Analytical Dimensions of Legitimacy

To enable empirical research of legitimacy in a context like Afghanistan, I want to propose such a multidimensional analytical understanding. First, in line with Weber, I advocate investigating people's *needs and beliefs*, which underpin their perceptions and expectations with regard to authority. This helps us to understand why people think that an authority has the right to exercise social control or why it is at least useful for them if it does. Following Weber, a person may believe that a rational-legal, traditional, or charismatic authority has the right to exercise social control. But a person's belief in what is right may also emerge from religion, another ideology, such as capitalism and communism, or values that cannot be categorized easily according to ideologies. Second, we should look at what *aspects of authority* people's needs and beliefs relate to and determine specifically the referent objects of their perceptions and expectations. This allows us to deal more flexibly with the complexities of conflict-torn spaces than the common approaches, which, based on Weber, view authorities as coherent entities or systems. While an authority's instrumental legitimacy is linked to its actions, which address people's needs, people's beliefs may also be linked to other aspects of authority, such as what an authority stands for.

The literature on legitimacy in rational-legal contexts suggests that input, procedures, and output are relevant aspects of authority. However, due to the outlined fluidity of authority in a conflict-torn setting,[65] a different range of aspects of authority may matter in such contexts. People might be concerned with an authority's *actions*, in terms of its "output" as suggested by Scharpf or,[66] building on psychology literature, in terms of its de facto behavior, practices, and modes of interaction—either institutionalized as procedures or unregulated.[67] Alternatively, people may believe in an authority's right to exercise social control because of its *history* of how it gained authority. Another aspect of importance might be what an authority stands for, the *idea* of authority—for instance, expressed through its formal or de jure institutions, symbols, personality, official narrative, or communicated ideology—when assessing its legitimacy.[68] For example, in their work on the Democratic Republic of the Congo (DRC), Hoffmann and Vlassenroot, illustrate how nonstate armed groups evoke notions of state discourse to build legitimacy, knowing that it addresses the idea of what people view as legitimate.[69] While some authorities might be coherent actors, with all of the aspects being aligned, in other cases, there might be gaps among actions, history, and what an authority stands for. But this is by no means a comprehensive list. There may be other aspects of authority that matter for people, which need to be developed inductively.

Combining the two dimensions of beliefs of the subjects on the one hand and a disentangled view on authority with various aspects on the other, a more detailed picture of legitimacy evolves (table 1.1). For example, people may believe that an authority has the right to exercise social control because they perceive the way it gained authority to be democratic, resulting in what Scharpf calls "input legitimacy."[70] But people may also

TABLE 1.1 DIMENSIONS OF ANALYSIS: ASPECTS OF
AUTHORITY VS. BELIEFS AND NEEDS, EXAMPLES

	Substantive legitimacy	Instrumental legitimacy
Authority's actions	E.g., belief in right to exercise social control because authority's practices align with religious values	E.g., usefulness of exercise of social control because of authority's provision of goods and services
History of gaining authority	E.g., belief in right to exercise social control because actor gained authority in way that aligns with traditional values	—
Idea of authority	E.g., belief in right to exercise social control because authority's code of law aligns with democratic values	—

consider an authority to be legitimate because they perceive its de jure institutions to be in line with their traditions. Or people may consider the behavior to be instrumentally useful or, more substantively, right, because it aligns with their religious beliefs.

Looking at legitimacy in the context of ongoing armed conflict necessarily poses the question of the relationship between legitimacy and physical force or violence.[71] Going beyond Weber's focus on tradition, charisma, and rational-legality as sources of legitimacy, the suggested framework enables us to go deeper in exploring this relationship. While I consider legitimacy and violence as the use of force underpinning coercion to be distinct sources of authority, they can be connected in several ways. Conceptually speaking, the use of force is not just a source of authority; it is also an action of an authority. Hence, violence can directly affect both instrumental and substantive legitimacy. Arendt prominently argues that "violence can destroy power; it is utterly incapable of creating it."[72] But looking at the relationship between legitimacy and violence in a conflict-torn space suggests that the use of force may also help an authority with the construction of legitimacy. Violence could potentially help establish output legitimacy, for instance, by illustrating an authority's ability to provide security against a threat.[73] However, as coercion and legitimacy are two distinct sources of authority, the ability to exercise force is not required to build legitimacy. For instance, community authorities may rely on legitimacy only or apply nonviolent and more indirect forms of coercion, such as social pressure.

By analyzing the extent to which people's perceptions with regard to different aspects of authority match their expectations, we can draw conclusions on the legitimacy of different authorities. To comprehensively assess legitimacy, it is necessary to ask what matters the most for people, also including perceptions of coercion, as the complementary source of authority. For example, people may consider a community authority to be coercive because of its violent actions in the present, even though they view the process of how it gained power to be legitimate for traditional reasons. Conversely, people may consider the state to be legitimate because of its democratic procedures, accepting its insufficient output or even its sporadic coerciveness.

It is worth noting that the dimensions of substantive and instrumental legitimacy are not static but are subject to constant change. Legitimacy is always in a process of transformation, construction, and deconstruction. The aspects of authorities change, as do people's needs, norms, and values, particularly as their societies change.[74] Such changes may happen frequently, particularly in a dynamic conflict-torn setting. In addition, people's experiences with and perceptions of an authority may also affect their expectations and ultimately what they consider to be legitimate. For instance, after positive long-term experiences with an authority, people's expectations with regard to future authorities may rise. Or, vice versa, long-term negative experiences with authorities may lower expectations, reducing the threshold of legitimacy. Scholars working on *adaptive preferences* illustrate that people adjust their preferences if they have limited options and may even become complicit in maintaining their own deprivation or suppression.[75]

Self-Perception of Authority

Finally, to gain a comprehensive understanding of legitimacy, I propose looking at the perception of authority from as many different perspectives as possible, including the self-perception of authorities. Beetham challenges Weber's understanding of legitimacy and rightfully points out that looking at people's beliefs narrows down the complexity of legitimacy to a single dimension. In contrast, he argues that "a given power relationship is not legitimate because people believe in its legitimacy, but because it can be *justified in terms* of their beliefs."[76] Ultimately, however, Beetham's definition—based on the justification of legitimacy only—is similarly one-sided.

Hence, I propose combining both approaches and analyzing legitimacy from two perspectives, not only focusing on the *perception of legitimacy*, the people's point of view, but also including its *self-perception of legitimacy*, the authority's point of view. Investigating the self-perception of authorities supplements the picture we gain from public perceptions. Building on Beetham's suggestion, by analyzing authority's self-perception, we can discover on what basis they claim legitimacy and justify their authority, how they portray themselves, and frame their actions, history, and idea of authority. But investigating the self-perception of authorities also provides us with a better understanding of their own interpretations and the reasons that underpin their actions. This allows us to put their authority into context, going beyond public perceptions.

To find out more about the authorities' view on legitimacy, we need to talk to individuals who are themselves authorities or are associated with them. We can distinguish different dimensions that provide insights into how they perceive their legitimacy. All of these can be analyzed through the lens of aspects of authority on the one hand and instrumental and substantive legitimacy on the other. First, we can investigate the *personal claim of legitimacy*, the reasons why an individual says that his or her authority is legitimate or that certain ways of exercising authority are legitimate. These personal claims of legitimacy may differ from *official* statements and claims of legitimacy that are linked to the idea of authority. But, in addition to claims, I propose to try to find out more about an authority's self-perception. There may be differences between what authorities claim and how they personally think about it. Hence, second, I suggest analyzing the *personal motives* of why a person joined or became an authority. Doing so voluntarily illustrates a high level of legitimacy, making it relevant to study the reasons and the extent to which they are instrumental or substantive. By looking at the motives, we can go beyond both official and personal claims and find out more about to what extent and why a person thinks that his or her authority is legitimate. Third, we can examine the reasons why a person assumes that their authority has *local legitimacy*. Again, this can provide us with a better understanding of legitimacy beyond claims of what a person thinks the people in their society think. Research may consider one or many of these dimensions. Even though, ultimately, we cannot always be sure what a claim is and what honest self-perception is, any insight beyond the official claim furthers our understanding of the authority's view on legitimacy.[77] We can then compare these dimensions of the authority's view on legitimacy with how the public perceives them, analyze to what extent the perspectives match, and explore the reasons that explain potential gaps between their own view and how others perceive them. On that basis, we can draw more nuanced conclusions on what underpins the authority's legitimacy and how substantive it is.

INTERACTIVE DIGNITY: THEORIZING LEGITIMACY IN CONFLICT-TORN SPACES

Our current unsatisfactory understanding of the role of legitimacy in conflict-torn spaces can easily be dismissed as an abstract scholarly problem. But the situation in Afghanistan between 2001 and 2021, which we will discuss in the following chapters, illustrates the significant implications for ordinary people and, accordingly, for peace- and state-building initiatives.

I use the proposed framework to analyze perceptions of people in Afghanistan that I explored through my interviews. The analysis of how people thought about the state, the Taliban, strongmen, and community authorities shows that what matters most for them and is a key mechanism or source of substantive legitimacy in Afghanistan, and possibly also in other conflict zones, is not covered by the fundamental theories on legitimacy and authority. It is what I call *interactive dignity*. The aspect of authority that most concerns people in Afghanistan are its actions, particularly with regard to how authorities *interact* with them on a day-to-day basis. The value-based expectation people have with regard to such interactions is one of *human dignity*. People expect procedures to be fair and practices to be respectful, reflecting a serving rather than an extractive attitude.

The analysis of people's views on different authorities in Afghanistan in the following chapters shows that they care little about *how an actor gained authority* and whether this happened through democratic, Islamic, or traditional procedures. For example, those emphasizing their support for their village elder rarely did so with reference to how he was appointed. Similarly, the *idea an authority stands for* matters surprisingly little in contrast to a commonly stated view on Afghanistan, which tends to emphasize a clash of big ideologies. But few interviewees were concerned with what authorities stood for or their institutions' formal aspects, whether it be the Afghan state's democratic and liberal constitution, the traditional character of community authorities, or the Taliban's religious claims.

Instead, people are most concerned with the *action* of authorities. Unsurprisingly, people in a conflict zone like Afghanistan often worry about and demand not only improved security and justice but also education, health, and other services, from the various authorities. However, it is not necessarily the output as such that matters. Much more important are the *modes of interaction*, people's day-to-day experience of an authority and its behavior, and the way authorities interact with them. For instance, in the security sector, people expect coordinated approaches, which involve the community, address their concerns, and ensure that people are treated with respect on a daily basis. Meanwhile, behavior that is perceived as corrupt, extractive, abusive, or disrespectful undermines the legitimacy of an authority. This matches findings in psychology literature on policing that illustrates the role procedures of interaction play for legitimacy in rational-legal settings.[78] But interactions appear to be even more important for legitimacy in conflict zones. In the absence of rational-legal structures that connect input and output on the macrolevel, people hope for accountability on the microlevel in their day-to-day lives.

The importance of interaction adds to the understanding of legitimacy proposed both by Weber and Bourdieu. For example, adding to Weber's conceptualization of legitimacy, the finding suggests the importance of procedures beyond rational-legal contexts. Meanwhile, in contrast to Bourdieu's work that focuses on structural objective relations within fields, the finding suggests that interactions possibly matter more than acknowledged by him—at least in the context of a dynamic political order with competing authorities.[79] Regardless of whether we accept Bourdieu's view on interactions as being shaped by and merely expressing underlying structures, the finding suggests that the way interactions are conducted is an important form of symbolic capital and, hence, legitimacy. Structural factors may, for example, determine how police officers interact with civilians. Nonetheless, the way this interaction is conducted affects the legitimacy of the state.

Modes of interaction are important for instrumental and substantive legitimacy. People compare the experienced interactions to their needs-based expectations, which include *costs*, *predictability*, and *convenience*. For example, in some parts of Afghanistan, the Taliban constructed instrumental legitimacy by providing courts that were easy to access, free of charge, and followed understandable rules. In addition, people have value-based expectations with regard to interaction in the form of basic *human dignities*, such as *fairness* and *respect*. Such value-based expectation, which underpins substantive legitimacy, rests on the hope of being treated as equal citizens. Especially in court cases, for instance, fairness matters. Many interviewees demanded that parties should be treated equally, regardless of their status or networks, and that it should not be possible to win a case through bribes and influence. In some cases, the Taliban were also more successful in responding to this expectation than the Afghan state, as most people considered its courts to be highly corrupt.

The idea of interactive dignity also sheds further light on the relationship between violence and legitimacy. Crucially, as Arendt notes, violence often undermines legitimacy. The experience of violence is exceptionally memorable and often traumatic, having a lasting impact on the perception of the responsible authority and undermining its substantive legitimacy. The book shows that if an authority fails to provide security despite having the ability to do so, it can similarly undermine its legitimacy. Hence, for instance, the Taliban used large-scale attacks to delegitimize the state. Here also, the symbolic effect of violence matters—as suggested by Bourdieu. For example, large-scale attacks in Kabul were not only physically violent, but they also affected a wider population and contributed to a sense that the state could not protect its citizens.

Meanwhile, perhaps counterintuitively, violence and the ability to use force can also help authorities to construct legitimacy. Most importantly, the experience of violence with one authority can legitimize another authority. That will become especially clear in the reasoning of some of the interviewed Taliban fighters who joined the movement and took up arms against the state after experiencing violence perpetrated by state actors. The same experience further illustrates that the ability to exercise force can help to construct legitimacy, as people joined the Taliban to be able to fight the perceived source of injustice. Furthermore, authorities that control force have an opportunity to construct legitimacy by exercising force in a way that matches peoples' expectations of being treated with dignity through respectful day-to-day interactions that provide a sense that security is given equally for everyone. However, this demands a very restrained use of violence.

Beyond modes of interactions, there is another aspect of authority that the interviewees paid considerable attention to—an *authority's attitude*. People have substantive, value-based expectations with regard to the attitude of authorities, hoping for authorities to be serving the public rather than being driven by self-interest or by serving foreign interests. For example, community authorities and the Afghan army were often described as serving the public in my interviews. Also, the perceived attitude of an authority is ultimately tied to its actions. In order to judge an authority's attitude, people relied on their experience of interacting with them. Authorities that are perceived as living up to the expectation of interactive dignity are also considered to be serving the public. Meanwhile, for instance, a police officer demanding bribes is viewed as being self-interested and failing to serve the public.

Finally, even though people appeared to care little about the idea of authority, they did believe in the *idea of the state* as an abstract concept and hoped for a state to govern again in the future. While interactive dignity may be the first and most essential step for the construction of legitimacy in Afghanistan, in the long-term, they seemed to expect a Weberian monopoly of force and *rational-legality*. This finding leaves some room for optimism with regard to efforts of establishing the state as one overarching legitimate authority in Afghanistan. However, as long as the state fails to live up to people's expectation of interactive dignity, it is bound to fail in constructing a monopoly of the legitimate use of force.

Hence, this book illustrates that the beliefs and values that underpin people's expectations are not linked to any of Weber's ideal types and that they also do not rest on religion or another ideology. Instead, people have a very basic expectation of being treated with dignity, as equal citizens, in day-to-day interactions.

2

THE STATE

"The police uniform you are wearing is not yours, it is the trust of the people."

General in the Afghan National Police, Kabul City, 2015

Hopes for Afghanistan were high in 2001. After decades of violence followed by the Taliban regime, there was an opportunity to build a new state with a monopoly on the legitimate use of force that lived up to the expectations of Afghanistan's citizens and other nations. As I write this, hopes have faded, and the Taliban have again taken control of the state. In the years leading up to 2021, the international community's expectations regarding the success of "state-building" started to wane. Large parts of rural Afghanistan were outside of state control, and the Taliban frequently attacked people in cities, including Kabul. Even territories that remained under the control of the state often had to compete or arrange themselves with other authorities, such as elders, councils, and strongmen.

The state that existed from 2001 to 2021 was fragmented, and its de jure formalized structure and hierarchy frequently failed to translate into practice. Different branches often seemed to be in conflict, following competing agendas or the commands of individual strongmen. Lacking a monopoly of force and a functioning bureaucracy, the Weberian conceptual understanding of the state is one of limited use. The state nonetheless continued to play a key role in the political order of Afghanistan. There was an army that fought insurgents and tried to expand the state's level of monopolization of force; there was a police force that patrolled the streets; people elected members of Parliament, who then decided on new laws that some people obeyed; and there was a government that interacted with other countries around the world. But did people consider this state or any of its branches to be legitimate? Or did people ultimately perceive the state only as a coercive authority, hidden behind the façade of democracy?

Over time, various individuals and groups have controlled the state in Afghanistan, advocating different ideas of authority and claiming legitimacy based on different ideologies, including monarchical tradition, communism, religion, and democracy. This chapter begins with a brief overview of the history of competition for control of the formal state structures in Afghanistan and looks into how different rulers and governments have tried to construct legitimacy. Building on interviews, the chapter then investigates how the Afghan public perceived the state and contrasted it with the self-perceptions of state actors. Thereby, the chapter analyzes the state's legitimacy in light of perceptions surrounding security and conflict resolution, which correspond with different branches of a Weberian state. The chapter first looks at the Afghan National Security Forces (ANSF),[1] which were meant to provide security and enforce the laws as part of a bureaucracy that was subordinate to the executive branch of the state. Secondly, specifically through the lens of conflict resolution, the chapter looks at the judicial sector, courts, and prosecutors who implemented and interpreted the laws. A third section is about the legislative branch, the members of Parliament, who made the laws.

At the time of my research, people in Afghanistan had to deal with the state in its 2001–2021 form on a regular basis, particularly in the urban areas of the provinces. However, most interviewees did not think of the Afghan state as one system that was underpinned by one governing principle. Instead, people often had very different views on the different types of state actors. For instance, many people considered the Afghan National Army (ANA) to be legitimate, but not the Afghan National Police (ANP) or the state's courts. My findings suggest that personal experience lies at the heart of these differing perceptions; the way each entity exercised authority and interacted with people on a daily basis determined perceptions of its legitimacy. People expected fair procedures, respectful behavior, and an attitude of serving the country, and they perceived most state actors as corrupt and driven purely by their own interests. Nonetheless, while the state authorities failed to live up to people's expectations in practice, people still believed in the idea of the state.

THE ROLE OF COERCION IN KABUL'S HISTORY

Since Kabul became the capital of Afghanistan in 1775, it has been the central stage of the power struggles over the formal Afghan state structures. The main players on this stage have been various influential families vying for control of the country. But these internal power struggles have also been closely linked to geopolitical conflicts, making imperialism a common theme of the city's modern history—the Anglo-Afghan Wars during

Western colonialism, the Soviet invasion during the Cold War, and the presence of Western military forces after 2001 who were fighting the "war on terror". The constant contest of various foreign and Afghan authorities over power resulted in frequent periods of insecurity for the city's citizens.[2]

Dost Mohammad of the Barakzai Durrani family took control of Kabul away from the Sadozai Durrani family in 1826. The Barakzai dynasty would largely retain control until 1973 except, for instance, during the period of British occupation during the First Anglo-Afghan War, 1839–1842, when British-Indian troops reinstated the Sadozai Durrani dynasty. King Amanullah of the Barakzai dynasty (r. 1919–1929), influenced by ideas from Europe, was determined to "modernize" Kabul. In the 1920s, he reformed the constitution, built Kabul's Western-style landmarks, Darul Aman Palace and Tajberg Palace, and propagated a Western dress code. King Amanullah's successor, Mohammed Nadir Shah (r. 1929–1933), abolished many of the reforms to accommodate the more conservative factions. But Nadir Shah's son, the last king of Afghanistan, Zahir Shah (r. 1933–1973), reinstated Westernization in the forms of a constitutional monarchy, more rights for women, large-scale development projects, and even a zoo that still exists. Though most of Afghanistan remained rural, poor, and conservative in its culture, a more liberal, Western lifestyle developed in parts of Kabul. Photographs from the 1950s and 1960s show women wearing skirts in the office or in bathing suits at the pool of the Intercontinental Hotel, which sits on one of Kabul's hilltops. Hippies from Western countries who could afford overseas trips in the late 1960s often visited Kabul, as it was a popular stop on the "hippie trail" from Europe to India.

King Zahir Shah's reign ended in 1973 when his cousin, Mohammed Daoud Khan, seized power. The pro-Soviet People's

Democratic Party of Afghanistan (PDPA) had put him in place. He established a republic, proclaiming himself president. However, Maley notes that Daoud, unable to claim legitimacy on the basis of tradition, increased the use of coercion, for instance, by building a large prison—Pul-e Charkhi, which remains the country's main prison.[3] Daoud was critical of his party's dependence on the Soviet Union, and members of the PDPA killed him and his supporters in the Saur Revolution in April 1978. The position of the chairman of the presidium of the revolutionary council was created, replacing the presidency. After a brief transition period, Nur Muhammad Taraki, a founding member of the PDPA, took over the post but was killed in September 1979 on orders from his former friend and ally, Hazifullah Amin. Amin was chairman for three months. Both Taraki and Amin requested military support from the Soviet Union. When Soviet troops entered the country in December 1979, Amin reportedly believed they had come to support him. However, they did not trust Amin, and he died at the hands of Soviet troops in the Tajbeg Palace in Kabul.[4]

In the years that followed, several groups in the country took up arms to fight Russia with the support of Western countries, channeling money and weapons through the Pakistani Inter-Services Intelligence (ISI). The Mujahedin groups were centered around "jihadi" leaders and commanders, such as Ahmad Shah Massoud, Gulbuddin Hekmatyar, Abdul Rashid Dostum, Abdul Qadir, and Burhanuddin Rabbani (see chapter 3 on strongmen). In the early 1980s, most of the fighting occurred in the rural parts of the country, sparing Kabul from the immediate effects of the conflict and leading many to take refuge there, resulting in a growing urban population in the capital. However, in the late 1980s, attacks on Kabul intensified, and a large number of civilians were killed. Human Rights Watch reported from Kabul that sometimes twenty rockets, many purchased with U.S. funds, struck Kabul every day.[5]

After the Soviet troops left Afghanistan in 1989, the pro-Soviet government of Mohammad Najibullah continued without direct external military support. Following the collapse of the Soviet Union in 1991, it also went without financial support. Indeed, the Najibullah government remained in power and managed to control Kabul until April 1992, when he asked the UN for asylum and moved into their compound. Mujahedin forces subsequently took over the city.

Competing Mujahedin groups turned Kabul, in particular, into a battleground. The city was heavily bombarded, destroying many buildings and the infrastructure that provided water and electricity. Atrocities against civilians in the city, a horrendous scale of executions, abductions, torture, and sexual violence followed the collapse of Najibullah's government.[6] In addition, the Taliban began bombarding the city early in 1995, making conditions worse than they had ever been. The Taliban had begun as a group of Deobandi madrassa students and quickly expanded their influence from Kandahar in the south of Afghanistan to other provinces (see chapter 4). They blocked the road into the city, and there was no electricity and minimal food by the end of 1995.

Civilian deaths in Kabul between 1992 and 1995 have been estimated at one hundred thousand.[7] In September 1996, Mujahedin commander Massoud and his forces, who were controlling Kabul at the time, left the city in the face of another Taliban offensive. The Taliban captured Kabul, killed Najibullah, and established the Islamic Emirate of Afghanistan. The Taliban took over the government offices and appointed their own ministers. People in Kabul began to slowly recover from the war in a comparatively stable and secure environment. However, the

Taliban's rules banned music, required men to grow beards, and demanded that women wear burqas and not attend school or go to work. Meanwhile, many of the Mujahedin commanders joined forces and created the United Islamic Front for the Salvation of Afghanistan, also known as the Northern Alliance, to defend the north of the country against the Taliban.

Once U.S. President George W. Bush launched the war on terror after 9/11, Afghanistan was soon targeted in Operation Enduring Freedom in October 2001. Western forces conducted airstrikes on targets in Kabul and supported the Mujahedin commanders of the Northern Alliance and their militias in taking over the city. The Taliban quickly withdrew from Kabul in early November to the south of the country, where the fighting continued. When the Taliban appeared to be defeated in December 2001, the victorious commanders of the Northern Alliance met with representatives of the international community in the German city of Bonn to discuss the future of Afghanistan, excluding any members of the Taliban. The result of the conference was the Agreement on Provisional Arrangements in Afghanistan Pending the Re-Establishment of Permanent Government Institutions, which is often simply called the Bonn Agreement. In it, the participants outlined a road map for the first steps to building a new Afghan state on the basis of "the principles of Islam, democracy, pluralism and social justice."[8] The UN Security Council supported the process and established the International Security Assistance Force (ISAF) by Resolution 1386 in December 2001 "to assist the Afghan Interim Authority in the maintenance of security in Kabul and its surrounding areas."[9] Furthermore, international donors pledged $4.5 billion for the reconstruction of Afghanistan at the Tokyo Conference in January 2002. And at the G8 conference in Geneva in June 2002, the participants further agreed on a "lead nation approach" to support the "state-building" process, assigning responsibility for different sectors in Afghanistan—the United States was assigned the army; Germany, the police; Italy, the judiciary; Britain took charge of counternarcotics; and the UN, demobilization.

The first step agreed on in Bonn was an emergency *loya jirga* (grand assembly of elders) to decide on a transitional government to take over the responsibilities from the interim head of state, Burhanuddin Rabbani. The meeting of representatives from all districts, including nomads, refugees, and the interim administration, took place in June 2002. Afghanistan's last king, Zahir Shah, opened the meeting at which Hamid Karzai was elected president of the transitional administration. The second step was a constitutional loya jirga in December 2003. This lasted until January 2004. After a long discussion the delegates accepted the presidential system Karzai had proposed and a catalog of rights, including equal rights for men and women, freedom of speech, protection of minorities, and an independent human rights commission.[10]

Kabul experienced a few peaceful and liberal years under the government of Karzai, who was formally elected in late 2004, the presence of ISAF, and a large amount of foreign aid. Some people dressed in Western clothes, and alcohol quickly became easily available. Kabul became a buzzing urban space with more than four million inhabitants, enormous traffic jams, polluted air, and widespread poverty. But there were also vibrant cafés, restaurants, art galleries, night-lit wedding halls, and a critical media landscape. Meanwhile, in many rural parts of Afghanistan, instability was growing again once the Taliban reorganized and had begun fighting as an insurgency (see chapter 4). The ISAF mandate was extended again and again with further UN Security Council resolutions and attempts to expand its presence by establishing provincial reconstruction teams (PRTs)—"small teams of military and civilian personnel working in Afghanistan's provinces to provide security for aid workers and help humanitarian assistance or reconstruction tasks" across the country.[11] And while divisions of the U.S. forces were part of the ISAF mission, the United States continued its own combat mission in Afghanistan to fight the war on terror. Karzai was reelected for a second term in 2009. But at that time, the security situation in Kabul had begun to deteriorate again. The Taliban increasingly launched attacks in Kabul, often killing large numbers of civilians, and their influence began to expand. People in the city reverted to dressing in traditional Afghan clothes, shops stopped selling alcohol, and foreigners heavily limited their movements. The Obama administration initiated a "surge" aimed at pushing back the insurgency movement with increased U.S. troop numbers. However, it only escalated the conflict.

The 2014 presidential election resulted in a stalemate between Ashraf Ghani and Abdullah Abdullah. Ghani was a technocrat who had worked as an academic and World Bank official in the United States before returning to Afghanistan in the early 2000s. Abdullah used to be a member of the Northern Alliance and had close ties to Burhanuddin Rabbani and Ahmad Shah Massoud. Under international pressure, Ghani and Abdullah formed a so-called National Unity Government. While expectations for progress and peace were high in the city during the election, frustration grew in the streets of Kabul in the following years as the people's hopes failed to materialize.[12] In 2014, the transition of the responsibility for security in Afghanistan from ISAF to the Afghan security forces, the ANSF, that began in 2011 was completed. The Western military's Resolute Support Mission replaced ISAF in 2015, and foreign troop numbers in the country decreased significantly. Similarly, funding for development projects began dwindling, contributing to both an increasingly weakened economy and rising unemployment. While the 2019 presidential elections again resulted in a stalemate between Ashraf Ghani and Abdullah Abdullah, even ensuing in two parallel swearing-in ceremonies by both as presidents, Abdullah ultimately conceded in exchange for a 50 percent share of government positions.

Meanwhile, the United States started directed negotiations with the Taliban and, under the Trump administration and its Afghan American chief negotiator, the special representative for Afghanistan reconciliation, Zalmay Khalilzad, agreed to a full withdraw from the country. In February 2020, the United States and the Taliban signed the Doha Agreement (Agreement for Bringing Peace to Afghanistan) in Qatar. In the agreement, the United States promised the full withdrawal of international military forces from Afghanistan within fourteen months (by May 2021) and the initial release of five thousand Taliban prisoners, followed by all remaining Taliban prisoners, from Afghan government prisons. In exchange, the Taliban promised to refrain from attacking U.S. forces, to release one thousand prisoners, and to participate in intra-Afghan negotiations with the Afghan government.[13] The agreement was widely seen as predominantly driven by U.S. domestic politics, fulfilling U.S. President Trump's promise to "bring home the troops" ahead of the U.S. election in 2020. The release of Taliban prisoners was delayed by the Afghan government, which was not a party to the United States-Taliban agreement, first demanding a comprehensive ceasefire that would also protect the ANSF.

Ultimately, intra-Afghan negotiations between the Afghan government and the Taliban began in September 2020. However, they quickly stalled while the war between the ANSF and the Taliban continued. Following the election of Joe Biden as the new U.S. president in late 2020, the Afghan government gained fresh hope that the international military could be kept in Afghanistan longer to support its fight against the Taliban. However, the government was disappointed when, on April 14, 2021, Biden announced an end to the "forever war" and committed to a full and unconditional withdrawal of U.S. forces by September 11, 2021, only exceeding the timeline promised to the Taliban in Doha by four months. Commenting on the withdrawal, a U.S. official noted, "Probably, this is all going to shit. But we also have confidence . . . that no one's going to give a shit."[14]

Following Biden's announcement, the Taliban launched a large-scale military offensive against the ANSF while continuing to refrain from attacking U.S. installations and forces as agreed. Districts fell at unprecedented speed—even though, in many districts, the Taliban only had to formalize their already existing influence by taking the governors' compounds. In July 2021, in the middle of the night, without informing its Afghan partners, the United States vacated its last major remaining base, Bagram Airfield, just north of Kabul City, concentrating its forces at the U.S. embassy and the airport.

Soon after, the Taliban began capturing provincial capitals. The first city, Zaranj, the capital of Nimroz Province in the remote southwest of Afghanistan, fell on August 6. The next day, Sheberghan in northern Jowzjan Province fell. On August 8, the Taliban took Kunduz, Sar-e-Pul, and Taloqan. The Taliban's advancements resulted in a domino effect, and within days the Taliban took all provincial capitals. Seeing the international partners leave shook ANSF morale. They had already lived without regular salary payments, and agreements with the Taliban promised amnesty. Entire cities surrendered without a single shot fired.

On August 15, 2021, the Taliban entered Kabul. President Ghani and his loyal supporters, National Security Advisor Hamdullah Mohib and Chief of Staff Fazel Fazly, fled the country by helicopter. While the Taliban established control in the city and entered the palace, desperate civilians tried getting onto evacuation flights out of the country—in some cases even hanging on to the wheels of departing flights. On August 29, 2021, a U.S. drone strike targeting a suspected Islamic State Khorasan Province (IS-K) suicide attacker in Kabul City killed a man who had been working for a U.S. aid organization and his family, including several children. It was a grim reminder of the toll civilians in Afghanistan had to pay for the U.S. war on terror, usually in remote rural areas far away from the media attention in Kabul. The Bureau of Investigative Journalism estimates that between 333 and 878 civilians were killed in drone strikes in Afghanistan between 2015 and 2020 when the number of airstrikes was already much lower than in previous years.[15] The next day, on August 30, the last U.S. military planes left the international airport in Kabul.

Resistance to the Taliban continued for another week in Panjshir Province, which the Taliban failed to capture in the 1990s. Finally, the Taliban claimed full control of the country on September 6, but the war did not end. IS-K continues to conduct attacks, and armed resistance to the Taliban evolved again.[16]

THE ROLE OF LEGITIMACY: RELIGION, TRADITION, AND PARTICIPATION

Afghanistan's history of state authority was not only written in blood; many rulers also tried to build state legitimacy once they had conquered Kabul by applying various other strategies.

The changing official names of the Afghan state illustrates how diverse the ideologies have been and on what basis the state claimed legitimacy: Emirate of Afghanistan (1823–1926, established by Dost Mohammad Khan), Kingdom of Afghanistan (1926–1973, established by Amanullah Khan), Republic of Afghanistan (1973–1978, established by Mohammed Daoud Khan), Democratic Republic of Afghanistan (1978–1987, established by the PDPA), Republic of Afghanistan (1987–1992, established by Mohammad Najibullah), Islamic State of Afghanistan (1992–2001, established by the Mujahedin), Islamic Emirate of Afghanistan (1996–2001, established by the Taliban) and Islamic Republic of Afghanistan (2001–2021).[17]

In the early twentieth century, ruling elites attempted to construct a national identity that transcended ethnic or other divisions with the purpose of legitimizing the monarchy as the ultimate authority for "all Afghans."[18] In addition, rulers invoked religion and tradition. Particularly striking in the more recent history of the Afghan state is the use of loya jirgas. Such assemblies can be portrayed as both a tradition and as a way of facilitating public participation. Barfield illustrates how Amanullah Khan (1919–1929) decided to use loya jirgas to ratify his laws, claiming legitimacy on the basis of treating people as constituents rather than subjects.[19] A few months after Amanullah was overthrown in 1929, Nadir Shah became the new king even though he was not a descendant of the governing dynasty. Not being able to draw on the "tradition" of a dynasty, he had a loya jirga to elect him as a new leader to legitimize his rule. In fact, no jirga had chosen a ruler since 1747. And even in 1747, when Ahmad Shah Durrani became king, the jirga was more likely a military gathering that only aimed at creating the image of consultation and, hence, public legitimacy.[20] While successfully inventing a "tradition" to become the king of Afghanistan, the

authority of the state under Nadir Shah remained limited, particularly in rural areas of the country. Barfield points out that
when people talked about the state or the government, "they
often quite literally meant the local government compound—a
place rather than a concept."[21] On passing out of its front gate,
and particularly after leaving the road that led to it, "government
ceased." The government's representatives in the villages, *arbabs*
and *maliks*, were often considered to be corrupt. Instead, wealthy
strongmen with good political networks were the main authorities in rural Afghanistan.[22]

After removing Nadir Shah and ending the monarchy, the
pro-Soviet PDPA claimed legitimacy on a secular and communist basis from 1978 onward. Even the Soviet advisors opposed
the PDPA's speed of implementing new rules in rural Afghanistan, where communist land reform, the cancellation of debts,
women's rights, and the abolition of dowries were highly dis-
ruptive.[23] Barfield argues that the PDPA failed to recognize
that the success of previous governments in Afghanistan rested
on ignoring rural populations instead of confronting them.[24]
The approach resulted in widespread resistance in rural areas,
and it legitimized the Mujahedin movement to fight the state.
The drawdown of Soviet troops in 1988/1989 lessened President
Najibullah's access to coercion, and he realized that he needed
more legitimacy to maintain his authority. He called a loya
jirga to ratify a new constitution in 1987 and modified it again
in 1990, replacing the communist terminology with Islam and
nationalism.[25]

As the Taliban took over (the first time), they reclaimed
legitimacy on the basis of religion, emphasizing that Islam
was their only ideology and implementing Islamic Sharia law.
But they often had limited knowledge of Islam. Instead, their
policies were mixed with rural traditions, most importantly
the Pashtunwali, the Pashtun's cultural code (see chapter 5).

This increased their legitimacy in certain rural areas, particularly those where Pashtuns dominated. However, urbanites especially saw them as conservative extremists.[26]

After the 2001 intervention, representatives of the international community and the Afghan elite quickly agreed on the desired institutional result of the "state-building" process—a centralized state with a legitimate monopoly of force. In contrast to the previous attempts at constructing state legitimacy in Afghanistan, the population of the country was not the only audience. It was also necessary to legitimize the military intervention internationally.[27] Thus, the state had to promote the claim of democracy and human rights as well as tradition, religion, and nationalism. The new Afghan state was called the Islamic Republic of Afghanistan, a label claiming legitimacy on the basis of both religious and democratic values. In addition, the former king, Zahir Shah, returned to Kabul to provide the new state with traditional authority.[28] The loya jirgas again became a tool to combine citizen participation while incorporating established traditions.

The constitution of 2004 was widely recognized by the public as being genuinely democratic, not only in a procedural way of having an elected government but also in a substantive way by emphasizing equal rights and freedom of speech. But, beyond claiming legitimacy on the basis of ideologies and value systems, the Afghan state also invested in service delivery—again, with international support. The strategy of the international military in the country reflected the idea of constructing legitimacy through actions by providing services, such as security. For example, according to the *ISAF Security Force Assistance (SFA) Guide*, "by definition SFA is a unified action . . . in support of a legitimate authority. Legitimacy is vital, as the Afghan population must perceive the ANSF as capable of long-term success."[29]

Over the years, the interest of the international community in building legitimacy in Afghanistan declined. The counterinsurgency objectives of the U.S. military were often at odds with the idea of state-building. When the influence of the Taliban started to grow, U.S. counterinsurgency objectives again became more dominant and were viewed as important to "protect the gains"—with force, if necessary—meanwhile accepting that civilian casualties undermine the state's legitimacy.

Fearing a growing Taliban influence and withdrawal of international forces, essentially leaving the Afghan government to fight for itself with little support, former President Ghani increasingly focused on maintaining his authority through coercive means, fighting the war against the Taliban. However, he continued claiming legitimacy on the basis of being elected while also drawing on supposedly traditional loya jirgas, in particular, to illustrate public support for specific decisions. For example, Ghani held a loya jirga to discuss the agenda for a peace process with the Taliban in April/May 2019 and, again, before releasing Taliban prisoners in August 2020, a decision he had been pressured into through the U.S.-Taliban agreement.

Furthermore, Ghani extensively tried constructing legitimacy by delivering goods and services on the community level. The Taliban, however, well aware of this strategy, tried to stop the interventions on the community level in areas under their influence that they considered to be part of Ghani's plans. For instance, following the COVID-19 outbreak in 2020, Ghani initiated the dastarkhan-e-milli (National Dining Table) program to gain popular support by providing food to poor families across the country, including in Taliban-controlled areas. The program was funded through two World Bank initiatives: the Citizens' Charter (see chapter 5) and the COVID-19 Relief Effort for Afghan Communities and Households (REACH) program. As the Taliban also viewed the World Bank to be a long-standing ally of Ghani, they threatened NGOs (nongovernmental organizations) with letters to stop implementing initiatives that were part of Citizens' Charter and REACH.[30] This illustrates the risks of Ghani's strategy of building legitimacy through service delivery, especially when using the humanitarian response for such political goals.

Hindsight reveals that the various attempts at legitimacy construction yielded mixed results. Reports by the Asia Foundation show low and often even further decreasing confidence in all government institutions in Afghanistan. Tadjbakhsh and Schoiswohl argue that the government failed to construct a belief in the new state or to advocate for more public participation beyond elections.[31] Goodhand, Suhrke, and Bohse find that Afghans understood elections "as an arena of intense competition between politico-military elites over access to rents, resources and positions" instead of being about legitimacy.[32]

There is little consensus as to what the Afghan state could have done to enhance its legitimacy more successfully. Quantitative, survey-based studies focus almost exclusively on service delivery, indicating an instrumental understanding of legitimacy. For instance, Sabarre, Solomon, and Van Blarcom conclude that "perceptions of security are key indicators of legitimacy scores."[33] Scholars and practitioners with a more substantive understanding of legitimacy often argue that for successful state-building rational-legal structures have to be improved, particularly with regard to elections.[34] Meanwhile, Maley emphasizes the importance of instrumental legitimacy, noting that "legitimacy in a fraught and fractious situation will be highly dependent upon the capacity of a new system, and of powerholders within it, actually to deliver the goods."[35] Others claim that local customs are crucial, pointing to what Weber would call "traditional legit-imacy." For example, Liebl writes that Pashtuns tend to accept any government that members of their ethnicity control, that Pushtun *jirgas* (councils) sanction, and that follow the basics of the cultural code Pashtunwali.[36] Similarly, a USAID study claims that "legitimacy begins with empowering the local level with traditional decision-making processes and from there, slowly establishing links with the Weberian rational-legal insti-tutions of the state can ensure accountability."[37]

Conversely, other scholars point out that tradition alone does not confer legitimacy. Barfield and Nojumi argue that, historically, the government delegated authority to nonstate actors acting as mediators for grievances on the local level. According to their analysis, "This system was highly functional and grounded in local perceptions of fairness and trust. It crossed ethnic, linguistic and tribal boundaries with ease because it was in the interest of all parties to cooperate."[38] Similarly, Roy argues that the "Afghan identity is based on a common political culture." He suggests three criteria that the state in Afghanistan needs to fulfill to be con-sidered legitimate: building on the concept of Afghanistan being an independent Muslim territory, acting as a mediating broker between competing groups, and providing basic services.[39]

Over time, rulers and governments in Afghanistan have defined tradition, religion, and participation in varying ways in their efforts to construct legitimacy. In addition, the provision of basic services has played a role and is a particularly prominent theme in the literature on the legitimacy of the Afghan state and in the development and state-building efforts of the international community.

To gain a better understanding of what underpinned the Afghan state's (lack of) legitimacy and how such an issue could be addressed, this chapter will look more closely at what people expected the state to do, whether people thought the state was living up to these expectations, and how this related to the perception of those who represented the state. Thereby, the chapter moves away from looking at the state as a coherent unit defined by its ruler or government and instead investigates the people's perceptions of the state in three different sectors—security, justice, and legislation.

EXECUTIVE BRANCH—THE AFGHAN NATIONAL SECURITY FORCES

When a new Afghan state was set up in 2001, its security sector was highly fractionalized, reflecting the divisions in the country after an invasion by Northern Alliance commanders and militias. The ANSF came out of the Bonn conference's decision to establish a national security force in December 2001. Initially, many commanders agreed only to withdraw—not to dissolve—militias from urban areas. The lines between militias and the state's security forces remained blurry in the following years. Commanders of the Northern Alliance enlisted their militias with the state's forces, allowing them to get their salaries paid and turning them into strongmen within the state structure (see chapter 3).

ANSF began with six thousand soldiers in 2003, but then grew considerably. By 2019, the ANSF had a strength of around three hundred thousand.[40] It was a voluntary force, in contrast to the 1980s when the Afghan security forces relied on conscription. The ANSF consisted of the Afghan National Army (ANA), the Afghan National Police (ANP), the Afghan Local Police (ALP), and Afghanistan's intelligence agency, the National Directorate of Security (NDS). The Afghan media reported daily on the ANSF's fight against the Taliban. While the Afghan government stopped releasing figures on battlefield casualties, in 2018 some officials estimated that on average thirty to forty members of the security forces got killed every day—a figure that likely increased in the following years, as media reported on more than five hundred security forces killed in some weeks. Meanwhile, the fighting also took a toll on the civilian population. The ANSF were responsible for killing and injuring thousands of civilians every year.[41]

However, Jalali suggests that most of the Afghan public supported the ANSF because they saw its soldiers as public servants committed to establishing peace in the country.[42] An Asia Foundation survey conducted in 2015 partially validates this claim, putting overall public confidence in the ANA at 80 percent, with 60 percent perceiving it to be "honest and fair."[43] The survey also indicates that people in Afghanistan often have varying perceptions of different state security actors. Confidence in the ANP and perception of it as honest and fair was considerably lower, at 70 percent and 44 percent, respectively. Only 44 percent thought that the ANP was helping to improve security.[44]

Similarly, in the interviews I conducted, many people expressed their overall disappointment with the state's failure to provide security. Most saw the ANP in a negative light, although they viewed the ANA and the NDS favorably. Perceptions of the Afghan Local Police were mixed, ranging within provinces from support to hatred. The interviews illustrate how these differences in perception evolved and why people were more supportive of the ANA and NDS than the ANP and the ALP.

The Afghan National Army

The ANA was the biggest force within the ANSF. One frequently encountered convoys of armored ANA vehicles in the countryside and their ubiquitous sand-colored Ford pick-ups in urban areas. Their active role was to fight insurgents on the battleground of rural Afghanistan, particularly at the fringes of state-controlled territories. In urban areas, their presence appeared to be a symbol of security and state authority. However, the influence of insurgents in Afghanistan increased over the years, with rural districts increasingly falling to the Taliban and frequent violent attacks in the heart of Kabul.

The defense of Afghanistan against external threats is a recurrent theme in the country's history. After all, Afghan fighters have fought three wars against the British Empire. Popular uprisings were often an element of such resistance, and Afghanistan's armies have rarely monopolized the legitimate use of force. The size of the army has fluctuated across time. For instance, it is estimated that it was about fifty thousand strong during the Second Anglo-Afghan War, before dropping to around eleven thousand due to recruitment problems in the 1920s.[45] After the end of King Amanullah Khan's reign in 1929, the Afghan army introduced conscription, and it quickly grew to seventy thousand. As Pakistan became independent in the course of the partition of British India in 1947, a fight over the Durand Line—marking the border with Afghanistan—gained momentum. The Soviet Union quickly became the biggest donor of military aid to Afghanistan after Pakistan joined the side of the United States in the Cold War. In addition to funds, aircraft, and other military equipment, the Soviet Union offered training for a large number of Afghan army officers. The army reached ninety-eight thousand in the late 1960s.

However, factionalism started to grow, reflecting the divided political order of Afghanistan in the late 1970s. During the subsequent occupation, desertion was common within the Afghan army, which was supporting the Soviet fight against the Mujahedin. And in the civil war, which followed the Soviet withdrawal, many more soldiers joined the rival Mujahedin commanders.[46] When the Taliban took control of large parts of Afghanistan, the last remnants of the army collapsed and were replaced by Taliban fighters in the south and Mujahedin militias in the north. After the Taliban appeared to be defeated, the army was reestablished by presidential decree as the Afghan National Army (ANA) at the second round of talks in Bonn in 2002:

> With the blessings of the Almighty, the Islamic Transitional State of Afghanistan (ITSA) hereby decrees that the Afghan National Army (ANA) shall be established. . . . The ANA will not exceed 70,000 soldiers. . . . The organization and staffing of the ANA and the MoD will take place on the basis of individual merit and in accordance with accepted principles of balance among different ethnic groups and establishment of trust among all the citizens of this country. . . . Military formations, armed groups, and any other military or paramilitary units that are not a part of the ANA shall be prohibited.[47]

While President Karzai made an effort to monopolize power and go beyond the 2001 Bonn Agreement, which only banned militias from Kabul, no officially published document specifies the ANA's mandate in more detail. Under U.S. guidance, new forces were recruited and trained in the following years, with the United States alone spending $62 billion on the Afghan military from 2002 to 2014.[48] According to Giustozzi, the international community wanted to weaken strongmen, centralize power, and reestablish a monopoly of force. In a bid to quell the concerns of neighboring Pakistan of the new state's friendliness to India, their vision was of a deliberately minimalist force that would have limited armor, artillery, air support, and training in modern tactics.[49]

But when the insurgency gained momentum around 2006, the strategy slowly changed. The U.S.-led training mission American Combined Security Transition Command—Afghanistan was integrated into a NATO Training Mission—Afghanistan, and the training shifted from creating a light infantry toward smaller units that could conduct counterinsurgency operations.

ANA's size of roughly 160,000 to 190,000 soldiers in 2020 far exceeded the original plans from 2002[50]—although the numbers were inflated with "ghost soldiers" that only existed on paper but were paid nonetheless.[51] In addition, the ANA was poorly equipped. While the ANA often relied on old Humvees, the unarmored Ford Rangers I observed also continued to be a major way of deploying to battle.[52] Meanwhile, the monthly basic salary of a low-ranked ANA soldier was around $165 to $200.[53]

Across the provinces, most Afghans I talked to in 2014/2015 looked favorably on the ANA, describing them as the main provider of their security. There were no noticeable differences in different geographic locations or in different social groups. This statement by shopkeeper Fahim from Char Asiab District in the rural south of Kabul Province was typical: "The ANA have established security in the entire area."[54] Farid from Herat City said, "I am very satisfied with the work of the ANA."[55] Shamsia from Mazar-e-Sharif in Balkh told me that "the ANA plays an important role for the security of our people and our country."[56] "The ANA keep us safe" was a frequent statement.[57] Even some participants who lived in Taliban-controlled areas and preferred the Taliban justice mechanisms over the state's emphasized the positive contribution of the ANA to their security.

Most interviewees stressed that the ANA was serving the people or the Afghan nation as the reason for viewing the force positively. For example, Khyber, an NGO worker from Jalalabad in Nangarhar, said that the "ANA are real servants of the

Afghan people,"[58] and shopkeeper Najibullah from Surkh Rod in Nangarhar explained that "the ANA is really serving the people."[59] Hajji Mohammad Dara Noor, a provincial councilor in Nangarhar, claimed, "The ANA is the only defender of the people and our welfare. The people support them."[60] And Ghulam Ali from Dehdadi in Balkh said, "We trust the Afghan forces because they are working for us day and night. They are our brothers."[61] Most people that I talked to saw the ANA as a group of people working in the public interest while sacrificing their own personal interests and accepting a low salary and a high risk. For instance, according to the mechanic Farhad from Mazar-e-Sharif in Balkh, "Afghan forces are doing their duty, for . . . around 12,000 Afs [about $180].[62] They are serving the country and sacrificing their lives."[63]

The perception of the ANA as a serving—rather than coercive or oppressive—authority was closely associated with observations of their behavior, especially among participants in rural areas. Most interviewees said that the ANA generally conducted themselves well. Real estate dealer Abdul Kareem from Mazar-e-Sharif told me, "Our Afghan forces are very talented and professional. They have a good behaviour with the people."[64] In answer to my question about who should be providing security, Humayon, from Enjil District in Herat Province, who was unemployed at the time of the interview, said, "The security in the district should be provided by our military because they are active and have a good way of behaving with the people here. We like them."[65]

Participants' standard of good behavior largely referred to not being corrupt. For instance, civil society activist Samar Gul from Jalalabad explained, "I like the ANA since they are free of corruption and are doing good things."[66] Torkhan from Surkh Rod District in Nangarhar was even simpler about it: "I like the ANA . . . because they are not involved in corruption."[67]

Shopkeeper Aminullah from Herat City called the ANA "clean people," meaning that they are free of corruption.[68] At the same time, coordination with communities garnered good feeling. Hajji Nazar, the head of a village in Behsod District of Nangarhar, declared, "I always support the ANA because they come to me every week for a regular meeting to discuss security provision in the district."[69] Wakil from Enjil District in Herat also emphasized that ANA officials "ask us on how we can work together to ensure security." He also said that his community was "proud to have such a brave military."[70]

The few critics did not question the ANA's intentions or approach but claimed that they were not properly equipped to do their jobs. They also commented on how other, more harmful authorities influenced the ANA. Some said that the government did not provide the ANA with the right equipment. For example, Mohammad Sharif, an employee of an NGO in Mazar-e-Sharif, told me that the "Afghan forces are working hard. But they need more support, otherwise they will be weak."[71] Another resident of Mazar-e-Sharif, student Nazir Hussain, explained, "Everybody knows that our security forces lack the right military equipment to defend themselves against the enemies and stand up against them."[72] Similarly, shopkeeper Obid from Khogyani District in Nangarhar Province said passionately, "The capacity of the army is quite low as they don't have heavy weapons. The Taliban have access to heavy weapons, which allows them to accurately hit targets at a distance of 1,800 metres while the Afghan forces can't do anything about it."[73] Malik Shukrullah from Surkh Rod in Nangarhar said bitterly, "The ANA are loyal and are the real defender of people's lives and honour. But unfortunately, the government is not serious in supporting them."[74]

Another critique, voiced less frequently, was that the Taliban and foreign intelligence agencies infiltrated the ANA to harm the country. For example, Mohammad Zubair from Enjil District in Herat claimed, "The ANA are not 'pure' and even the Taliban find their way in. We witnessed Iranian agents with fake Afghan National ID cards and passports serving in our ANA for years, and Pakistani agents do the same."[75] Similarly, school principal Hajji Muhebullah from Surkh Rod in Nangarhar said, "I trust the ANA, but unfortunately there still are a lot of spies among them."[76] Some people, especially from more rural Taliban-controlled or influenced areas, saw the ANA as a source of insecurity, viewing them as a threat to civilians. For instance, Wais from the more rural part of Beshod District in Nangarhar stated, "Here in our area only ANA officers have guns and sometime they have fights with the Taliban and other insurgent groups. The government shouldn't let ANA soldiers come here with their weapons."[77]

At the time, the widespread support for the ANA reflected a feeling that the ANA served the country and the people, and soldiers made personal sacrifices to protect the public. The public behavior of the ANA seemed to contribute to this perception in a fundamental way. Interviewees from rural areas described the ANA interacting with communities in a friendly manner, talking to the people and discussing the security situation to coordinate responses instead of trying to make money through bribery in their interactions. This ultimately resulted in a high level of trust and support. In urban areas where the interaction with the ANA was more limited, the absence of negative behavior resulted in a positive view. Public support was so extensive that it was not the ANA but the wider state that was blamed for the ANA's failures. These recognized failures are likewise consistent with the literature on the ANA, which considers the army to be poorly equipped and trained.

The Afghan National Police

The Afghan National Police (ANP) was the second important security force in the country. It was also heavily shaped by foreign countries. Germany established the first "police training center" in the country in 1935 and supported it until World War II.[78] During the war, Turkey provided assistance; after the war, Germany resumed its supporting role. In the 1960s and 1970s, during the reign of Mohammad Zahir Shah, both the Federal Republic of Germany and the German Democratic Republic provided funding and trained the Afghan police force.[79] With the Soviet invasion and the Mujahedin's fight funded by the West against the Soviet forces, civilian policing broke down in many parts of the country.[80] A new police academy was established in Kabul in 1989, still under President Najibullah.[81] However, when the Mujahedin took over Kabul and the civil war started in 1992, the academy was closed again, and there was no longer an organized police force in the country. When the Taliban took over Kabul in 1996, they replaced the legal framework for policing established in 1973 with Sharia law, interpreted by the Taliban's Department for the Promotion of Virtue and Prevention of Vice.[82]

After the military intervention in 2001, Germany was assigned to be the "lead nation" in assisting with setting up and training a new police force, which became the ANP. Germany introduced an extensive training plan for police officers based on European-style civilian policing, but they only supported the initiative with limited instructors to implement it.[83] As a consequence, the number of trained Afghan police officers remained low. To deal with the problem and to support the German officers in building a civil police force, the European Union Police Mission (EUPOL) was set up in 2007. At the same time, the

United States was training police officers as part of its Combined Security Transition Command–Afghanistan program. Without vetting, the program recruited and trained officers for five weeks by English-speaking instructors from a private security company.[84] The U.S. program was integrated into the NATO Training Mission-Afghanistan in 2009, but it followed a different curriculum from EUPOL, providing military training instead of elements of community and democratic policing.[85] Conducted on a much larger scale, many police officers went through the U.S. and NATO military-style training, while only a few, mainly higher-ranking ones, were trained in civilian policing by EUPOL.

According to official accounts, the ANP consisted of about 120,000 police officers,[86] who were expected "to perform all police-related activities in order to restore and uphold the local social order, rule of law and the protection of human and gender rights."[87] The monthly salaries of the ANP were matched to those of the ANA in 2009, meaning patrolmen more than doubled their salaries from $70 to $165. NATO acknowledged that "the ANP suffers from recruiting issues, literacy, corruption, insider threats, and a lack of effective Non-Commissioned Officers."[88] Dodge illustrates the scale of corruption, with police officers demanding bribes at every checkpoint but also having to pay up to $50,000 themselves for a promotion.[89] A 2020 *New York Times* article illustrates how the police maintained their established practice of demanding bribes from trucks at checkpoints even on highways largely controlled by the Taliban. For instance, in a case in southern Afghanistan, police tossed a box with a rope from a hilltop outpost that all truck drivers knew they had to fill with AFN 5,000 (about $65).[90]

There were various units and departments within the ANP, such as the Afghan Border Police, the traffic police, the Afghan

Anti-Crime Police, the Afghan Civil Order Police, and the fire-fighters.[91] However, the ANP's main branch was the Afghan Uniformed Police (AUP), which covered a broad range of responsibilities.[92] NATO's *ISAF Security Force Assistance Guide* from 2014 states: "The AUP provides a non-specialist law enforcement and security capability at the district, provincial and zone levels. . . . In general, the AUP performs general policing and law enforcement tasks, conducts community policing from a police sub-station, performs routine traffic duties, and performs patrols and mans static and mobile checkpoints in order to promote public safety and to deter, detect, and interdict criminals. The AUP fill the role of community police."[93]

The guide doesn't mention it, but the police also fought insurgents, much like the ANA did. The limited training in civilian policing coupled with the growing strength and expanding territorial control of the Taliban cemented the role of the police as an auxiliary counterinsurgency force. Becoming responsible for security in 2014, the Afghan government continued the U.S. approach of using the ANP more for military objectives rather than for civilian policing. Often, the ANP was the first line of defense, manning remote checkpoints and attempting to push back Taliban attacks in the countryside. Hence, the ANP suffered high casualties. For example, between 2001 and 2016, more than eighteen thousand police officers were killed in Helmand Province in southern Afghanistan, where much of the fighting with the Taliban took place.[94]

During my research, the ANP was a very visible actor in government-held territories. The patrolmen, usually dressed in light blue military-style uniforms, staffed the numerous checkpoints, guarded buildings, and patrolled the streets in government-controlled areas. Their Ford Rangers were green and had machine gun mounts that were usually empty. Despite their

visibility and naturally closer interaction with the public than
the army, the Asia Foundation's survey data suggests that people's confidence in the ANP was lower, with less than half of
the population thinking that the ANP contributed to improved
security. I spoke to both policemen and civilians about this. My
findings mirrored those of the Asia Foundation while also providing an explanation.

"THE UNIFORM AS THE TRUST OF THE PEOPLE": SELF-PERCEPTIONS OF THE AFGHAN POLICE

I met Sabawoon from Jalalabad in Nangarhar in June 2015.
He said he had become an officer with the ANP to support
himself and his family, noting, "without a good salary nobody
would be working for the police. . . . Most people join the army
or police to solve their economic problems. Few people want
to serve the country if they don't need to solve their economic
problems. Personally, I do it for the salary."[95] He enjoyed his job
for a while, but during our interview, he complained, "Today
we have very basic problems. Sometimes there is no salary or
not even food." Furthermore, he felt unsafe: "We face security
problems the most. We are targeted by warlords, Taliban, and
other insurgents." He also felt that civilians increasingly had a
low opinion of officers. "The people's perception has changed,"
he said. "They respect the police less than in the past because of
problems in the system."

General Rafeeq, a more senior police officer in Kabul, had a
longer view of the subject than Sabawoon, and he agreed that the
perception of the police had deteriorated recently.[96] He started
working as a police officer during the Soviet occupation in September 1979 and had been an officer whenever possible ever since.
I asked him if the perception of the police was different in the
past and why it might have changed. He described a condition of

mutual trust he observed when he was a child: "My uncle was the *malik* [village leader]. . . . When the government wanted to summon people, a policeman came to the village, only with the belt of his uniform and a list of people. He would stay at the malik's place for the night and then, the next morning, he would give the list to the malik. The malik then collected all people mentioned on the list and sent them away with the police officer."

By contrast, he described: "Today the police are going in large groups, with a lot of guns. They use force and loot people's houses. Today the police officers have no faith and loyalty to the country or Islam." Rafeeq emphasized the scant training his colleagues were receiving and the fact that multiple countries have taken it over:

> In the past, when people were recruited for the police, they were trained for six months. The training was about the code of conduct, culture, Islam, and so on. But it was not about fighting at all. Today the officers receive a brief training. Then they have to fight. Americans, British, Afghans—they all have their own training centres. In the past, the training was only conducted by Germany. Today it is a two-week training. Then the officers are called "experts of the battlefield." I did a much longer training and have 35 years of experience and still don't call myself "expert of the battlefield."

Rafeeq also felt that conscription and good management had made the police better in years past:

> In the past, any male turning 22 had to join the military or police for two years, regardless of where they were from. There were no tribes, we were a unity. Today the US says, we want x Pashtuns, y Uzbeks and so on in the forces, regardless of their age. That divides the people. In the past, we had more of a national identity.

Today, everyone belongs to some warlord. The ALP [Afghan Local Police] is a good example. It's not a national police force. And even in Kabul most police officers have a criminal record. For example, the police beat people selling vegetables on the street, asking them for money. Corruption hurts the weakest.

Rafeeq recalled, "When I was trained, we were told, 'The police uniform you are wearing is not yours, it is the trust of the people.' That is a huge responsibility. The price of a uniform is low, but it has a high value. You can make an [expensive] uniform for 32,000 Afs [about $480], but it is worth nothing."

"IF YOU SEE THE POLICE ON THE STREET, YOU WANT TO TURN AROUND": PUBLIC PERCEPTIONS OF THE ANP

Reflecting on the contrast between views of the ANA and the ANP that predominated among interviewees, Bahir from Jalalabad in Nangarhar Province, who was unemployed at the time, joked that only the ANA was actually able to provide security. "The ANA is doing a good job. If there was no ANA, the ANP would leave their pants behind and run to escape as fast as they can."[97] School principal Hajji Muhebullah from Surkh Rod District in Nangarhar said it more simply, "I don't trust the ANP at all."[98] People in both of these areas agreed that the ANP was failing in its job, including providing security. Ziarmal, a cab driver from Jalalabad, criticized, "Because there is more crime happening on Fridays the police don't usually patrol our area then."[99] Some of the interviewees linked the inability of the police to provide security with the involvement of warlords and strongmen. Civil society activist Jamil explained, "The security situation in Jalalabad has become worse because the police are used to guarding warlords."[100] According to him, they didn't have time to do actual policing. Instead, their commanders may even use them as coercive and extractive forces to harm civilians. Another common complaint was that the police granted the warlords impunity. Jamil explained that the police were always "silent" if an issue affected warlords or if a warlord was responsible for criminality. Gulagha, a university student, said that police were simply "not capable of facing the warlords."[101]

Beyond their inadequacy as police, interviewees highlighted other extractive behaviors. Corruption and extortion were the most frequent complaints about the police. Mirwais, a laborer from Surkh Rod District, said that he and his family were paying 300 Afs [about $4.50] weekly in protection money and were not even receiving security in exchange.[102] Similarly, Bahir complained, "The police are busy extracting money from the people. . . . They also illegally sell the fuel they get from the government for their vehicles. And in general, the police do not act impartially."[103] Gulagha said that it was very common for police to extract money at wedding receptions. In Afghanistan, people often shoot guns into the air at wedding receptions as part of the celebration. In his example, the police had rushed to the scene upon hearing gunshots in the hopes of extracting money from guests. But when they realized that an actual murder had taken place, they left quickly.[104]

Mechanic Rahmanullah from Jalalabad told me about an incident in his family: "Some of my relatives had a fight with their neighbours. The police came and imprisoned my innocent relatives. So, I went to the police and they told me 'I got this job to make money. So, if you don't give me money I am not going to release them.'"[105] Halim, a tailor from Surkh Rod, told me, "The people don't call the police because they are afraid of the headache it might cause for them later."[106] A number of interviewees accused the police of being involved in robberies and kidnappings and using their government-issued guns and cars for criminal purposes. Overall, many interviewees saw the ANP as a criminal actor that contributes to violence.

One of the most devastating stories of the dangers of interacting with police came from Mohammad Nazar from Dehdadi in Balkh Province:

> I had a sister who committed suicide when she was 37 years old. I was at work and my younger brother was at the bazaar. Suddenly, my brother-in-law called and asked me to come home. There he told me that my sister was dead. [My younger brother and I] decided to take the body to our own home village in Faryab Province. All our relatives came and we put the body in the car. Suddenly police officers showed up, asked us what had happened and said, "You two are involved in this case." They arrested us and we couldn't bury my sister. I told my uncle to do so. We were in prison for forty days and couldn't attend the funeral. They finally released me, but my brother is still in prison. They asked for a bribe of 50,000 Afs [about $750], but we don't have that much money. Now he has been in prison for many years. He is not getting any education and nobody is paying any attention to him anymore.[107]

Interviewees' negative perceptions of the ANP often became apparent when asked what they thought about the police in comparison to the army. For example, the shopkeeper Farid told me, "The ANP lacks training and is corrupt. I would suggest that the ANA should take over control of the checkpoints in the city as they are able to recognise what is right and what is wrong."[108] Masoud, who works in social media, stated, "To ensure security I would recommend that the government replace the ANP with military troops. The military is far more educated than the ANP. And the ANP doesn't have a good behaviour towards the people, compared to the army. I have experienced both of them before. Therefore, I only trust the military."[109]

Many interviewees concurred with Parwiz and Qadiri's claims and Rafeeq's comments to me that training was the key distinction between the ANP and ANA. But others argued that people think ANA is less corrupt only because they have had less interaction with the army.

Bashir, an investigation attorney working for the Ministry of Interior Affairs in Kabul and overseeing the work of the police, had a low opinion of the police, saying that most of them "do what they want. They neither follow orders, nor do they respond to the needs of people. They arrest whom they want and release them once enough money has been paid." But he felt that the army was better largely because they had less opportunity to be corrupt. "The army works in the mountains and deserts. They interact much less with the people so there are fewer problems and far fewer complaints. They simply have a better image because they interact less with the people. For instance, if you see special forces on the street you want to approach them to take a photo with them. If you see the police on the street, you want to turn around and go another way. If somebody is drunk, the police will take 500 Afs [roughly $7.50] and let him go. The army wouldn't get involved as it's not their job."[110]

Likewise, Elyas from Herat City told me, "The ANA and particularly the special forces are strongly supported by the people. The ANA is always at a distance from the people, while the police are among the people. The strongmen have involved the police in corruption. Otherwise the police would not be corrupt."[111]

But despite their dissatisfaction, most people I talked to admitted that having a police force was important, and policing was necessary. NGO employee Khyber said, "If there were no police, we wouldn't be able to stay where we are even for seconds."[112] A civil society activist placed the blame on the presence of warlords. If they were wiped out, he said, "ANA, ANP, and NDS would become strong enough to provide security." Malik Shukrullah, the head of a village in Surkh Rod, envisioned a future with greater coordination, which he said would be "the best source of security."[113]

There were some people who were positive about the ANP. While most residents of Nangarhar Province were critical, interviewees in Behsod District were overall satisfied with the work of the ANP. For instance, tribal elder and medical doctor Mohammad Jamil from Behsod told me, "All the people here are very satisfied with the ANA and the ANP."[114] NGO employee Subhanullah said, "The police are very fast here in Behsod. If an accident happens they arrive within a few minutes."[115] And Hajji Nazar, the head of a village in Behsod, pointed out, "There is a police station close to our community and they patrol our area, especially at night. If the police station . . . didn't exist, the security situation here would be as bad as in Khogyani [a district in Nangarhar Province, which was considered to be very unsafe at the time of the interview]."[116] In line with Rafeeq's comments and those of Malik Shukrullah, when asked about the reason for the success of the police, many people referred to their practice of coordinating with the communities. For example, Hajji Nazar explained, "ANP and ANA provide security and the local people help them."[117] Similarly, shopkeeper Ghaniullah stated, "We help the ANP and ANA to provide security."[118]

I encountered a similarly positive perception of the ANP in the rural district Farza in Kabul Province. Everyone I talked to in Farza felt surprisingly secure and satisfied with the work of the police and considered them to be as good as the army.[119] For instance, Rahim, a shopkeeper in the district center, said,

"We like all security forces in the area and I always supported them."[120] Abdul, an interviewee from Karim Qalla village, said, "We are convinced by all security forces because they are the main source of security."[121] According to the interviewees, there were only around fifty police officers in the entire district. Like those in Behsod District, they credited coordination between the police and the people for the efficacy of the police. Naqib, one of the community authorities, explained, "Security reinforcement is designed in a way that involves all community members. . . . Security is the result of close cooperation between the people and police, while neither of the parties would be able to achieve security alone."[122] Similarly, the principal of a local school, Hamid, said that "security is provided by both people and police."[123] Another interviewee summarized, "As there are only fifty police officers, they couldn't provide security without the support of the people."[124] This cooperation was extensive. The head of the development council explained the nature of this collaboration: "We [the community members] patrol the main road ourselves. If we see suspicious individuals or groups we chase them, report them and, if we realise that they might escape before the police arrive, arrest them ourselves."[125] In addition, the people in Farza viewed the composition of the police as a success factor, combining local expertise with external neutrality. Hamid explained to me that "the ANP consists of residents from this area as well as some outsiders. Having people from this area in the police force helps to assist the police in finding the right targets."

Therefore, despite the large-scale level of dissatisfaction with the police, a divided picture evolves. The case of Nangarhar exemplifies the reasons for the apparently widespread negative perception. Here, many people thought the ANP was not only not living up to the expectation of being a source of security but was also actively contributing to the lack of security. According to the people I talked to in Nangarhar, the police were too afraid of strongmen to protect people or to investigate crimes in which they were, at times, complicit. This resonates with the self-perception of the police officer in Kabul who told me that he feared both insurgents and strongmen. Some people accused the ANP of robberies, and almost everyone complained about their corrupt behavior aimed at making money instead of dealing with people's problems. While the influence of strongmen in Nangarhar might be particularly strong, most people I talked to in Herat and Kabul were also afraid of the police and tried to avoid any contact with them, assuming that the police might try to extract money from them. This corrupt behavior indeed appears to be the main factor undermining people's trust in the police. So, while the ANA is considered to be working in the public interest, serving the people and the country, the ANP is seen as being driven by self-interest—a corrupt actor that uses its authority only to extract money. This public perception aligned with the police officers' perception. They acknowledged the high level of corruption and explained it with reference to substantial flaws in the recruitment and training process.

Thus, there was a big gap between the perceptions of the people and the official description of the police as a "law enforcement" agency and "community police" who are supposed to provide security. The perceptions further illustrate the danger of a police force that is trained to fight insurgents, protecting only the Afghan state, while being incapable of doing what people expect the police to do—deal with criminality and provide security for the people on a day-to-day basis. In the following years, political violence and violent crime continued to skyrocket in urban areas, including in Kabul City. In 2020, the population of Kabul even considered criminality to be the main problem.[126]

Conversely, the cases of Behsod and Farza show how different the perception of the police can be if the police behave differently. Farza District appeared to be a zone with few visible security measures while having widespread perceived security. This resulted partially from a lower threat level in terms of insurgent attacks than interviewees in Kabul experienced. However, while this factor was out of the control of Farza's citizens, they also worked hard to ensure security in the district. They considered the ANP to be a source of security, serving the community. This perception seemed to be driven by a collective interest and ability to provide security for the community, which included the police. People trusted the police and felt respected, and the police officers appeared to be interested in providing security for the people in the district, which was also their home.

The Afghan Local Police

Even though the Afghan Local Police (ALP), which General Rafeeq mentioned above, was also called "police," it was a very different kind of actor from the ANP. According to its mandate, it was not supposed to police in the ordinary sense of protecting people from criminality and ensuring law and order but to provide security by fighting insurgents in rural parts of the country, like the army. In contrast to the ANA and ANP, ALP officers did not necessarily wear uniforms and were sometimes difficult to recognize. On a trip to Chimtal District in rural Balkh Province, a group of armed people on motorbikes surrounded the car I was riding in with my colleague. We first assumed they were insurgents or criminals but only realized later that they were members of the ALP and that they were trying to help and protect us by surrounding our car.

Officially, the ALP was described as an "Afghan government-led, village stability-focused program." It was set up in 2010 as part of the surge, when the United States committed to additional troops in Afghanistan to push back the Taliban. The idea of the ALP was to support the surge by "training rural Afghans to defend their communities against insurgents and other illegally armed groups."[127] In light of the limited success of the ANP's rational-legal ideals approach, U.S. designers of the program shifted their focus to cultivating traditional legitimacy. Proponents of the approach argued that community self-defense was a long-standing Afghan tradition, making the support of local opposition to the insurgency a cost-effective and legitimate way of extending the influence of the ANSF.[128]

Based on the official guidelines, community authorities were supposed to identify trustworthy people who would then get vetted by various branches of the Afghan security apparatus.[129] Afterwards, the recruits were equipped, trained, and paid a monthly salary of around 60 percent of the ANP salaries.[130] The ALP was integrated into the command structure of the Ministry of the Interior, with the district chief of police acting as a superior to the ALP district leader.[131] While initially portrayed as a temporary force of ten thousand patrolmen, its size grew and reached almost thirty thousand in 2015.[132]

According to NATO, the ALP "ensures the security of local community and paves the way for reconstruction, development, and political stability."[133] The ALP appeared to be living up to expectations in some parts of the country; it was often ALP forces that were standing at the frontlines to fight insurgents. But with a low degree of training, makeshift equipment, and limited backup from the ANA, they also suffered a high number of casualties. In 2016, the ALP directorate in the Ministry of Interior put the number of deaths, injuries leading to leaving the force, and desertions at approximately five hundred per month.[134]

In addition, as Gaston describes, irregular actors were difficult to regulate.[135] Many ALP units were de facto militias, acting in the interests of local strongmen or power brokers instead of working for communities and protecting them.[136] Several reports describe extortion, abuse, torture, and murder of civilians.[137] Sedra summarizes that the ALP provided "an umbrella of legitimacy for illegal armed groups."[138]

The two places where I conducted interviews and respondents had experience with ALP in 2014/2015 were Chimtal District in Balkh Province and Nangarhar Province. Here, a considerable number of people I talked to had regular dealings with the ALP and had strong views about them. These views varied a lot.

On the one hand, a number of people from different districts of Nangarhar expressed their satisfaction with the ALP, praising their role in providing security. For instance, Ziba from Jalalabad told me, "They secure the villages and suburbs,"[139] while Farida, a student from Surkh Rod, explained approvingly, "The ALP provides security in areas that are far from the central government." Similarly, Stoor from Behsod District commented, "The ALP has played a positive role here. They managed to remove the Taliban from the area."[140] Medical doctor and tribal elder Mohammad Jamil said, "In our area only the ALP owns guns and they don't use them if it is against the law. The have a regular patrol in our area and provide security."[141] Hajji Mohammad Dara, a member of Nangarhar's provincial council, noted that "the local police have proven to be quite effective in facing insurgents, including the Taliban. They serve the people and try to ensure that the people are secure. . . . The lives of the members of the local police are particularly endangered. . . . The Taliban's first enemy is the local police. The Taliban would prefer to kill one ALP rather than ten ANP officers. I would suggest increasing their salary."[142]

On the other hand, an even larger number of people severely criticized the ALP. Malik Shukrullah, head of a village in Surkh Rod District, said, "The local police are involved in all kind of illegal activities, therefore I am against their presence in our district."[143] Unemployed Khalid from Khogyani District said, "The local police only take care of their personal enmities and revenge."[144] Hajji Aziz from Surkh Rod perceived the ALP as an initiative to militarize the country: "The Ministry of Interior is continuously distributing licenses to carry weapons. That has increased the number of kidnappings, robberies, murders and other illegal things."[145] People impugned the officers in the ALP. For example, Khalid explained, "People hate the local police as all of them are homeless and addicts, who are involved in all kinds of illegal activities."[146] Similarly, Karimzay, a carpenter from Behsod, claimed, "I don't like the ALP because they are addicts and illiterate. And sometimes they cause trouble for people over very small issues."[147] Wais said, "I am not happy with [the ALP]. If they weren't here, we would have a peaceful life. They behave and treat people in an outrageous way."[148]

Prosecutor Abullah from Jalalabad had a more balanced perspective. "The ALP are only trained in a technical way. They don't know the constitution and they are often very young. In some areas they provide security, in other areas they are a source of insecurity. For instance, in Laghman [province] the government would have been smashed without the ALP. But then, in other parts of the country, they kill for sugar cane—for example, in Kunduz. Sometimes they deliver great results. Sometimes they are only destructive."[149]

The role of the ALP varied a great deal in different parts of the country, reflecting the low degree of monopolization of force and the consequently high level of fractionalization in the "security sector," causing respondents to have a variety of experiences with the force. The dynamics of the local political order shaped what the ALP did and how they did it—and, therefore, how people perceived the force. In some parts of the country, these dynamics incentivized the ALP to work for the public and contribute to an improved perception of security. In such places, the ALP worked like community police, just as a "local police" is expected to do, providing security for all community members—as the ANP did in Farza—or at least to protect a community against insurgents. Conversely, and as the interviews illustrate considerably more prominently, in other parts of the country, local people were frequently ignored.[150] Instead, strongmen controlled the ALP and used them for their own political agendas or to make money.

The ALP program ended in December 2020 with the plan of retiring one-third and integrating the remaining officers into the ANP and the Afghan National Army Territorial Force, a similar imitative within the ANA.[151] This resulted in widespread fear of former supposedly retired ALP forces, armed but left without a salary, becoming even more abusive and extractive. Meanwhile, the integration of the remaining former ALP members into other forces turned out to be difficult, as most of them had not been trained at all and often resisted to being posted elsewhere in the country as the ANA demanded.

The National Directorate of Security

The NDS was the major domestic and foreign intelligence agency in Afghanistan. Naturally, its work was less visible than that of the army or police. However, the NDS did not always

work in a clandestine way. People saw glimpses of it in the form
of black Ford Ranger pick-up trucks, often with camouflage
netting and menacing-looking soldierlike officers. Around the
NDS offices in Kabul's central district, Shar-e Now, and on
Great Massoud Road, one could easily spot plain-clothed officers who carried radios wrapped in scarves and reported suspicious movements.

Literature on the NDS is comparatively scarce, but the
agency can be seen as the successor to the Khedamat-e-Atlaat-
e-Dawlati (KhaD, the State Information Service). In 1978, during his brief reign with the support of the People's Democratic
Party of Afghanistan, Taraki created the Afghan Security Service. It was renamed KhaD in September 1980 after the Soviet
Union invaded Afghanistan. The Soviet Union's intelligence
agency, the KGB, heavily invested in and trained the KhaD.
Under the guidance of KGB agents trained under Stalin, the
KhaD gained a reputation for violent torture and murder.[152]
Mohammad Najibullah was director of the KhaD from 1980 to
1985 before becoming president of Afghanistan in 1987. Reportedly, prisoners saw him execute other prisoners by beating and
kicking them to death.[153] According to Andrew and Mitrokhin,
the KhaD played a key role in the Soviet War by infiltrating
Mujahedin groups and convincing them to support the Soviets
or turning them against other Mujahedin groups.

The agency had been called the National Directorate of Security since the fall of the Taliban regime in 2001. Its mandate was
defined by a presidential decree, which remained secret. The
NDS reported directly to the president and had an estimated
size of fifteen to thirty thousand in 2007 (the official numbers
remain classified). In its 2007 report, Amnesty International
describes the NDS as violent and unaccountable, detailing

reports of torture, other ill-treatment of detainees, and "a culture of impunity" for abuse.[154]

Mustafa, an NDS officer working in Kabul, agreed to an interview in the summer of 2015. He was concerned about the secrecy of our meeting and did not want to come to my house or be seen with me in public. Instead, we decided to do the interview in the car while driving around in the city. Mustafa had mixed views of the NDS. He felt that sometimes it was a force for good that improved security in the country. But he also felt that corruption and patronage were major problems. He said that within the agency, promotions were awarded based on influence and even "blackmailing others." However, he pointed out that the system of patronage within the NDS had to be seen within a bigger picture of a north-south divide along ethnic lines. As a Pashtun, he felt at a disadvantage. He said:

> Higher officials are selected on the basis of their tribal affiliation and Tajiks dominate the NDS and they try to make the Pashtun areas look bad. They ship weapons. They burn schools and make sure that the Pashtun areas don't develop. For instance, they spent USD 35,000 on organising a meeting with all the high-rank officials from Khost [a predominantly Pashtun province], inviting nominees for the cabinet and MPs. Meanwhile they paid for a suicide attack to kill all of these people. We [at the NDS] have the evidence. . . . If high-ranked Pashtun authorities are targeted they do not interfere. If, however, low-rank Tajiks get targeted, they take it very seriously.

There was no way for me to verify such accusations, but he certainly felt that the operations of the NDS were determined by clientelistic politics and that they did not treat all threats equally.

Most members of the public I talked to did not have a distinct opinion of the NDS. Those who did, however, were mainly positive. One reason for this could be fear, although the support appeared to be genuine. The most positive opinions came from people living in government-controlled parts of the country that were considered less secure, such as Nangarhar. For instance, Parwana, a teacher from Jalalabad, said that the agency "plays the best role in the country."[155] Nidah of Kama District, in close proximity to Jalalabad, offered this praise: "The NDS detects criminal and insurgent activities and by doing so brings peace."[156] And local elder Mardan from Herat stated, "Compared to the other security forces, the NDS most successfully contributes to security."[157] Another aspect of the NDS that many people emphasized was their work in the national interest, like shopkeeper Fazal from Jalalabad: "The NDS keeps the nation secure."[158] But a number of interviewees pointed out that while the NDS was doing a good job, it required more support from the government. For example, civil society activist Samar Gul said, "I am happy with the NDS as they have had great successes. But they need to be equipped better and be more active."[159] Meanwhile, most interviewees acknowledged that they had not interacted with the NDS at all.

The NDS also gained a reputation for operating in a particularly violent way, often with direct support from the United States. The so-called zero units and the Khost Protection Force (KPF) were used for night raids and other operations against suspected insurgents. Even though these units were formally part of the NDS, they were backed by the CIA, which recruited, equipped, and oversaw them.[160] The KPF, for instance, which covered southeast Afghanistan, operated out of the CIA base Camp Chapman in Khost. Human Rights Watch documented widespread abusive behavior. In particular, the KPF was found to fatally shoot civilians during search operations.[161] According to UNAMA, in 2019 "Search operations caused 360 civilian casualties (278 killed and 82 injured) with approximately three-quarters of the cases caused by NDS Special Forces, Shaheen Forces and the Khost Protection Force, all of whom are supported by international actors."[162] It was zero units that protected the outer parameters of Kabul airport during the last days of the U.S. withdrawal when the Taliban had already entered the city. In some cases, they allegedly demanded bribes to allow people through the airport gates to get on evacuations flights.[163] The United States then prioritized their evacuation, reportedly flying out seven thousand commandos and relatives.[164]

Mashal's reporting suggests that the NDS was viewed to be highly coercive and dangerous in those areas where such operations happened. Ruthless proceedings and high numbers of civilian casualties increased support for the Taliban in those predominantly rural areas where such operations took place.[165] However, elsewhere, this violent behavior was barely noticed or viewed as necessary to push back the influence of the Taliban.

It is clear why the NDS was a very polarizing force. People who had something to say about the NDS praised it in many of the same terms as they praised the ANA, describing it as a good security provider that protected and served the nation. Their statements were vague and general, likely because the NDS operated with limited visibility in the public domain and because most people had not interacted with the force much. But the positive public perceptions stand in contrast to the experiences of those who had to interact with the NDS during often violent operations, which were not discussed much by the wider public. While Mustafa's critical voice and internal view might very well be an exception based on personal grievances, it still indicates that the NDS was not only a subordinate agency but also an active player in the political dynamics of Afghanistan, which did not always act in the public's interest.

The Legitimacy of the Afghan National Security Forces

The interviews show that people had distinct views on the different branches of the ANSF, resulting in different assessments of authority and legitimacy. The ANA had actual authority—an ability to exercise social control—in state-controlled territories. While there were exceptions, most people I talked to considered this authority to be legitimate rather than coercive. Across the state-controlled areas of the country, people were supportive of the ANA not because they were forced to be but because they were convinced that the ANA was a source of security. In some cases, even people from Taliban-controlled areas, where the authority of the ANA was merely potential, shared this view. People considered the ANA to be useful, and they emphasized their loyal and committed attitude and noncorrupt behavior. The interviewees appreciated the ANA's coordination with communities, which included them in the process of security provision. Many people also mentioned that they had trust in the ANA. All of this indicates that the ANA had quite substantive legitimacy in Afghanistan based on values relating to attitude and how to behave and interact with the people in the right way. A central benchmark for the "right" attitude, reflected in behavior, appears to be the perception of serving the public, not the individual. In the case of the ANA, people widely agreed that it actually worked for the people and the country, at the cost of personal sacrifices, having what Jalali calls "a strong commitment to the mission."[166] In urban areas, where people did not interact with the ANA much, an absence of negative behavior supported this perception. But even though most people perceived the ANA positively, that was not the case for everyone. Critics complained that foreign agents and interests compromised the ANA's dedication to serving the public, and some others in rural areas considered the ANA to be threatening civilian lives.

The ANP was perceived very differently. In Nangarhar and across the other provinces I looked at, most people had strikingly negative views on the ANP, living up to what Perito describes as the "weak link" in the security sector due to the coercive nature of its authority.[167] The overall public disapproval of the police did not appear to be based on a general rejection of the concept of policing, as people displayed an expectation that the police would provide security for them. The failure of the police to achieve security in Afghanistan only partly explains their negative perception. Far more than about the actual "output" of the ANP as a security force, people referenced the processes of how they were policed and the way the police delivered this output and behaved on a day-to-day basis when interacting with the people. The ANP were particularly close to the people, interacting a lot with the public in daily life, and it was through this interaction that the people formed their views of the police. But the ANP did not live up to the expectations of the people in terms of what these interactions should look like. People complained about the high level of corruption of the police officers, who would try anything to extract money from the people when given a chance to do so. The behavior resulted in the overall perception of the police as a source of insecurity instead of being a security provider. The police officers I talked to were similarly dissatisfied, not claiming legitimacy but admitting that the motive for becoming a police officer was simply about making money, not serving the public, and complaining that officers were not properly trained to interact with people. For instance, Ahmad, an officer, was well aware that people didn't consider him to be a legitimate authority.

The cases of the districts Behsod and Farza are intriguing exceptions. Here, people were supportive of the police, as they felt they were heard and included in the process of security provision. This illustrates how important it is for the legitimacy of the police to focus on interactions with civilians, creating a perception of working in their interest, not against it. According to General Rafeeq, Afghan police officers had been trained to do this in the past.

The difference in people's perceptions of the ANA and the ANP also reflects their different functions. As the army's duty was to deal with threats from outside and to fight insurgents, and as the soldiers often lived in bases away from the urban centers, the army was at a greater distance from the people and, thus, had few opportunities to extract money from them. Conversely, while helping out on the frontlines, the police were also responsible for law and order internally, and they directly intervened in the day-to-day life of the people. For instance, they would search people and impose fines, providing ample opportunities to ask for bribes. And, with less personal interaction between the people and the army, at least in the more populated areas, the perception of the army was probably not always based on personal experiences but influenced by second-hand information and media reporting, which tended to praise the role of the army.

The behavior of ANA soldiers in state-controlled territories, including urban centers like Kabul, likely also garnered support. Being armed, they could abuse the public and top up their salaries through bribes, but they did not do so very much, likely increasing the public's appreciation of them. Hence, having the ability to be coercive but not being abusive was, indeed, a driving factor of the army's legitimacy. In addition, levels of violence continued to be high across the country during my research, and people perceived the army as an actor that coordinated its approach and worked with communities to ensure security. Finally, the positive perceptions surrounding the army were even prominent in the parts of the country that were not fully state-controlled, and some people who preferred the Taliban for public services, such as justice, nonetheless considered the army to be a source of security. Therefore, while media reporting and the kinds of duties certainly matter, it can be concluded that there was an actual difference in the behaviors of the police and the army and the kinds of interactions they had with the public. This difference in behavior explains why the two actors were perceived so differently. The self-perception of the interviewed police officers and the case of Farza, where people perceived the police positively, further supports this understanding. In Farza, the police constructed legitimacy by working with civilians to increase security. In other words, close contact between people and the police can be an opportunity to create a positive perception, but it also has hazards.[168]

Several factors could explain the differences of the ANA and the ANP. Corruption seemed to be systemic in the police force. Many officers had to pay a monthly fee to their superiors therefore needed to make money through bribes. But the recruitment process also appears to be critical. In a vicious cycle, the police attracted people who reinforced the public's perception that the police hired people who couldn't find any other jobs and were often already marginalized from society. Due to failures in the selection process, many even had criminal backgrounds. Making money, also through bribes, appeared to be the main incentive for people to join the police. This further undermined the image of the police and made it less attractive to work there. The short training of police officers focused on handling weapons was also problematic and did not counteract the (perceived) flaws of the recruitment process. It prepared them to be an auxiliary counterinsurgency force rather than a police force that knew how to prevent and investigate crime or interact with people in a courteous and principled manner. Therefore, police officers might have been cheap fighters, but they were not trained to police. Nonetheless, there were exceptions. In several cases, police forces made headline news in Afghanistan by stopping suicide attacks and serving the public at the cost of their own lives—such as an attack on Al-Zahra Mosque in Kabul in June 2017.

Views on the Afghan Local Police were significantly more varied than those of the ANA and the ANP, which were almost uniformly good and bad, respectively. But, as with the ANA and the ANP, the day-to-day behavior of the ALP, and the attitude it reflected, appears to play a key role in explaining these differences. In some parts of the country, people considered the ALP to be useful, and they praised its members for risking their lives to protect the people. Hence, the ALP possessed a high degree of legitimacy, even in a substantive way. But, in other parts of the country, people perceived the ALP in an even worse light than the ANP—as drug addicts and criminals who threatened people and behaved in a predatory way. People thought that ALP members only cared about their personal interests, and they viewed it as an authority that relied on coercion. Thus, the ALP, in actuality, was the weakest link of the security sector. The dynamics and the differences of the local political orders and the use of the ALP by strongmen for their personal agendas play a major role in explaining why ALP units behaved so differently, resulting in very different perceptions depending on which community one approached. But it certainly shows that what is supposedly "traditional" is not necessarily legitimate in the eyes of the population.

In contrast to the other branches of the ANSF, people had vague views regarding the secretive NDS. Reporting suggests that those who had to interact with the NDS were treated in a rather coercive way, heavily undermining the organization's legitimacy in the eyes of this specific group of people with direct experience. Even the NDS officer I interviewed was suspicious of his own agency and its political role. However, most people in the general public who voiced an opinion on the agency were very positive about it, perceiving it to be serving and protecting the country, despite a lack of personal experience. People were particularly vocal about the NDS in areas that were more insecure and where the agency was perhaps more visible. This illustrates that security actors can construct a degree of even substantive legitimacy without directly interacting with people as long as harmful behavior is considered to be necessary to deal with a threat, or, as was more prevalent, it remained invisible and did not become part of the public discourse.

Looking at the Afghan state through the lens of security demonstrates that people expect the state to provide security in a way that is beneficial for the public—not for individuals within the security sector. People were clearly dissatisfied with some of the state actors in the security sector, particularly the police because of their extractive and corrupt behavior, and considered them to be coercive rather than legitimate. However, the expectation that the state would provide security also shows that there is a substantive belief in the *idea of state authority*, not because of its constitution or de jure institutions, but on a more general and abstract level as a *concept*. More specifically, the belief in the idea of policing can even be read as a belief in state bureaucracy and rational-legal structures.

The importance of the idea of the state as a concept—in contrast to its history and practices—and as a legitimate authority reflects findings from other conflict zones, such as Hoffmann and Vlassenroot's work on the Democratic Republic of the Congo.[169] In the Afghan context, the state, simply because it was the state and not an insurgency, already had favorable starting conditions for constructing legitimacy. In practice, however, agents of the state often did not live up to people's expectations of how security needed to be provided on a day-to-day basis, failing to match their idea of state authority and ultimately undermining its legitimacy.

THE JUDICIAL BRANCH

In keeping with the idea of looking at the Afghan state through different lenses, it is also worth exploring perceptions of the judicial branch of the state that was formally responsible for conflict resolution. The courts were where people experienced the laws and legislation of the Afghan state. But throughout Afghanistan's recent history, there have been a plethora of actors offering conflict resolution based on different codes of laws, giving rise to a pluralist body of jurisprudence.

Conflict resolution did not only occur in the state's courts. The ability of the state to impose its code of law and exercise symbolic violence remained limited in many rural parts of Afghanistan, and different actors competed in the wider political order, offering conflict resolution on the basis of different codes of law. Instead of going to the state's courts, some people resolved conflicts within their extended families or took cases to community or religious authorities and other locally influential individuals who could also be formally part of the state system, such as district governors. In addition, the courts of the Taliban had increasingly gained influence across Afghanistan in the years leading up to 2021 (chapter 4). Different actors applied different codes of law or interpreted the same law in different ways, resulting in a high degree of legal pluralism. Religious authorities may have applied the Islamic Sharia law. Community authorities may have used Sharia law or applied "traditional" customary law (chapter 5). However, understanding of the Sharia and traditions also varied spatially. Hence, there was also a parallel existence and competition among different codes of law.

Even the central state applied different ideologies across time. In the late nineteenth century, the state used only Islamic law, but over time they incorporated more and more new secular laws.[170] While the state's laws were supposed to be in line with Islamic principles, the state asked the judges to prioritize its laws over religious ones if the laws were in conflict.[171] King Amanullah instituted many secular laws in his attempts to modernize the country. The constitution developed under his authority still referred to Islam as the state religion, but it introduced the protection of other religions. He promoted the rights of women and abolished child marriage, which incited objections from the tribal elite and religious leaders.[172] His successor, accommodating both progressive and religious interest groups, introduced separate secular law and Sharia faculties at Kabul University. Graduates in Sharia law were hired for general fields as judges, while graduates from the secular law faculty were hired in more specialized commercial and administrative courts.[173] Afghanistan's last king, Zahir Shah, again increased the role of secular laws. While Islam remained the state religion, the new constitution stated that Sharia law only applied in cases that secular law did not address.[174] Regardless of the changing constitutions, however, the court system at that time was widely considered to be slow and corrupt.[175]

The communist PDPA went a step further, eradicating religious and traditional vocabulary from the constitution, banning women from wearing veils, and enhancing women's rights through laws on marriage.[176] "Popular committees" were introduced to resolve legal disputes, but the intelligence agency KhAD was often the only de facto judicial power, arresting, detaining, and executing people.[177] Barfield argues that governments that attempted rapid change, such as that of King Amanullah and the PDPA, heavily undermined their legitimacy, as people felt they were abandoning Afghan values.[178] The Taliban then introduced Sharia law as the state's only valid code of law.[179] However, while the Taliban's legal system was framed in terms of Islam, its interpretation was also heavily influenced by rural customs. For example, while Sharia courts had sole authority to sentence a murderer to death, the executions often reflected the influence of tradition in that they would give the victim's family the opportunity to shoot the prisoner personally.[180]

In 2004, Afghanistan adopted a new constitution, defining the basic values and setting the framework for future laws and their interpretations. Islam was defined as a central pillar of the jurisprudence: "No law shall contravene the tenets and provisions of the holy religion of Islam in Afghanistan."[181] In addition, the idea of a progressive and democratic state was anchored in the constitution: "The state shall be obligated to create a prosperous and progressive society based on social justice, preservation of human dignity, protection of human rights, realization of democracy, attainment of national unity as well as equality between all peoples and tribes and balance development of all areas of the country."[182]

The constitution further defined the structure of the court system: a supreme court, courts of appeal on the provincial level, and primary courts on the district level. There were 364 district courts and forty-five city courts in 2010.[183] However, at that time, sixty-nine were not operational due to security reasons, indicating that nonstate authorities oversaw conflict resolution in these areas.[184] By 2021, many more district courts had been closed. For example, when conducting research in Faryab Province in 2019, most district courts in the province had been shifted to the provincial capital, Maimana, for security reasons. But even where the courts were operational, challenges remained. Competition was ongoing among secular, religious, and customary laws and their interpretations. Barfield documents that even though the Afghan constitution and the state laws were aligned with international standards, interpretations of Sharia law and customary law, which sometimes also conflicted with each other, often superseded written laws at the local level, especially in rural contexts.[185]

But what did the people think about the justice sector? Were they dissatisfied with the state's court system because the judges applied a code of law they did not agree with? The Asia Foundation's perception data indicate that few people went to the formal courts to settle disputes.[186] Meanwhile, many observers saw the judicial system as a crucial part of establishing the legitimacy of the Afghan state.[187]

My own investigation of the perceived legitimacy of the courts began with interviews of an investigation attorney at the MoI in Kabul and a prosecutor in Nangarhar.[188] Bashir, the investigation attorney, described his job in 2015 as "the investigation, interrogation and provision, of files for the courts in cases that are related to officers mandated by the Ministry of Interior and are related to their job, such as corruption, fraud, bribery, murder, taking advantage of weapons, and civilian complaints about the police."[189] Asked about the biggest challenge, he said:

> It is the corruption of the authorities. It is very organised now. It's a bigger problem than the Taliban or Daesh [IS-K]. . . . The problem of corruption has become worse since 2001. In 2001, nobody in the villages knew what a bribe was. Now it is very common. All ministers are foreign [meaning that they hold a second passport]. They don't love the country and are only here to extract money. Two big steps need to be taken. First of all, one has to take away the privileges of the so-called "jihadists" [meaning Mujahedin commanders]. Secondly, we need to find the right and most qualified people for each job. For instance, the aviation ministry was given to somebody with a background in agriculture, because he is a "jihadist." We need to start at the top. It's organised crime, . . . which trickles down and destroys the country. . . . Ninety-five per cent of the positions at the MoI are paid for. There are different rates depending on the rank.

Wondering how he, as a government employee, perceived the justice system of the Taliban, I asked him if he thought that they were less corrupt than the government. Bashir replied, "They are corrupt in their own way. Actually, the Taliban and the government are very similar. As soon as someone becomes a minister in the government they buy a house, have three or four women, and so on. All for their personal benefit! It's the same with the Taliban. They take hostages and collect *ushr* [tithe on agricultural produce] and use the money for their personal benefits."

In a second interview with a member of the de jure state's judicial system, I talked to Abdullah, a prosecutor at the prosecution department in Jalalabad.[190] Abdullah investigated robbery cases. According to him, insecurity was the most serious existential problem in Nangarhar and had been growing steadily, particularly over the past few years. Asked about his perception of how the public perceives prosecutors like him, he responded, "The people have a very negative view of prosecutors. A person might be sent to jail for ten years due to the work of the prosecutor. The family and tribe will think that it was corrupt but have no evidence. Or a person might be sentenced to death. Then you can give a bit of money to the prosecutor. So, some people think that all prosecutors are corrupt. They do not perceive prosecutors to be doing law enforcement. That's a massive problem. Many prosecutors actually ask for money directly in the first stage of the investigation." He described himself as unusual because he is not corrupt because "of my financial circumstances," indicating that he was not financially dependent on the job. He felt that his job paid a comfortable salary, "but people have high standards," and that they try to obtain via taking bribes and other extractive processes.

Neither man viewed the sector where they worked as imbued with much legitimacy. According to their reports, the systemic corruption in the justice sector was a bigger threat to the state than the Taliban.

Public Perceptions in Rural Afghanistan

While most people I talked to did not view the Afghan state as one system, they did not distinguish much between the entities or actors of the judicial system—such as courts of different kinds and varying instances—but viewed it as a whole. They often referred to any kind of conflict resolution bodies of the state as "the government." Also, the public perceptions of the state's judiciary system were similar across the four provinces where I interviewed people. However, there were some differences between the rural parts of the provinces and their urban centers. These differences were particularly evident in Nangarhar and Herat provinces, in the far east near Pakistan, and in the far west at Afghanistan's border with Iran.

In the rural parts of the provinces, the state's conflict resolution mechanisms played a subordinate role (something I address in more detail in chapter 5). Courts were often remote and difficult to access. Most people I talked to in 2014/2015 told me they would choose informal mechanisms rather than go to the official courts. For example, property dealer Hajji Kamran from Enjil District in Herat Province explained, "The people first take their cases to elders or shuras [councils]. Only if they can't solve the case, do we take the case to the government."[191] Ghulam, a community authority from Kushk Robat Sanghi in Herat Province said, "To solve conflicts, we first take the case to the leaders of our cluster of associated villages. If they can't solve the conflict, we take the case to the religious leaders. And if they can't solve the case, we take it to the government."[192] This phenomenon was not restricted to Herat Province but was equally prominent across rural Afghanistan. For example, in Surkh Rod District, in rural Nangarhar, school principal Hajji Muhebullah also said that people in his community only take a conflict to the formal government justice system if the local councils can't settle it.[193] An exception to this was in the case of large-scale conflicts and bigger crimes. Hajji Kamran from Enjil in Herat explained, "In all cases we first refer to a shura. Unless it's a case of killing or death. Then we observe the rules of the government's formal system."[194] I observed a similar pattern in rural Nangarhar. Here, Nader, a teacher in Surkh Rod District explained, "Micro cases are solved by the local councils while macro ones are taken to the office of the district governor."[195]

The interviewees across the provinces viewed corruption in the formal system as the main reason for their preference for informal conflict resolution mechanisms. Particularly in Nangarhar Province, this complaint came up frequently. For example, manual laborer Mohammad Nasim from Surkh Rod complained, "The first option [for conflict resolution] is always local councils. And the second option is the government. But the government is very corrupt and all of its employees are involved in corruption."[196] Driver Abdul Wahab from Behsod told me, "The formal justice mechanisms in our province that work according to the law are more corrupt than the traditional mechanisms."[197] A number of people in Herat Province also made this point. For instance, Ghulam, a village leader from Kushk Robat Sanghi, summarized his view: "People trust the informal system because the community leaders are closer to the people than the government and the community leaders are less corrupt than the government."[198]

Nonetheless, there also were more balanced perspectives, acknowledging corruption in all systems. Often, community authorities required both conflict parties to pay a deposit that is only returned to them if the conflict does not reignite in a set amount of time, a practice called *Machalgha*. A number of interviewees, however, complained that the full amount was often not returned. Referencing this practice, Karimzay, a medical doctor in Behsod District, complained, "In the traditional mechanisms of conflict resolution there are other forms of corruption. The bribes have different names, such as *Machalgha* and *Shirini* [sweets]."[199] Other respondents in Herat Province made similar remarks. For instance, Jalil Ahmad, a high school student from Enjil District, explained, "Both the formal and the informal system are corrupt. Therefore, in either system the results are often not fair."[200] At the same time, interviewees thought that the informal mechanisms still offered certain advantages, like being a bit less corrupt or faster. Karimzay concluded, "The formal justice mechanisms are usually even more corrupt than the informal mechanisms."[201] A carpenter named Burhanuddin, also from Behsod, argued, "I think that both the formal and the informal conflict resolution mechanisms are corrupt, . . . but the informal one is at least fast."[202] Mahmood, a doctor from Kushk Robat Sanghi in Heart, explained, "Poor people don't even have enough money to travel to the centre of the province for conflict resolution. So, they prefer the local councils."[203] Hajji Nazar, the head of a village in Behsod District, said that, as a consequence, the role of informal conflict resolution has been increasing in his village: "Before 2001, we were not involved in solving people's conflicts. But now, day by day, our role in conflict resolution is growing as people don't take their cases to the formal justice system because of the high level of corruption."[204]

Due to this perceived high level of corruption in the formal conflict resolution system, some of the people I talked to in Nangarhar acknowledged advantages of the Taliban's justice system. For example, Nidah, from Kama District, who worked at the Directorate of Women's Affairs, told me in 2015, "Today's system is less transparent than during the time of the Taliban."[205] Wais from Behsod District told me, "If the local councils can't solve a conflict, we would never go to the government because they are so corrupt. We would go to the Taliban in the area instead." And, even a civil society activist argued, "The Taliban's conflict resolution mechanism is less corrupt and solves conflicts much faster than the government's."[206] Indeed, chapter 4 shows how the Taliban successfully used their justice system to construct legitimacy.

Clearly, most respondents did not rely on the state to settle disputes. People only used the state system once they had tried all other available options or if they couldn't avoid it—for instance, in the case of killings or if the issue was related to the state, like the public provision of healthcare. The reasons for the choice of alternative mechanisms were the corrupt procedures in the state's court system and the resulting costs, its slow pace, and the unpredictability of the outcome. Even though some people acknowledged that the alternative actors providing conflict resolution were also corrupt, they were considered to be either less corrupt or at least faster than the state. From 2015 onward, this view intensified further, and a growing number of people used Taliban courts instead of the formal justice system.

Nonetheless, people considered the state responsible for conflict resolution. For example, mechanic Nematullah from Enjil said, "The government should solve conflicts. It's their responsibility."[207] Aziullah, a shopkeeper also from Enjil, argued, "In the future the government needs to solve conflicts and disputes of the people."[208] The perceptions in Nangarhar were phrased in a similar way. Torkhan from Surkh Rod told me, "It is definitely the government, which—together with the courts—has to solve conflicts."[209] And Stoor, who was unemployed at the time of the interview, summarized: "The government should help us to solve conflicts in the future."[210] Thus, the prominent role of community authorities in conflict resolution related to a sense that the state was not playing this role effectively, not a preference for traditional mechanisms.

Public Perceptions in Urban Afghanistan

In contrast to the rural areas, in the urban centers of Herat and Nangarhar provinces, more people told me that they used the official judicial system. In Herat City, the second-largest city of the country, which has been shaped by Persian culture and is famous for the large variety of grapes, Khalid, an oil seller, said that he goes "directly to the government's courts" if he has a conflict.[211] Shahnawas from Jalalabad, the urban center of the east that has been more influenced by Pashtun culture and produces delicious pomegranates, described it as a normal thing for "some people [to] solve their conflicts through the formal justice system, such as the police and the courts."[212] A shopkeeper from Herat City, Elyas, explained his case to me: "I am currently involved in a conflict with the head of [an organization] in Herat province. I took the case to the government's office, but so far, the case has remained unsolved. Now I am waiting for reforms in the formal system. Then I will take my case there again and hope that it finally gets solved."[213] The largest group who saw the court system in a positive light lived in Herat City.

Others shared the frustration of rural Afghans. Fridon, who runs a juice shop in Jalalabad, explained: "We are poor people and don't have access to the high-level conflict resolution bodies. If we want to take a case there, we have to bribe many people. It's very corrupt; they hire all of their relatives."[214] Also, civil society activist Jamil protested that bribes are common, "The formal government system is very corrupt. They wouldn't miss a single chance to get bribed from all involved parties."[215] Unemployed former ISAF employee Bahir told me that "most conflicts in the formal government system are only solved after paying a great number of bribes to the attorney general's office and to the court."[216] Abdul Wahab, a teacher from Herat City, complained, "If I take a case to the government, it doesn't matter if I am guilty. One always has to pay."[217] And civil society activist Mujibullah from Herat told me: "I had never been involved in any conflicts. But recently I was called to the attorney general's office for the first time in my life because somebody identified me on some photo. The prosecutor fortunately was a good person. I told him: 'Please don't make me familiar with the attorney general's office culture.' Fortunately, he accepted and didn't bother me further."[218]

In some cases, it was clear that people in cities used the courts because they had fewer alternative options for conflict resolution. In Jalalabad, NGO employee Khyber said, "Within villages most conflicts are being solved by local councils and influential people, while within cities almost all conflicts are taken to and solved in the formal justice system."[219]

On the other hand, some urban dwellers could take their cases to informal conflict resolution bodies. For instance, manual laborer Zakerullah in Jalalabad said, "For conflict resolution we first speak to our tribal elders. If they can't solve our problem we take the case to the formal conflict resolution bodies in the areas, like the district government, the police or the attorney general's office."[220] Similarly, Rahmanullah argued, "If we have a conflict we take the case to the tribal elders or the mullah of the mosque. Only if they are unable to help we approach the formal conflict resolution bodies."[221] Even more interviewees appeared to have access to community authorities in Herat City (an entity I describe further in chapter 5). For instance, Shoaib from Herat City, who was unemployed at the time of the interview, explained, "If there is a conflict, we usually take it to our community leaders. They solve conflicts in a fair manner. And if they can't solve it, we take the case to the government court."[222]

In Herat City, the existence of informal conflict resolution mechanisms appeared to be a fairly recent phenomenon, which evolved in response to corruption in the court system. Parwiz, a cook, explained, "Ten years ago there weren't any shuras in the city. People took their cases to the district administration and the governmental offices. Now most people take their cases to local shuras."[223] However, while some demanded the extension of the influence of the councils, many people considered the state responsible for providing better conflict resolution. For example, university student Khair from Jalalabad demanded, "The government should get more involved in conflict resolution again. It would be much more effective."[224] Naimullah from Herat City proposed the following: "In the future the government needs to make an effort to solve the people's conflict instead of relying on local councils, since the government has the legitimacy of the people and has the authority to jail people or release them."[225]

People tended to make use of alternative conflict resolution options if they had the option, complaining about the high level of corruption in the courts and its slow procedures. In urban areas, more people used the courts because there were fewer alternative options. But even here, those people who did have access to alternative conflict resolution mechanisms tended to make use of them. In response to the problem of limited access, even newer informal conflict resolution mechanisms evolved. The juridical branch of the state was far from living up to the role the constitution describes as the only provider of conflict resolution. There was not only a competition of different bodies of laws but also a competition—or coexistence—of different authorities applying different codes of laws. Rather than fulfilling its mandate to ensure "equality between all people," the judiciary was considered to be the most corrupt actor in the conflict resolution sector. It is clear, however, that, as with the police, people would have preferred to have a functioning, state-sanctioned judiciary that meets their needs instead of having to rely on alternatives.

People's Demands for Justice

Looking at the state through the lens of conflict resolution reveals a deeply engrained frustration. As with the security sector, most people had personal experiences with the state's courts or had second-hand information from friends and family members. The overall perception resulting from such experiences is one of corruption. Almost all members of the public I talked to complained about the bribes they had to pay in the state's judicial system. This view resonates with the self-perception of people working within the courts who also considered corruption in the judiciary to be systemic and, in the case of Bashir, even compared it to organized crime.

In a way, not much had changed in the Afghan court system since the time of King Zahir Shah described by Barfield: it was slow and corrupt.[226] In rural areas, in addition to being perceived to be slower and more corrupt, the state's judicial system was also remote and more difficult to access than other authorities. However, people had access to and therefore used alternative conflict resolution mechanisms, indicating an overall low degree of legitimacy of the state's system. In urban areas, people had fewer options and, therefore, often had to use the state system. But the fact that their choice rested solely on a lack of alternatives again indicates a low level of legitimacy. People in cities were equally dissatisfied with the state because of the high degree of perceived corruption. As a consequence, alternative mechanisms also evolved in the cities.

The interviews indicate that the people's assessments of which authority to choose for conflict resolution rested on instrumental factors, such as accessibility, speed, and, more substantively, the perceived degree of corruption and the fairness of procedure—not, for instance, on which authority "traditionally" solved conflicts in the community. The perceived level of corruption indeed appeared to be the substantive cornerstone of the assessment of authorities in the judicial sector. A low level or absence of corruption was not only important to ensure a perception of fairness, based on equal treatment of everyone, but it also made the process more predictable. It undermines other potentially legitimizing factors, such as the tradition of a conflict resolution body or the ideology underpinning the code of law that is applied. Hence, the debate as to which code of law people want and consider to be legitimate, whether it is traditional, Islamic, or secular law, appears to be a secondary problem. It is far more important to people that any law is applied in a straightforward and noncorrupt way, making the process predictable and fair. But the state's judicial system was perceived to be neither fast, predictable, nor fair, and people avoided it wherever possible. Hence, it lacked both instrumental as well as substantive legitimacy.

It is worth noting, however, that, as in the context of security, many people considered the state responsible for conflict resolution. This again suggests that people had not given up on the state entirely and further emphasizes the importance and legitimacy of the idea of the state. People did not choose alternative conflict resolution mechanisms because they considered them to be more traditional or because they preferred Islamic law but simply because the alternatives appeared to be less corrupt or at least faster than the state. Many would have actually preferred the state's judicial system if the procedures were fairer, easier to access, or faster.

THE LEGISLATIVE BRANCH

An impressive new Afghan Parliament building constructed with Indian aid money was inaugurated in 2015, right next to Darul Aman Palace on the outskirts of Kabul. But, while the new Parliament was meant to be a symbol of a democratic

Afghanistan, the legislature felt remote for most people in the country.

As Afghanistan was governed by monarchs for most of its recent history, there was no clear separation of power and no independent legislative branch. Even though the kings had advisors and a bureaucracy to implement their decisions, it was the king who had the final say on laws. While Amanullah Khan used loya jirgas to ratify his laws in the early twentieth century, jirgas did not play a central role in law making. This changed when Mohammad Zahir Shah came into power and advocated for modernization. His constitution separated the executive, legislative, and judicial authorities. It was adopted in 1964 after being modified and approved by a loya jirga.[227] The Parliament consisted of two houses: the Wolesi Jirga (House of the People) and the Meshrano Jirga (House of the Elders).[228] The members of the House of the People were elected, while the members of the House of the Elders were appointed by the king or elected by the provincial councils.[229] Members of Parliament had the power to draft laws, and laws had to be passed by both houses and signed by the king to take effect.[230]

The new constitution, however, only lasted for a few years. In 1973, the monarchy was overthrown in a military coup and the two houses of Parliament were replaced by one assembly—the Melli Jirga—in 1977. After the Saur Revolution in 1978, a Soviet model was adopted, with a Revolutionary Council taking over the legislature power.[231] When President Najibullah felt in danger of losing power when the Soviet Union announced that it would withdraw its troops from Afghanistan, he drafted a new constitution in 1987 and adjusted it further in 1990. A National Assembly, consisting of the House of Representatives and the Senate, became the "highest legislative organ."[232] But when the Taliban came into power after the civil war, Parliament was abolished again, and final decisions were made by an Inner Shura, which was based in Kandahar and consisted of six members under the leadership of Mullah Omar.[233]

Afghanistan's post-2001 constitution, approved once again by a loya jirga, showed remarkable similarities to the constitutions of 1964, 1987, and 1990. The Afghan Parliament was called the National Assembly again, once more consisting of two houses: the House of the People and the House of the Elders. The House of the Elders consisted of elected representatives of the provincial and district councils as well as individuals appointed by the president.[234] Half the appointed members of the House of the Elders had to be women.[235] The members of the House of the People were elected by the people for five years, including at least two women from each province.[236] The National Assembly had to ratify laws and could modify them.[237] Like the government, members of the National Assembly could also make proposals for drafting new laws.[238] The House of the People had additional powers and could, for instance, decide on the state budget.[239]

Even though there were strong political parties in Afghanistan, such as Hezb-e Islami (chapter 3), they did not play much of a formal role in parliamentary elections between 2001 and 2021. Candidates and members of Parliament were not required to be members of a political party, and in the 2005 elections, party affiliations were not even mentioned on the ballot paper.[240] Members of Parliament were elected on the basis of a single, nontransferable vote (SNTV) system to exclude political parties, both as a means of quenching opposition to the new government and because political parties were often associated with violence.[241]

Research on the parliamentary elections in 2010 and the presidential elections in 2014 indicates that they, by and large, failed to construct legitimate state authority. Dodge illustrates how widespread voter fraud undermined the legitimacy of the electoral process.[242] Sharan and Bose describe how elections manifested power networks instead of enhancing the legitimacy of the state. Along similar lines,[243] Schmeidl argues that elections actually contributed to a growing gap between citizens and elites.[244] Only 43 percent of the people had confidence in their member of Parliament (MP) in 2015,[245] a rate that dropped further to 35 percent in 2016.[246] An additional challenge for elections in Afghanistan, and their ability to construct legitimate results, was the security situation. As the Taliban were consistently expanding their territorial control in Afghanistan, and as armed conflict continued in many other parts of the country, holding elections became increasingly difficult, and participation was limited to people from more urban state-controlled areas.

Following the 2010 elections, the Afghan constitution would have required the next parliamentary elections to be held in 2015. However, after turbulent presidential elections in 2014, President Ghani and then CEO Abdallah Abdullah decided to set up an Electoral Reform Commission (ERC) to recommend changes to the election process. When the ERC finally announced its suggestions in August 2015—such as strengthening political parties and improving the voter identification system—some accused them of being Abdullah's puppets.[247] Meanwhile, the people elected in 2010 retained their seats in Parliament. However, the attendance in the lower house was so low that in two-thirds of all sessions there were not enough lawmakers present to hold a vote on new laws.[248] A number of lawmakers were suspended after not attending twenty or more parliamentary sessions in a row.[249]

Finally, elections were held in late 2018, and the new House of the People was inaugurated in April 2019; however, the legitimacy crisis continued. Out of the approximately 15 million eligible voters in Afghanistan, only 8.9 million registered to vote, and less than 3.5 million (about 23 percent) cast their vote.[250] Due to the security situation, few members of Afghanistan's rural population were able to participate in the elections and lacked representation in Parliament. Furthermore, Johnson and Barnhart point out that the SNTV electoral system resulted in a majority of people voting for losing candidates.[251] For instance, in Kabul Province, twenty-six of thirty-three elected House of the People members got less than 1 percent of the vote, and only 2.5 percent of the voters voted for the candidate who ultimately won. Johnson and Barnhart conclude that the electoral system left "Afghanistan with a parliament that is only tenuously tied to its electorate."[252]

SELF-PERCEPTIONS OF MPS

To gain an understanding of how MPs viewed their legitimacy in such a context, I interviewed several lawmakers representing Kabul, Nangarhar, and Herat in the House of People in 2015. I met Kobra Mustafawi, who represented Kabul Province, first. At her humble but crowded office in the outskirts of Kabul, she participated in a long interview of several hours. When I entered, the main room on the ground floor was packed with petitioners, and she appeared to be busy dealing with them. When the crowd began to thin, we went upstairs to a more informal room on the top floor of the building. She told me about her motivation, the challenges she had been facing, and why she thought people voted for her. In response to my initial question on her life story and how and why she became a member of the Afghan Parliament, she told me:

> My father was killed during the Russian invasion, and I was his oldest daughter. My father didn't have any sons. My mother

always wished I was a boy and could fight against enemies. My father was well educated, an established academic and a political figure and his seat couldn't be left empty. His weapon was his pen and I didn't want it to be put down. . . . As a girl, I couldn't hold a weapon and fight against the Russians. So, I picked up the pen and studied. I migrated to Iran, where I had a harsh daily life. But I continued my education. My husband is from Maidan Wardak province, where women are not accepted at all in society. But I fought and was finally nominated for the elections. My husband was always criticised by the people from his province for letting me run in the election and for not doing so himself. I proved that I could do it, and was elected because I was serving my village, my people and district. I always wanted to serve the entire nation, without considering colour and ethnic differences. I started by printing a number of photos and business cards. I announced my strategy and plans. People trusted me and voted for me because they noticed that I wanted to serve groups, not individuals. I wanted my society to become like Europe, well developed, where all citizens have equal rights and where people are treated equally before the law. I dream of the same type of society.

Kobra Mustafawi also shared her views on what she thought distinguished her from warlords and why people support her:

Afghans no longer support those types of people [warlords]. Afghans support people like me who accept development, education, technology, good relations with the international community, and democracy. I fight for my children's rights. Currently, my girls are attending a medical school, and I want them to grow stronger and liberal like me. With the power of education, warlords can't harm my daughters, me and my sons. The only thing they can use against my knowledge is force. I was once kidnapped by the Taliban and later on released in exchange for one of their men. And I witnessed the harsh life in Iran. I don't want my children to have the same bitter experience. With all my powers, I will prevent that from happening. I would fight for my ideology, against the Taliban, against ISIS, against warlords. If I don't work in my own country, who would? If I don't even build my own house, who would build the country? I have a diplomatic passport and so do my children. I can send them to any foreign country to study. I also have the financial resources to do so. But I want them to grow up proudly in their own country.

She described to me in detail how she was kidnapped, an experience that had clearly left marks. Her passion and determination to change Afghanistan and work for the people whom she represents despite all personal risks and challenges left a lasting impression on me.

Not any less memorable was my interview with the MP Ramazan Bashardost. Bashardost is, perhaps, one of the most famous MPs in Kabul Province, known for his accessibility and vocal criticism of corruption. He spent many summers living and working in a tent across from the Parliament building to protest the inaccessibility of the government. He was without any security measures and accessible to anyone. Instead of driving a convoy of heavily armored vehicles, he drove a small car that was very recognizably painted in the colors of the Afghan flag. Living in Kabul, I would often see his car parked on the roadside and Bashardost talking to the ordinary people who approached him. He also gained the attention of the international community when, working as minister of planning in 2004, he suggested expelling international aid organizations from Afghanistan for their involvement in corruption. Bashardost ran for president in 2009, coming in third behind Karzai and Abdullah

Abdullah—despite not having backing by any of the rich or influential people and relying on public donations instead.

When I met Ramazan Bashardost in July 2015, he emphasized that he wasn't an MP anymore. He explained that, according to the Afghan constitution, it was time for new elections (which were subsequently delayed further until 2018). When asked about why he thought people supported him, he emphasized that he always continued being an ordinary person and treating everyone equally:

> I am not a good man. But I am not a bad man either. People see bad men every day. MPs waste their power, they have big luxury cars, they do land-grabbing, they don't pay rent for their houses. Afghan leaders unfortunately often become bad men or women when they are in power. I am not a good man, but I stayed an ordinary man. When I became the Minister of Planning, it was a chance for me to get money, a car, power—to be very different from ordinary people. But as a minister, I stayed like the ordinary people. . . . I didn't use my salary, I gave it to the restaurant at the ministry for instance. And the employees at the ministry said, "It's incredible, the ministers before always took a share of our money. And you give us your money." . . . In the restaurant, I used the same tables, the same chairs, the same cutlery as everyone else and ate the same food. . . . But usually people change if they gain such a position, then they are not men and women of the people anymore.

Sitting in his cramped office, he further emphasized the importance of remaining accessible and treating people equally:

> The door of my office is always open. [As a minister] I saw a man who wanted to talk to me but was stopped by the security guards. I saw a fight outside and asked what the matter was. The security people said "Minister, he wants to see you, but he has no

appointment." I said, "That's not a crime." . . . Afterwards I told security, "Any Afghan who comes to the ministry and wants to see me, you must think that person is the king of Afghanistan. Because if there are no people, there is no ministry. And if there is no ministry, there is no minister." I was a minister for nine months and I have been an MP for 10 years now. I haven't been able to do much good for the people in practice. But they can see that at least I am not doing anything bad. I am against corruption, there is no discrimination, regardless of whether people are Shia, Sunni or Pashtun, Muslim, American. . . . Many say and have slogans that they work for the Afghan people, but in fact they do not. . . . It is an absolute honour for me that also Pashtun or Tajik people trust me, not just Hazara. . . . People claim that I am a good man. I am not. But I am not a bad man. That's a big difference. I haven't achieved anything big like Gandhi or Abraham Lincoln. . . . But I am not a bad man. I don't want to do bad things against people. That's why people trust me.

While Bashardost's critics accuse him of populism, he came across as very convincing. He believed that qualities such as accessibility, empathy, and honesty are needed to represent the people of Afghanistan.

I conducted a similar interview with Mirwais Yasini, an MP from Nangarhar Province, in April 2014. He invited me to his house in the heart of Kabul, on Ministry of Interior Road, neighboring the compound of the European delegation. At the beginning of the interview, I asked him about his life story and how he became a member of the Afghan Parliament. He explained:

I was born under miserable conditions. However, my family is middle class. My father was a district and provincial attorney general. So, we were an educated family. . . . Because we were a political family we had to flee right after the Communist Coup in 1978 to Pakistan before the Russian invasion. . . . I was there mostly in Jihad. I went to Paktika, Nangarhar, Torabora and that area. And I was present when the first Russian was captured close to Dushaka. . . . We took him to Peshawar. His name was Mikhael Simonovitch, from Volgograd, a 21-year-old pilot. So, in 1986 I was working with the Mujahedin in Pakistan. In 1987 I escaped to Europe, to the States as an Afghan Jihadi activist. And in '87 I joined the International Islamic University, which was a very famous institution in Pakistan. . . . And again, I was involved in the Afghan opposition at that time. And with the social activities and a little bit of business. And during the Taliban time I went to Europe and the States a lot and came back to Pakistan, where I stayed until 9/11. . . . I became the first deputy speaker of the constitutional Loya Jirga. Then I was involved in the election of Karzai in 2004. . . . I became the First Deputy Minister at the Ministry of Counternarcotic. I resigned and went to the parliament. . . . And for two consecutive years I was the first deputy speaker. . . . Later I became the speaker. And I am still a member of the parliament today.

We sat in his garden for a long time and often got carried away in the course of the interview. In fact, we were still talking when elders from Nangarhar Province, whom he had invited for dinner, arrived. He invited me to stay, and we continued talking through dinner. Toward the end of the more formal interview part of the meeting, I asked him about the basis of his support and why he was elected. After thinking for a while, he responded:

I am not a thief. I am not involved in corruption. I always stayed with my people. I didn't tell them lies. And I know the people and I know how to communicate with the different levels of the people. How you can talk with educated or less educated people. With the literate class, illiterate class, different languages, different clans. If you talk to different Pashto clans, you require different skills. And if you go to Uzbeks, Turmens, Hazaras, Tajiks, and, thank God, I do believe in humanity and I do believe in my Afghanhood. That under the skies of Afghanistan, every clan, sectarian, religious, men, women, they have the same rights. . . . All Afghans have to feel that they are equal citizens. . . . So, I expressed that particularly in the past fourteen, fifteen years . . . and that is why people trust me.

Yasini, certainly in contrast to Kobra Mustafawi, was from an older generation that was shaped by the Jihad against the Soviet Union. While his statements were perhaps less passionate, he nonetheless emphasized similar values—most importantly, the importance of equality.

Another MP I talked to was Ahmad Behzad from Herat Province. He was one of the MPs who was suspended after a prolonged absence.[253] We met at his Kabul house in August 2015, and it was the most formal of all the interviews with the MPs. We stuck to questions and answers, and the interview rarely developed into a conversation. Talking about his life story, he briefly explained how he had been elected as an MP after working as a journalist after the fall of the Taliban regime. When I asked why people supported him, he suggested:

People were looking for fresh faces. During my election campaigns, I found that people were looking for fresh faces who could guide them into the new era, while my rivals were all very famous personalities, with Jihadi and military backgrounds. One of the reasons people voted for us was that we were fresh faces and we had new promises for people. Before that, I was working as a news reporter. But Mr. Ismail Khan, who was the provincial governor, kicked me out of Herat. When I came back to Herat, I ran for Parliament. In fact, the vote I received in the elections was a clear rejection by the people of the Ismail Khan type of personality. This showed that people have entered a new era and have selected new forces with new ideas, although later situations started worsening gradually.

The interviewees' ideas about why they had popular support and won elections essentially depict why they believed people considered them to be legitimate. Bashardost emphasized the importance of remaining an ordinary person when becoming a leader and being accessible to everyone. Yasini similarly believed he got elected because of his loyalty to the people, his ability to talk to different kinds of people, and his fight for an equal Afghan society. But Yasini's description of himself as a jihadist who won the people's favor by fighting the Soviets contrasts with Mustafawi's reference to liberal values, feminism, and family tradition and Behzad's portrayal of himself in opposition to jihadists in Herat, such as Ismail Khan. Both Mustafawi and Behzad portrayed themselves as a new generation fighting the old jihadists and warlords with political means. Meanwhile, their stance against corruption was a common theme across all interviews with MPs. Ultimately, much like when people praise soldiers for putting country first, all four portrayed themselves as people who are fighting for a better society.

PUBLIC PERCEPTIONS OF MPS

Few people across the provinces expressed distinct views on MPs. A notable exception, however, was Nangarhar, where

many people had strong views. The opinions of most interviewees there painted a very different picture. They considered
MPs to be threatening warlords, causing insecurity, and being
involved in criminal activities. For example, Hajji Aziz from
Surkh Rod claimed: "In addition to the Taliban, there are a
large number of illegally armed men in the city that commit
crimes in the night. These illegally armed men are supported
by Hajji Zahir [Qadir, see chapter 3] and [other] members of
parliament. They always drive in convoys of many cars and with
dozens of illegally armed men."[254]

Hajji Muhebullah from Surkh Rod's concerns about Parliament were entwined with his distrust of the police: "Because
nobody collects all the illegal weapons and disarms the warlords,
security provision is very difficult. Most of the police officers work
for MPs and the heads of departments."[255] NGO worker Khyber
argued that some MPs were criminals: "MPs and members of
the cabinet use their authority to cut down forests illegally and
are involved in drug trafficking." In addition, he saw connections
between MPs and insurgency groups: "A number of government
authorities cooperate with insurgents, which carry out suicide
attacks. Unfortunately, even some MPs are among them."[256]

Other interviewees were not quite as negative. They did,
however, criticize the MPs' detachment from their reality. University student Gulagha from Jalalabad pointed out, "The MPs
move around in bullet-proofed vehicles. And through the thick
glass probably everything looks fine and good."[257] And unemployed Bahir, also from Jalalabad, assessed, "In the last two years
I haven't seen any member of parliament coming to our place. In
the dark night they are busy with prostitutes from Tajikistan and
during the day they sleep."[258]

Some people in Nangarhar also complained about MPs not
being accountable. Khyber argued, "In my opinion, the MPs

in power are not the ones who were elected on the basis of the people's votes."²⁵⁹ Hajji Shahib Mohammad Dara, a member of the provincial council in Jalalabad, told me, "The MPs won the elections because they cheated. They make laws and can have the right to call the government to justice. But nobody can call them to justice."²⁶⁰

Across all provinces, not just in Nangarhar, people protested that MPs only cared about them around election times and did not live up to the promises they had made once they were in power. Arbab Ahmad, a community authority in Enjil District in Herat Province, stated, "I contacted Mr. Qata Ali, MP. I asked him: 'Wasn't it you who called me twenty times per day during the elections and asked me to call people for him. Wasn't it you who was begging for votes by giving food to the people?' And now he doesn't even pick up the phone if I try to call him."²⁶¹

Tailor Halim from Surkh Rod said, "The members of parliament haven't done anything for us yet. Once they are elected they will not care about the people anymore."²⁶² And Asadullah from Char Asiab in Kabul Province complained, "Many people promised us that they will help us to fight unemployment. The MPs, the provincial council. But nobody is doing anything about it."²⁶³ Nonetheless, in Kabul Province a number of people made one notable exception: Ramazan Bashardost—who many described as taking people's concerns seriously.

Generally, the perception of MPs seemed to reflect how they appeared in public: distant, driving around in armored cars, accompanied by armed security guards. The idea of MPs "not caring" was widespread across both urban and rural areas and across provinces. The people's main concern appeared to be that MPs were not working in the public interest, only for themselves. Not encountering MPs much and not considering them to be of any relevance, in most provinces under study, few people had distinct views on MPs at all. The civil society activist Jamil summarized, "In my opinion there is no Afghan parliament at all, as all of its members only care about their personal business."[264] In Nangarhar, the views on MPs were often even more distinct—many people thought that MPs not only "did not care" but that they were actually harmful warlords, unaccountable to no one, who used force to extract money.

In contrast to the security and justice sector, there appeared to be a considerable gap between the public perceptions and the self-perception of MPs. Having been elected, the MPs I talked to appeared to be more confident about their own legitimacy than authorities in the security and justice sectors. They assumed to have local support because of their ideas of authority—being a jihadist or fighting jihadists with political means—and, in one way or other, bringing Afghanistan forward.

Meanwhile, most members of the public I talked to had little interest in what ideas the MPs stood for. Those with a distinct view on the elected lawmakers thought that they were not working for the people but only for themselves; this was more important than their policies. The lack of support voiced in the interviews indicates a low level of legitimacy, in line with the findings of scholars like Sharan and Bose.[265] The perception that lawmakers do not care about the people seemed to be driven by the limited interaction between MPs and people and the distance of MPs from the community level, not being visible and only showing up at election times. Their work appeared to be too intangible for many people.

The behavior of MPs in Afghanistan and the character of their work as such are not unusual, as there probably is little interaction between people and MPs in most countries. However, the consequences were more extreme. While people in many countries may also feel distant from their lawmakers, the interviewees, in this case, did not feel connected with or represented by their MPs at all, thinking that the MPs' work had no impact on their lives. However, there were exceptions. For example, people like Kobra Mustafawi and Ramazan Bashardost made an active effort to be as accessible as possible. Bashardost in particular was therefore known and viewed positively. He was perceived to practice what he preached, living up to the claims he made. A different kind of exception was Nangarhar, where people thought that MPs had a negative impact. These participants described the elections as rigged and considered MPs to be unaccountable, using their power for their own benefits and not caring about the people. Nangarhar was viewed as a province run by strongmen in control of all branches of state power, exploiting people with impunity.

CONCLUSIONS

For many people in Afghanistan, the state was an actor entirely external to their lives, nothing more than a potential authority. They had no relationship with the state and were not subject to its social control, as they lived in areas where the state had no ability to have an impact on their lives—for instance, because their area was controlled by the Taliban. This trend further intensified over the years until 2021, with a growing number of especially rural populations living beyond the reach of the state. However, in most of the areas where I conducted interviews in 2014/2015, the state still had some impact on people's lives, at least through the use of coercive means. This did not give the state or its component parts legitimacy, though. The only entities of the Afghan state covered by my research that were seen as substantively legitimate by many were the army and, to some extent, the NDS. People tried to avoid taking their cases to the courts and stayed clear of police officers. They perceived these institutions in their form at the time as illegitimate and, particularly in the case of the police, coercive.

The perceptions of the three formal branches of state authority in Afghanistan indicate that the main referent object people based their assessment of legitimacy on was how they perceive the authority's *behavior in day-to-day life*. People judged behavior on the basis of shared values—not just usefulness—expecting authorities to behave in a fair or inclusive manner. For instance, the way people viewed the army illustrates that its procedures were far more important than its "output," "service delivery," or "performance." The security situation in Afghanistan was fragile, and people did not witness significant success in the army's fight against the insurgency. Instead, people judged the army by looking at its coordination when providing security.

Based on how people perceived the behavior and procedures, they drew conclusions about an authority's invisible *attitude*. Therefore, they saw the ANA as serving the nation. Drawing on Bourdieu's understanding of legitimacy, we can say that this attitude is a form of symbolic capital, capital that is spontaneously recognized as legitimate. Similarly, people viewed MP Bashardost as taking their concerns seriously and serving the public because he met people as equals and with empathy. Meanwhile, as the courts' procedures were considered to be corrupt and unfair, people who worked in the justice sector were viewed as extractive and nepotistic. Nonetheless, in addition to these substantive, value-based judgments, more instrumental factors also mattered. These factors were particularly prominent in the case of conflict resolution, in which people were also concerned about the accessibility of courts and the speed of conflict resolution.

In most cases, the perceptions and assessment of an authority's behavior were based on *personal experiences*. The direct interactions between state authorities and people with resulting personal experiences were particularly prominent in the cases of the police and justice system. The chapter shows that people perceived the state authorities' behavior at the time of their interview as corrupt and extractive, and therefore illegitimate. Most state actors were viewed as being driven by greed and self-interest instead of a desire to serve the public. An exception was Farza District, where many people perceived the police's process of providing security to be inclusive and its behavior to be fair and supportive. However, in addition to such value-based assessments of the authorities' behaviors, more pragmatic and instrumental factors also mattered. In the justice sector, it was not just fairness that people expected, but the courts also had to be accessible and as fast as other authorities offering conflict resolution. The case of Bashardost shows that even for MPs, it was important to be accessible.

In the absence of personal interaction and experience, several other factors become relevant. One is the *visibility of an actor*. In the interviews, people tended to have stronger views on those actors who were present in their day-to-day lives. For instance, the ANA did not actually interact much directly with the people in cities. But it was very visible, resulting in strong perceptions. Similarly, people had stronger views on the NDS in areas where it was visible. Conversely, many people simply did not care about the Afghan Local Police because it played no role in their lives. And MPs, at least those who rarely visited their constituencies and could afford tough security measures, remained distant and invisible in their armored vehicles, even when they were geographically close, and did not play much of a role in the lives of most people.

The *visibility of the actor's behavior* may be important as well. While the army certainly exercised force and killed people, and the NDS was accused of human rights violations, most people did not witness this behavior. Some perhaps even perceived it as legitimate given the level of security threats in the country. But people's comments suggest that lack of visibility was a more important driver. People did not refer to the hidden behaviors of which they were unlikely to approve. Thus, there is no reason to suppose they excused it.

Because authority within the Afghan state was considered to be dispersed, legitimacy also appears to be linked to the extent to which an actor was perceived to have an independent *ability to have an impact*—if it was seen as an actual rather than a potential authority. Without a perceived ability to have an impact, the ability of state authorities to construct legitimacy faded. In the case of the ANA, which had the ability to exercise coercion against people in state-controlled territories, the *absence of harmful interaction* was interpreted in a positive way and the behavior of the authority was considered to be good. Conversely, in the case of many MPs and courts, in the absence of a perceived ability to have an impact and a lack of accessibility, people were more indifferent. The different examples this chapter addresses show that authorities that have coercive means can construct legitimacy by acting according to the formal rules and *not using coercion in arbitrary, unpredictable, or extractive* ways. Finally, the absence of limited personal experience, second-hand information from friends and family members, as well as media reporting played an important role. This likely contributed to the positive image of the ANA and the NDS. After all, the narrative of the ANA as serving the nation was so powerful that even some people in Taliban-held areas bought into it.

Crucially, the Afghan state was not seen as a system; its entities and branches were viewed independently. Thus, there was little connection between Scharpf's "input" and "output" dimensions of state legitimacy. While the "output" side of the state, the executive and judicial branches, were seen as legitimate under certain circumstances, the "input" side, the elected MPs, had little to no legitimacy. Moreover, in some parts of the country, people associated MPs with coercion and warlordism. Hence, the democratic structure of the Afghan state did not actually ensure the accountability and "promotion" of democracy, which was part of the state-building agenda. Without accountability at the state level, people cared about accountability on the personal, microlevel in day-to-day interactions with the state. If state actors were able to show that they cared about the interests of the people and served the public, they could construct substantive legitimacy, as the case of Bashardost shows. He ensured accountability on the microlevel. In the absence of a systemic view on the state, this legitimacy could barely spill over to other branches of the state.

Using Bourdieu's language, the Afghan state also consisted of "fields"—like those states that monopolized force successfully. However, people considered these fields to be largely disconnected, and the Afghan state failed to be much of what Bourdieu describes as a "meta field." Instead, all fields within the Afghan state were subject to the dynamics of the wider political order— the real "meta field" in Afghanistan that also included several other authorities, such as strongmen, the Taliban, and community authorities.

Meanwhile, there appeared to be a widespread belief in the *idea of the state*. While the formal features of the state—its constitution, laws, and general structure—did not seem to provide the state with much legitimacy, as the features did not translate into perceived practices and the experienced reality of its citizens, people did hope that "the state" would govern the country again in the future. Further research is necessary to explore people's understanding of a future state, but it can be assumed that their idea of the state was based on a monopoly of force and, most likely, rational-legal structures. This assumption is supported by people's belief in the police as an institution, regardless of their dissatisfaction with the way it currently works.

The people I talked to within the judiciary and the security sectors appeared to have a reflective self-perception. They considered themselves to be part of a corrupt and extractive system that they couldn't change and resulted in little local legitimacy. Conversely, the MPs I interviewed displayed more agency and appeared to be more confident in their own legitimacy as representatives of the people. While my small sample is not generalizable, it may indicate that employees in the security and justice sectors were exposed to people's expectations on the microlevel and had to balance these with those of a corrupt system, while MPs did feel legitimized by the elections on the "input" side of the state system.

However, the findings also show that the Afghan state was successful in constructing a national identity. Legitimacy, for many, rested on the perception of an authority serving the nation—not specific ethnic groups. Traditions like the Pashtunwali and religion appear to matter to a lesser extent, in contrast to what some strands of literature argue.[266] In a way, the findings seem to support the prominent claim in the literature that improved service delivery can construct legitimacy, as suggested by Maley.[267] Most people I interviewed certainly expected services, such as security and conflict resolution. But instead of discussing solely *what* services matter to address people's needs, much more attention needs to be paid to *how* services are delivered to address people's values. In the moment of service delivery, the state interacts with its citizens, who have value-based expectations of what interaction should look like. In line with Barfield and Nojumi, such local expectations and perceptions of fairness and trust were similar across the country and not specific to certain ethnic or linguistic groups.[268]

To construct more substantive legitimacy, the Afghan state—regardless of whether it is controlled by an elected government or, following August 2021, the Taliban—has to focus on the procedures of how "outputs" are delivered, consider to what extent security provision is perceived to be inclusive and makes people feel more secure, and to what extent conflict resolution is perceived to be fair. The state needs to address expectations like these, which are not limited to specific groups or segments of the population, but are shared irrespectively of, for instance, ethnicity, age, gender, and economic status.

As the Taliban were expanding their territorial control within Afghanistan, the authority of the state was reduced to a potential one for a growing number of people, making it increasingly difficult for the state to construct legitimacy through interactions. Nonetheless, there is hope for a future state to be legitimate, if it treats people with the dignity they demand, as people continue to believe in the state as an idea.

3

STRONGMEN AND WARLORDS

"They have weapons and power. They can do any illegal activity, whenever they want to."

Woman in Khiwa District, Nangarhar Province, 2015

I n December 2015, the decapitated heads of suspected IS-K fighters were displayed on a main road in Achin District of eastern Nangarhar Province. Local militia forces loyal to Hajji Zahir Qadir had taken revenge for the alleged beheading of four members of their group. While some people described the victims as civilians who were only suspected to be IS-K fighters because they were from the same area as many members of the movement,[1] Hajji Qadir posted photos of the severed heads on his Facebook page and explained to reporters that local communities were fed up with IS-K's presence, asking "Do you think if they behead you, you cook them sweets?"[2]

Hajji Zahir Qadir is an influential member of the Arsala family and was a powerful strongman in Nangahar Province at the time of my research. I use the term "strongmen" to refer to those who, like Hajji Qadir, were perceived to control considerable armed forces on the provincial or national level.[3] While different strongmen dominated different parts of Afghanistan, all of them were known for their use of force and coercion, resulting in frequent accusations of human rights violations. For example, *The Guardian* reported on how Abdul Rashid Dostum, a strongman from Jowzjan in northern Afghanistan, dealt with prisoners of war in 2002: "They were taken to Qala Zaini, a mud-walled fortified compound on the outskirts of the [Mazar-i-Sharif]. There Gen Dostum's soldiers crammed them into shipping containers. When they protested that they could not breathe, the soldiers told them to duck down, then fired several Kalashnikov rounds into the containers. 'I saw blood coming out of the holes,' an eyewitness who refuses to be identified said."[4]

An estimated four hundred to three thousand imprisoned Taliban fighters died in Dostum's shipping containers in the Qala Zaini massacre.[5] In 2014, Dostum became the vice president of Afghanistan and, in 2020, was promoted to marshal, the highest rank in the Afghan security forces.

Meanwhile, Gulbuddin Hekmatyar, whose stronghold is in the east, is also known as the "butcher of Kabul" because of his indiscriminate shelling of the city during the civil war in the 1990s. The United States and the Pakistani intelligence agency ISI heavily funded his efforts in order to oppose the Soviet occupation.[6] After the 2001 intervention, he took up arms against the new government and the international presence in Afghanistan. While the population of Kabul considers him a war criminal, he signed a peace agreement with the government in 2016 and returned to Afghanistan from exile in May 2017 after being granted judicial immunity for past crimes.

We see strongmen primarily through the lens of the atrocities and human rights violations they commit. This makes it difficult to imagine that men notorious for war crimes may have gained legitimacy among the people. It is, of course, possible that what authority they have locally rests solely on fear of coercion. Indeed, Giustozzi defines warlords as people who control territory with military force in the absence of legitimacy.[7] But while strongmen are commonly seen as the driving force behind and major profiteers of armed conflicts, they were not only able to adapt to the changing political circumstances after 2001, they often even managed to expand their influence.[8]

In this chapter, I investigate the role of strongmen in Afghanistan between and 2001 and 2021 and the source of their authority and legitimacy. The chapter focuses on the case study of Nangarhar Province, where there was an ongoing competition among several strongmen. In addition, it looks at the case of Balkh Province, where at the time of my research, one strongman, Mohammad Atta Noor, who was also called "king of the north," was clearly in control. In Nangarhar, I explore the role of the former governor, Gul Agha Shirzai, who is known as "the bulldozer," and Hajji Zahir Qadir, who also was the deputy speaker of the Afghan Parliament at the time. Both of them agreed to be interviewed and shared their own perspectives with me. In the case studies, I investigate how these strongmen perceived themselves and their own legitimacy and then compare their views with those of the citizens.

The chapter shows that strongmen, in contrast to their own claims, remained first and foremost coercive authorities. Nonetheless, their control of force also enabled them to build legitimacy to varying extents. In Nangarhar, Shirzai and Qadir claimed substantive legitimacy on the basis of their work for Afghanistan, their good behavior and way of interacting with the people, and their family tradition. However, the public often had a different view of them. Most people I talked to perceived strongmen as coercive authorities with little legitimacy who were driven by personal interests alone, seeing them as sources of insecurity and blaming them for corrupt and extracting behavior. Only people who directly benefited from their influence and services spoke of them positively. In Balkh, Noor managed to monopolize force to a large extent, and the province remained comparatively stable for a long time, which many people appreciated. But because Noor, as an individual, was in control of the exercise of force, he was also feared, particularly by civil society activists. He was known to create insecurity to achieve his personal goals. There are few indicators that Shirzai, Qadir, or Noor constructed widespread substantive legitimacy. However, they certainly constructed a degree of instrumental legitimacy, which primarily rested on their abilities to provide services to supporters and, in the case of Noor, a degree of stability. Nonetheless, lacking substantive legitimacy, the authority of strongmen can quickly fade if their ability to control and exercise force or to provide services diminishes.

STRONGMEN GOVERNANCE

International involvement in Afghanistan long empowered warlords and strongmen. Hekmayar was only one of many Mujahedin commanders who relied on Western funding during the Soviet occupation. Taliban rule limited the influence of strongmen to areas in northern Afghanistan, but U.S. funding was renewed as part of the international intervention in 2001. Hence, Maley even categorizes strongmen as "American warlords."[9] Dostum received funds from the United States and the CIA to support his fight against the Taliban.[10] The Guardian points out that American Special Forces likely knew about the Qala Zaini massacre at the time.[11] Their capture of Kabul and other Taliban-held cities and territories cemented the influence of strongmen, which in the following twenty years was not only exercised through force but also through the government system of which they were part, giving them greater formal authority.

The type of authority that I refer to as strongmen has existed for centuries and is possibly as old as humankind.[12] Scholarly interest began in the 1990s amid a growing realization that individuals commanding militias play key roles in the wars of the globalized world. Research on people like Charles Taylor in Liberia[13] and competing warlords in Somalia[14] provided the analytical basis for investigating how the international intervention in Afghanistan in 2001 empowered various individuals to fight against the Taliban.

Even though the term "warlord" prevails in the academic literature, I prefer to describe individuals who have authority as *individuals*, resting primarily on the independent command of armed forces,[15] more neutrally as "strongmen." The terminology also recognizes that such authority, while originating in force, can nonetheless exceed the sphere of the battlefield.[16] In a way, strongmen were the epicenters of what some scholars describe as "network governance" in Afghanistan.[17] Even though strongmen had ties with community authorities, were often closely linked to the state—in fact, many had an official government function and title—and, in some cases, were also connected to insurgencies, they got their power from commanding militias or segments of the security forces, not those other arrangements.[18] For example, some strongmen commanded forces that were technically part of the Afghan security forces and were even paid by the state, such as the Afghan Local Police, but that nonetheless only followed the command of an individual strongman. In fact, many strongmen successfully managed to make their militias part of the Afghan security forces, substantially reducing the cost of maintaining their forces while maintaining control.

In the context of Afghanistan, they tended to have strongholds in certain provinces of the country while also influencing the national dynamics.[19]

The prevalence of strongmen as a distinct type of individual authority in Afghanistan makes them important to consider in any study of political order in the country. In our Bourdieu-inspired understanding of Afghanistan's political order as an arena of interaction for various authorities, strongmen played a key role. They simultaneously cooperated and competed with other authorities, most crucially the state, being part of the state while also trying to accumulate authority independently as individuals.

There has been an ongoing debate regarding the role strongmen play in the processes of state formation or state-building. Marten points out that strongmen have no incentive to contribute to state formation, as they benefit from corrupt state structures, insecurity, and a flourishing war economy.[20] Conversely, Giustozzi argues that in conflict-torn settings, "warlordism" is not necessarily the outcome of disintegration but can, on the contrary, also be a step toward order and monopolization of force.[21] Building on Elias's work, he suggests that after monopolizing force, strongmen will try to construct legitimacy to ensure stability.[22] Meanwhile, Malejacq concludes on a more balanced note that strongmen in Afghanistan constituted a different type of authority that could adjust to changing political circumstances while successfully resisting attempts of state centralization. In order to remain relevant in changing environments, strongmen constantly reinvented themselves and tried building local legitimacy.[23]

And, indeed, strongmen applied different strategies to construct legitimacy. Several researchers have shown that, in addition to coercion, strongmen relied on patronage networks, which gave them some instrumental legitimacy.[24] But strongmen also tried to build legitimacy within the general public beyond their immediate network of supporters. Mukhopadhyay shows that strongmen in Afghanistan used tax revenue and support from the international community to provide public services, including infrastructure, education, and healthcare, in addition to enriching themselves.[25] Malejacq's work illustrates that strongmen projected power in order to build legitimacy, trying to create an "image of strength" to portray themselves as sources of security and stability.[26] In addition, Murtazashvili notes that strongmen co-opted community authorities to gain more substantive traditional legitimacy.[27]

But did such strategies succeed? Could strongmen actually construct substantive legitimacy? And if strongmen were able to build legitimacy beyond their immediate patronage network, which strategies conferred that legitimacy?

STRONGMEN GOVERNANCE IN NANGARHAR

Nangarhar Province's political order was characterized by a considerable number of rival strongmen competing for authority. Without a doubt, a major player was Hajji Zahir Qadir from the Arsala family. The Arsala family was close to the king and already held some key government positions at the time.[28] During the Soviet occupation, the three Arsala brothers, Abdul Haq, Abdul Qadir, and Din Mohammad, became prominent Mujahedin in Nangarhar, one with Hezb-e Islami[29] and the other two with Hezb-e Islami Khales.[30] Abdul Haq and Abdul Qadir were part of the Mujahedin government after the fall of the pro-Soviet government in 1992. Both left the country by

2001; on his return, the Taliban killed Abdul Haq. Abdul Qadir and Din Mohammad, however, took control of Nangarhar from the Taliban.[31] Together with other Pashtun Mujahedin commanders they formed the Eastern Shura as a counterweight to the Northern Alliance. Abdul Qadir became minister of public works and vice president of Karzai's interim government but was assassinated shortly after in 2002. Din Mohammad became governor of Nangarhar and remained in this position until 2005. Abdul Qadir's sons, Zahir and Jamal Qadir, continued the family tradition. The former was a border police commander in Nangarhar and Takhar and ultimately moved on to become a member of Parliament (until 2018) and the deputy speaker of the Wolesi Jirga (lower house) in Parliament. He was frequently accused of drug smuggling.[32] Jamal Qadir became a member of Nangarhar's provincial council in 2009.[33]

The appointment of Gul Agha Shirzai as the provincial governor in 2005 interrupted the dominance of the Arsala family in Nangarhar.[34] Shirzai grew up far away from the central government in the southern province of Kandahar in a family uninvolved even in local government.[35] A member of Mahaz-e Milli during the Soviet occupation,[36] he was governor of Kandahar from 1992 to 1994. Karzai appointed him to the position in 2001 to neutralize the threat he posed as a commander of a militia that had fought against the Taliban with U.S. Special Forces backing.[37] Maley describes Shirzai as the "most spectacular example" of an "American warlord."[38]

After being accused of keeping the province's customs revenues for himself, Shirzai was removed in 2003 and became minister of urban affairs before becoming governor of Nangarhar in 2005. In contrast to the Arsala family, he did not have an established power base and access to the elite networks in Nangarhar, and he had to construct his authority from scratch. He did so by building relationships with commanders and groups that the Arsalas had marginalized.[39] He also tried to gain support at the community level by strengthening the roles of *maliks* and by appointing new ones when he was not successful in co-opting the existing ones.[40] In addition, Shirzai launched development projects with visible outputs, such as improving roads, parks, and mosques, and provided petitioners an audience, sometimes giving them money and occasionally trying to solve their conflicts. The corruption that had led to his removal in Kandahar continued, as he sought revenue to cover expenses through customs revenues, other invented taxes unevenly applied, bribes, and land-grabbing.[41] Nonetheless, he also gained international support and aid money, for instance, by claiming success in combatting poppy cultivation.

In addition to Shirzai and the Arsala family, there were other local strongmen, most prominently Hazrat Ali and Mohammed Zaman Ghamsharik. Both were former Mujahedin commanders and part of the Eastern Region Shura. Since then, they maintained a rivalry over authority and control in the province—with each other and the Asala family—but they also united when it was mutually beneficial. Mohammed Zaman was appointed as the deputy head of police in Nangarhar in 2010 but was killed soon after in an attack. His son, Jawed Zaman, succeeded him and became a key player in the province. Hazrat Ali was Nangarhar's head of police from 2003 to 2004 and later became a member of Parliament. Hazrat Ali and the Arsala family opposed Shirzai while he had the backing of Jawed Zaman. Jackson describes this struggle over power as the underlying reason for the frequent violence in Nangarhar at the time. For instance, Shirzai was accused of facilitating attacks on Kabul Bank in Jalalabad in 2011 and his opponents were seen as fomenting numerous public protests against Shirzai. In late 2013, Shirzai decided to run in the presidential elections in a bid that was ultimately unsuccessful. He resigned from his post as governor, effectively ceding control of Nangarhar to his competitors.[42]

GUL AGHA SHIRZAI, "THE SON OF THE LION"

I met with former governor of Kandahar and Nangarhar, Gul Agha Shirzai, at his house in Kabul in April 2015. Shirzai, a robust man in his early sixties with a deep voice, received me in the room where he keeps his radio collection, wearing a white *shalwar kameez* (traditional clothes). With visible pride and a great deal of confidence, he spoke of his achievements as an "Afghan hero."

We began our conversation by talking about his biography. He recited his résumé from his time as a government official in the 1970s, which included time in the tax department and a customs office. After the Soviet invasion, he said, "I consulted with my tribe and my famous father how to defend Afghanistan. I then started a Jihad. I fought the Soviets until the fall of the communist regime." Shirzai saw his father as a significant source of his own legitimacy. "During the fight against the Soviet Union, my father got the title 'Lion of Kandahar' in a battle at Malejad [in which he and many other members of the family died]. That's why the people now call me Shirzai, the Son of the Lion."

Shirzai also mentioned his father's wise leadership and contrasted his measured approach to seeking peace in contrast to some other actors:

During the war with the Soviet Union there were many rival groups of Mujahedin who were fighting each other. My father and

I didn't participate in this and didn't allow our tribe to fight other Mujahedin groups. We didn't fight rival groups in the 1990s and just wanted peace in Afghanistan. When the Soviet Union troops left Afghanistan, we proposed a peace plan. . . . We talked to different Mujahedin leaders, but unfortunately . . . they did not want the peace plan to be successful. After the fall of the Najib[ullah] regime . . . the people, the elders and Mujahedin came together and elected me as the new governor [of Kandarhar Province] of the Mujahedin government in 1992.

While the Taliban's rise to power depended in part on a claim to legitimacy on the grounds of fighting the corruption that was associated with strongmen like Shirzai, he saw it differently. Instead, he described himself as a promoter of peace and order: "When the Taliban entered Afghanistan there was intense fighting with Mujahedin groups. I didn't fight the Taliban, but left for Pakistan and had my own business. Again, I did not participate in the internal fighting between the Taliban and the Mujahedin."

Shirzai returned to Afghanistan in 2001 to fight the Taliban, but he emphasized that he did so at the request of the international community and that, in line with international humanitarian law, he did not kill outside the battlefield. "After 9/11, the international community, especially the Americans, asked for my support and I went to Kandahar again to help them. Karzai entered Afghanistan at the same time and went to Uruzgan [province], I went to Kandahar to fight. But I didn't kill any Taliban. Just on the battlefield I killed, but when I captured them I didn't kill them. Because this wasn't my goal."

Rather, Shirzai emphasized, "I was thinking about the future, the prosperous future of my people. And after we took Kandahar, Karzai proclaimed me as the first governor. So, for the second time I became governor of Kandahar. And I paid a lot attention to education in Kandahar, I also established a new university in Kandahar and after that I started to work on the structure of the government. I also did a lot of reconstruction work in Kandahar. I tried to build a new Kandahar, with new structures and a new government."

Shirzai's narrative emphasized that in entering the national government, he continued to work for his country's future:

> I prepared a comprehensive plan for development for the next few years, when I was Minister [of Urban Development]. And after that I was moved to the Ministry of Public Works. I worked there and also prepared a good plan for five years, what to do about the reconstruction of roads, etc. At that time, there was a road from Kabul to Paghman District, which President Hamed Karzai asked me to pave within two months. And I did it within 28 days. So, while the father of nation is His Excellency, the former King of Afghanistan, Mohammad Zahir Shah, Hamid Karzai gave me the title of "bulldozer." That's why people call me the bulldozer.

Shirzai described himself as an agent of peace in returning to Kandahar in 2003: "After that the security situation in Kandahar got worse. So, the president asked me to return to Kandahar, because the security situation wasn't good. So, I was appointed again as the governor of Kandahar. And after that I worked as a governor again, for about one year, and I started the reconstruction work in Kandahar."

He described his appointment as governor of Nangarhar Province in 2004 in similar terms:

> There was a demonstration in Jalalabad, in Nangarhar Province, and somewhere the Quran was burned, and the people

demonstrated. They burned the governor's house and a lot of people got killed or injured. Also, the consulate of Pakistan was burned. The situation was out of control. So, Hamid Karzai asked me to go to Nangarhar to bring the situation under control again. And I worked as a governor of Nangarhar for nine years. I started a reconstruction programme and invested USD 5.5 billion. The international community, especially America, the EU, Japan, India, Pakistan, all helped me and I did a lot of reconstruction work. I paved 2,480 kilometres of roads.

Here, Shirzai specifically contradicted the claim that he was removed from the governorship of Kandahar. He emphasized many prizes that he claimed to have won in connection with his work as governor of Nangarhar to further the narrative that he was needed there:

So, I was honoured with the medal of the Wazir Akbar, which is a very honourable medal in Afghanistan. And a presidential decree honoured me as a hero of reconstruction of Afghanistan. After that there was another presidential decree that announced that I was a hero of both peace and reconstruction. That's all my achievements. And after that, in 2014, I ran for presidency and resigned as governor of Nangarhar Province. Following that, I was elected as the "Best Person of the Year," twice. Radio Freedom asked people to vote for the "Best Person of the Year" and they voted for me two years running.

When I asked him more specifically about how he thought others perceived him and how he gained support both locally and internationally, he exhibited the same confidence: "I was able to bring the poppy cultivation in Nangarhar down to zero. That's why the international community gave me USD 10 million as a gift. I spent this money on the reconstruction and stabilisation of Nangarhar University. That's why the people of Afghanistan and also the international community respect me."

Shirzai contrasted his own performance with those of others: "And now you can see what the situation in Jalalabad is like, because I am not there. There is a lot of fighting, even inside the city. The security situation is not good. Probably, if it continues, Nangarhar may fall into the hands of the Taliban."

Welcoming me, a Western foreigner, into a room with sofas, he spoke of specific techniques he employs. "I know how to govern Afghanistan; that's why I was successful. I had good relations with the scholars, the religious scholars, with the elders and the influential people of Nangarhar. I was just sitting on the floor as they sit, together with them. And there were mullahs and religious scholars with them. When I see a mullah, I am a mullah. When I see young people, I am young, and when I see some people who are very smart, I am smart just like them. That's why everybody likes me."

Shirzai readily admitted that he hoped to play an important role in politics again: "I pray to God to also give me a chance to serve and unite the people of Afghanistan, and to be somehow helpful. . . . Now I am busy and am preparing a plan for a solution. Not a plan of reconstruction of Afghanistan but a plan for a solution. The problem with a solution." In other words, rhetoric about how Afghanistan needed reconstruction did not reflect a full understanding of what Shirzai thought he could accomplish. I asked him why he was so confident, and he said, "I have a lot of experience. I know how to do it. I live with the people, with the military, with the civilians. And I was governor for fourteen, fifteen years. I have experience and I know how to do it. And I have their support. . . . If we had a lot of heroes in the world then there would be no problems. That's why the people call me hero.

The hero of peace, the hero of reconstruction, the bulldozer of Afghanistan."

Shirzai clearly had authority as an individual—it was not linked to an organization, such as an insurgency group or the state. This is likely why his claims to legitimacy focused on his strengths as a person. To bolster his claims to legitimacy, Shirzai emphasized others' requests that he take on a certain role or responsibility, whether it be a domestic or foreign power, suggesting they recognized his talents and that he never sought power for himself, which might undermine his claim that "serving the country" and "bringing peace" were his primary motivations.

There are different dimensions to Shirzai's self-perception of legitimacy. He tried to portray himself as a heroic servant of the country, who was guided only by the greater good and not by personal interests. To construct a perception of himself at the local level that reflected an attitude of service, he focused on daily interaction with people, adjusting to their respective expectations of what interaction should look like. So, while he constructed instrumental legitimacy within different interest groups, eradicating drugs for the Americans and building infrastructure for the people at the local level, he also, and more substantively, considered values, particularly with regard to his attitudes and interactions.

HAJJI ZAHIR QADIR

Hajji Zahir Qadir, then deputy speaker of Parliament, also received me in one of his homes.[43] It was a more modest and casual setting than Shirzai's. Qadir referenced his family history immediately, saying, "I belong to a family which has been involved in politics not since yesterday or today, but for centuries." He referenced his great grandfather, his grandfather, his father, and his two uncles. His uncle Hajji Dean Muhammad, he said, had been his father's teacher. Muhammed had "been in politics since the beginning of Jihad and now our uncle is still alive but all of his students have died." However, it was his deceased uncle, Abdul Haq, who he believed could have been president. He said that Karzai would never have been the president of Afghanistan if Abdul Haq had been alive.

Zahir Qadir also referenced his own amassing of power from a young age: "I attended college in Pakistan. During our holidays, we went to fight the Russian Communist Regime [in Afghanistan]. Slowly, slowly, I became the commander of ten or twenty soldiers. And it got bigger and bigger over time. The time came, when I was 21, that I became the first young two-star general in Afghanistan. I was chief of the border police of four provinces at that time. During Jihad, when I was eighteen, I was in charge of 21,000 soldiers. There was no government. Everybody worked through parties, following senior individuals."

When the Taliban took control in the 1990s, Zahir Qadir was imprisoned with Ismail Khan, the later influential strongman of Herat in western Afghanistan.[44] He narrated his escape from prison to Pakistan via Iran and his struggles as he planned to return to his native country to fight the Taliban: "There was a shortage of money. And I remember I only had 200,000 Pakistani Rupees [about $2,000] and in 48 hours I collected my 1,000 soldiers and my 50 commanders in Pakistan. . . . I came with my soldiers, but also with a lot of problems and difficulties. There was no money, no food for eating, no ammunition, no guns, no weapons, no anything."

This incident suggested the confidence Zahir Qadir brought to command: "I crossed the border [to Afghanistan] with a lot of problems at 12 o'clock at night, I remember. The Pakistanis posted checkpoints at the border. They shouted at us to surrender and 'where are you going?' I smiled and told them to leave us [alone], 'You are 20, we are 1,000. And it's our country, not your country. I am going to my country. It's my business, not yours. If you want to fight, we are ready for fighting.' They understood and opened the way for us and we entered, and the Taliban at that time was in every town."

He emphasized his humane treatment of Taliban prisoners of war, saying, "I caught the 5th base of the Taliban. There were about 300 Taliban inside that base. When I caught them, they thought they would be killed. But I said 'no, all of us are Muslims and even more, we are humans. And humans need to respect each other.' And we were respectful. Okay, fighting is a different thing. But now my rules, our family rules, our Mujahedin rules are not to kill if you catch someone. I just took their guns and ammunition and gave them money and I told them 'you go, this is for your expenses.' But I kept their cars and weapons."

Zahir Qadir emphasized that soldiers followed him. "Slowly-slowly, they heard that I was in Afghanistan. When I entered Afghanistan at the beginning, there were 1,000 soldiers with me. But when I entered Jalalabad, there were 10,000 soldiers with me."

At this point, Zahir Qadir's father, Abdul Qadir, also returned to Jalalabad from Germany. Zahir Qadir outlined how he and his father supported Karzai to become president after Abdul Haq had died. He claimed they were the people who agreed to give up power in rural Afghanistan and to take up official positions in Kabul, while people like Dostum, Ismail Khan, and Atta Noor preferred to remain in the provinces. He referenced his father's assistance to Karzai at the loya jirga, where Abdul Zahir successfully convinced other candidates such as Rabbani and Qadir's cousin Hedayet Afzallah not to run for president. After Karzai became interim president in 2002, he appointed Abdul Qadir as the minister of public works and made him vice president. Soon after, however, his father was killed.

Zahir Qadir believed his father had a premonition of his own death.

> He told me to come to his house quickly. . . . He was looking very beautiful and his face was shining. . . . I went over and he told me "I have three things to tell you that you have to keep in mind. . . . First, make a friendship with my friends. Whether I am alive or dead." That was the first thing. And secondly, "anytime our people from Afghanistan are facing problems and knocking at your door at midnight you have to go out yourself and have to try to solve their problems." The third thing he told me [was,] "anytime you understand that you are so strong that you are hurting your people with your power you have to resign." I accepted his words. . . . But I was wondering why he told me this kind of things. Like he knew he was going to die.

Later that day, Zahir Qadir learned of his father's death from a Japanese television station, which called him and asked him for comment. Zahir Qadir explained how he tried to find those responsible for his father's death, investigating and arresting people himself.

> We caught some people who did the actual assassination. On one day I got all of them. And for two months we kept them with us and after that they were sent to the government, who asked me, "Please give these people to us, to take them to court." I collected

the proof from the investigation and gave it to them. . . . After some time, the chief prosecutor announced openly in the media that Hajji Zaman [Mohammed Zaman Ghamsharik], one of our commanders in the Eastern Region, had killed [my father]. But we didn't know who was above Hajji Zaman in all of this. There were many people acting above Hajji Zaman.

The death of Mohammed Zaman ultimately resulted in the breakdown of Zahir Qadir's friendship with Karzai. Mohammed Zaman, who had been taken to Kabul after the death of Zahir Qadir's father, was freed. According to his own account, Zahir Qadir promised Karzai he would not hurt Mohammed Zaman because Karzai had sought his support in the elections. However, he told me that he had warned Karzai that the grown children of people Mohammed Zaman had killed were ultimately going to kill him, but Karzai hadn't believed him.

And he [Mohammed Zaman] came to Jalalabad. . . . By the time one and a half months was up, he was dead. A suicide killer came and killed him, together with 18 other people. I remember three minutes later, President Karzai called me up, and asked me, "How are you, Khan?" He wasn't saying "Hajji" as usual, he was calling me "Khan." I said "I am okay, how are you?" He was telling me directly, "Khan, you killed him?" I asked, "Who?" He responded, "Hajji Zahman." I told him "It's the first time I am hearing it, from you. Listen, I told you at the beginning. Don't let him go to Jalalabad. If someone kills him then you will be blaming me. And now it has happened. And you are blaming me." . . . From then on the problems between me and the President started."

In the years that followed, Zahir Qadir's relationship with the Karzai administration deteriorated, and with it, his relationship with the United States and specifically the CIA. He reported that as head of the border police of eastern Afghanistan, without the president's authorization, he led a year-long fight with the Pakistani army that he felt was threatening to cross the border. The United States, he said, saw such actions as opposing its interests. In an echo of Shirzai, he noted, "But in reality, for me, my country, my people are important." Nonetheless, he lost his position as the head of border police in the east and was relocated to the north, where he became head of the border police for the provinces Badakhshan, Takhar, and Kunduz.

According to Zahir Qadir, he continued to face a power struggle. Much as he sought to fight drug trafficking, he felt that "international political games" were drawing him in. According to his account, his only chance of surviving these games politically was the threat of force:

> I did a lot of fighting there [in north Afghanistan]. There were smugglers I was fighting with. I seized a lot of drugs and these things. And the capture of drugs was not acceptable to some other people in Kabul. Because they were connected with them. At the time, Marshal [Fahem] was in a strong position and Atta Noor was Deputy Minister of MoI [Ministry of Interior]. I blocked their routes and it was not acceptable to them, because they were smuggling hundreds and thousands of kilos per day. I closed their benefit avenues. So, they tried a different way, portraying me as a smuggler. They caught some of my guys. For ten months my guys were in prison. I left my job and went back to Jalalabad. They were trying to catch me. At that time, Atta [Noor] called me and asked "Where are you? Can you come to Kabul? I want to meet you. Please come quickly." Some of my friends called me and said, "If you go to Kabul, you won't come back to Jalalabad. They will arrest you." I told them, "Don't worry."

I assembled my soldiers and I remember 170 cars full of ammunition and weapons. "Let's go to Kabul." And I called Engineer Ibrahim, he was deputy of the NDS, and told him, "I want to meet you for two minutes. I will not take any more of your time." He said, "okay." And I came to Kabul and I went there and told him, "I did not come to ask for help. It's not my habit to cry. This is the plan: I have 600–700 soldiers already in Kabul, with ammunitions and all kind of guns and weapons. If someone touches me, I will destroy Kabul in five minutes.". . . .

Then I came back from the NDS and came here [meaning his house]. And I called my commanders, [and said] a hundred trucks should go to the place where I was supposed to go. It's a place in Kart-e-Se [a neighborhood in Kabul]. The British were there, it was a place for the investigation of smuggling. I sent my hundred cars there and told them to surround the area. When you have surrounded the area, I will go inside. Our meeting was at 12.30 and they were ready to arrest me. My soldiers told me that they were there and controlling everything, so, "Now you can come." I went there with 70 cars. There were some Afghan soldiers and some people for the investigation. One lady was from the UK, one person was from the United States to investigate my case. It was a very big [laughing] problem. And they came out and asked, "That many soldiers and weapons? Where are they from? And whom do they belong to?" I said, "These are my soldiers and my weapons." "So why did you bring them?" I told them, "I told my soldiers I am entering the building at 12.30, if I haven't left by 1 p.m., kill everybody inside, including myself. Don't leave anyone alive." They were shocked. After 15 minutes, they had finished and let me go.

Zahir Qadir concluded, "There were political games going on. Not national, but international games. And I entered the international games but didn't understand them. But I was clean [innocent]. And if you are clean you don't need to be scared of anything."

After resigning from his position with the border police and moving back to Jalalabad, Zahir Qadir decided to run for Parliament and was elected. However, his conflict with Karzai continued. According to Zahir Qadir, for instance, Karzai refused to open the new Parliament, as he did not accept some of the newly elected MPs, arguing that there had been too much fraud in the process. "I gave a press conference and said 'Mr. President, it's not within your power. If you are closing parliament, we will be finished with you. I will finish you,' openly, I told him." Much as Shirzai had, Zahir Qadir emphasized that he won support that led others to tell him to seek power: "After that my friends recommended me as a candidate to become first deputy speaker [of Parliament]. I told them 'No, I am not ready. I am good as an MP.' Anyway, they selected me."

At the end of the interview, I asked Zahir Qadir about local perceptions of him and why he thought that people supported him. He referenced his family again. "Our family has the best people. My father, my grandfather. We have a long, good history. And we didn't hurt people. We were always working for the people."

He also emphasized that people follow him, although he made no apparent distinction between soldiers and civilians. "Whether I have been an MP or not, if I am sitting in my house, every day 1,000 or 2,000 people come to meet me. They are visiting me. In just 24 hours I can collect 100,000 people for a meeting if I decide to. It's not easy for the president. But in 24 hours my team and I can have a strong team, not just in Jalalabad, not just in the Eastern Region, but in all of Afghanistan, I can have such a team. But my team is an underground team, not out in the open. When I need them, they are doing their work. Because the government is scared of me."

Returning again to his family, he said, "If our family supports someone to be the President of Afghanistan, he will be the
President of Afghanistan. There are many reasons. We conduct
ourselves well with the local people, with our brothers, with our
family. We are listening to them, working for them, solving their
problems. That is crucial."

Zahir Qadir emphasized the force he commanded, referencing the number of soldiers he had and his history of calling on
them when he needed to. He was confident that the "government is scared" of him. On the other hand, he also highlighted
his legitimacy, which he considered to be stronger than that of
other strongmen and even the Karzai administration. This was
not only because of the influence of his family. He emphasized
that he put Afghan interests first and defended the country
against Pakistani and American influence and sinister machina-
tions. He said he was more responsive to attempts to consolidate
power in Kabul than other strongmen. He fought drug traffick-
ers, endured malevolent political games, and tried to achieve
peace and stability in the country. In contrast to Shirzai, Qadir
did not portray himself as a servant of the people. Instead, he
emphasized his own agency and leadership. But, like Shirzai,
he claimed that he sought to serve the interests of Afghanistan,
not himself. Thus, he narrated his history of standing up for the
integrity of the territory and constitutional rights—on the battlefield and in Parliament—whether it was against Pakistan or
the Afghan government.

Beyond that, he highlighted his work for the people and his
good behavior when dealing with them, reflecting the claim that
he worked for Afghanistan, not hurting people, but "listening to
them, working for them, solving their problems." Overall, Qadir's
self-perception of legitimacy rested heavily on values, making it
substantive. While he also provided services, he pointed out that

his legitimacy was based on procedural values, his day-to-day behavior with local people, and his attitude, especially his fight for national interests. It was these certain values that his father reminded him of before he was killed—friendship, engagement, and restraint.

Despite their many differences, Zahir Qadir shared with Shirzai a tendency to actively construct attempt construcing legitimacy on the local level, responding to needs and value-based expectations. He provided and financed public services, which enabled him to construct instrumental legitimacy. The two men also took this further by referencing the substantive, value-based dimension of legitimacy that was linked to what they believed to be right, particularly with regard to how to interact with people. While Qadir emphasized the importance of listening to people and solving their problems, Shirzai stressed the importance of his skill in adapting to different modes of interaction with different people.

"THE GOVERNMENT NEEDS TO DISARM THEM": PUBLIC PERCEPTIONS OF STRONGMEN

My conversations with civilians in Nangarhar suggest that strongmen had largely failed to establish legitimacy. They described strongmen like Shirzai and the Arsala family as connected to the government but acting outside the law, conducting land-grabbing and other forms of extortion, and acting with impunity. Some people also even speculated they were connected to Pakistan's Inter-Services Intelligence (ISI). Most interviewees considered strongmen to be intimidating drivers of insecurity. A few people were too afraid to talk to me about them, like the farmer Taher, who said, "I don't like to talk to you about the influential and powerful people here".[45]

The people I talked to in Nangarhar used different terms to refer to strongmen, including more descriptive ones such as "Jihadi commanders" and "influential people" along with more judgmental ones like "warlords." Regardless of the terminology, across the province and during the time I conducted my research, most interviewees considered strongmen to be intimidating drivers of insecurity. Rahmanullah, a mechanic, complained, "I think poor people can't influence the level of security. It is the powerful people in the province who cause security or insecurity."[46] Since Nangarhar lacked security, he had no respect for the strongmen. Bahir from Jalalabad, told me, "We know that all former Jihadi commanders are threats and are involved in causing insecurity."[47] A prevalent perception was that strongmen could easily ensure security in Nangarhar, but they wanted to maintain insecurity in the province to maintain their income from the war economy. For instance, university student Gulagha complained, "A secure environment can be risky for them. They therefore either directly or indirectly try to sabotage the security situation through their networks if they have the opportunity."[48]

Interviewees described the soldiers that the strongmen commanded as illegally armed. For example, Bahir explained, "They own weapons illegally and the government needs to disarm them as quickly as possible."[49] The fact that strongmen controlled parts of the "official" forces of the Afghan state, rather than conferring legitimacy on the strongmen, undermined the legitimacy of the state. Student Rohullah in Jalalabad told me that "the former Jihadi commanders like Gul Karim, former head of the police, Hazrat Ali, member of parliament, Hajji Zahir Qadir, brother of the former governor Hajji Mosa, and Hajji Jamal Qadir have a great number of both legal—government forces—and illegal gunmen and cause insecurity."[50] And Khyber, an NGO employee from Jalalabad, explained that when Jihadi commanders co-opted members of the ALP, they used the force's power to promote insecurity.[51]

The interviewees felt that strongmen threatened and exploited people for their own benefit. For instance, Khair from Jalalabad complained about the strongmen's conflict resolution procedures, which he perceived as unfair and corrupt. "Along with members of local councils and a number of influential people, it's the former Jihadi commanders who are involved in conflict resolution. But their authority is only based on their power, and the fear which they spread among the people. They use their power and take sides in conflict resolution."[52] Contradicting Shirzai's self-concept, interviewees, such as Nazar, the head of a council in Behsod District, noted that strongmen often did not even bother to treat them with respect.[53]

According to the interviewees, strongmen often did not even try to disguise their greed as public service delivery but simply took what they wanted. Along with many others, Khair openly condemned land-grabbing: "On the district level, warlords use force to either grab land or buy it off the owners against their will."[54] Najibullah, a shopkeeper from Surkh Rod District, said, "The main reason for insecurity is the presence and power of the former Jihadi commanders. These warlords or Jihadi commanders are involved in a big number of illegal acts such as land grabbing."[55] Teacher Mohammad Yusuf from Behsod stated, "The powerful people in the area take the land of the poor people."[56] NGO worker Subhanullah, also from Behsod, supported this claim, saying, "There was a big uninhabited area in our area. But now half of this area has been taken by powerful men, who fight each other up to the point that people get killed."[57] Ahmad, from the same district, who was unemployed, told me that land-grabbing often resulted in or fueled community conflicts on land distribution.[58]

People also saw the strongmen as the cause of many other criminal activities in the province. Student Gulagha said, "These circles [meaning strongmen] make their income from kidnappings, robberies, and murders."[59] Similarly, Rohullah explained, "The warlords own weapons illegally . . . and are involved in kidnappings and land grabbing."[60] An NGO worker from Jalalabad explained, "There is a ban on cutting down the forests. But some members of parliament and ministers use their power to continually do so. And they are involved in drug trafficking." He also described a protection racket that he thought was benefiting those strongmen controlling the local government: "On a weekly basis every shopkeeper at the bazaar has to pay 300 Afs [about $4.50] to Jalalabad's municipality. In total, this amount of money easily adds up to 200,000 USD each month."[61]

Just as connection with the state did not confer legitimacy on strongmen, people felt that it empowered strongmen to act with impunity. Unemployed Nadia summed this up. "They have weapons and power. They can do any illegal activity, whenever they want to."[62] And Nidah, from Kama District, told me, "They have weapons, and no one can fight them because they also are part of the government."[63] The university student went on to explain: "In Jalalabad city, the former Jihadi commanders and warlords have a strong presence. They use their links to the government . . . for kidnappings and land grabbing. This way they create an atmosphere of fear. For example, a former Jihadi commander prevented the construction of a second bridge in Behsod. It required special forces from Kabul to arrest him so that he couldn't cause problems anymore."[64]

Medical doctor and civil society activist Jamil similarly stated, "Providing security is the obligation of both the people and the government. But the problem is that the former Jihadi commanders are supported by government officials. Otherwise they wouldn't be able to create security threats."[65]

In keeping with the general skepticism about the police force, interviewees noted that even those forces that strongmen did not control were unlikely to question their authority. Bahir, a former local ISAF employee, claimed, "When the former Jihadi commanders cause trouble for the people and someone calls the police, they don't dare to interfere."[66] According to Jamil, because a large number of forces were occupied in guarding strongmen like Zahir Qadir they did not have enough capacity to ensure security for ordinary people.[67]

But the strongmen's authority did not only rest on militias and control of state forces. Many people I talked to described the strongmen's influences down to the community level, where they co-opted local structures. This complaint came up particularly frequently in Behsod District. For example, the carpenter Burhanuddin stated, "I don't like the local councils here because they have been created by powerful people in the area."[68] A civil society activist similarly complained, "Unfortunately, in some areas the warlords have reduced the prestige and honour of the local councils."[69] Other interviewees also claimed and criticized that strongmen used insurgency groups to defend their interests and mislead people when killing opponents.[70]

In contrast to the confident statements by Zahir Qadir of his utter opposition to Pakistan, many interviewees perceived all strongmen as being linked to the Pakistani intelligence agency. Wasiullah from Sherzad District referenced Shirzai specifically in connection to his charge: "Ten days ago a bomb exploded in front of Kabul Bank. I think it was planned by Pakistan. Similarly, three months ago a big attack happened on a football pitch in Paktika Province. These attacks are conducted by the ISI with the help of the powerful people in our country, like the last governor Gul Agha Shirzai."[71] Teacher Parwana summarized this popular perception, saying, "Insurgents, Taliban, and warlords are the people who cause insecurity and are a threat to peace. Most of them are controlled by foreign intelligence agencies."[72]

Consequently, many people said they wished to get rid of the strongmen. For instance, Jamil, a civil society activist, said: "Our essential need is the rule of law. If we had the rule of law there, the illegally-armed men would be wiped out."[73] Others were hoping for the Taliban to take over again, specifically because of the toxic effects of strongmen control. Zakerullah, a young man from Jalalabad, told me, "During the time of the Taliban, there were no influential people and there was no extortion in this area. But today the government can't control them anymore and all people hope for the Taliban to return."[74]

A tiny minority of people in Naranghar had positive views on strongmen. Shafeequllah from Jalalabad referenced traditional legitimacy from association with families who had power in the past and instrumental legitimacy from providing useful services. "There are two types of leaders in our city. One of them is leaders from certain families, who have a traditional role. The others are appointed formally by the municipality and receive a salary. Both of them provide services for the local people in the area. . . . I like the influential people because they are working for the poor people."[75] The farmer Haiatullah expressed similar feelings. "I like all influential people in our province because they help us if we have problems."[76] Most interviewees with positive views on strongmen emphasized their role in solving conflicts, suggesting

Zahir Qadir's strategy of accepting petitions had some success. Shopkeeper Abdul Sammad from Jalalabad explained that the strongman "is active in conflict resolution and solves our conflicts in a fair way."[77] Similarly, Hajji Nazar, the head of a village in Behsod District, named Zahir Qadir, and said he solved conflicts and provided security.[78] Abdul Wahab from Behsod District seemed to agree: "When we are involved in conflicts, we first of all refer the case to the influential and powerful people in the area [meaning strongmen]."[79]

Interestingly, no interviewees appeared to be on the fence or take a neutral stance. The limited number of positive views was based mainly on a perceived helpful role of strongmen and the services they were providing—resulting in instrumental legitimacy. Some people, however, did consider the authority of strongmen to be legitimate in a more substantive way. Zahir Qadir's conflict resolution procedures were his greatest source of legitimacy. It is striking that people particularly emphasized the notion of fairness. Some strongmen may have offered conflict resolution that was perceived as fair by all involved parties, not just the winners, as long as it did not affect their own affairs, enabling them to construct at least a degree of substantive legitimacy.[80] Overall, the divided picture left the impression that some selected people directly benefitted from the strongmen's influence and patronage networks. In contrast, most people felt insecure, threatened, or exploited.

People often described the actions of strongmen as "illegal," using the law as a benchmark. This indicates that, despite the strongmen's permeation of the state and the corruption of the system, they still believed in the law and the idea of a state with a rational-legal structure. Decades of violent conflict had not eliminated their strong views on which attitudes and behaviors of authorities were right and wrong. The negative perception of strongmen appeared to be the result of personal experience or second-hand information of the strongmen's behavior or of their forces, such as land-grabbing. These experiences undermined the claims the strongmen made.

Past research on Shirzai's time as governor indicates that people initially thought positively of him due to the services he provided.[81] This perception changed when he stopped providing services. Then, interviewees considered him to be just one of the many corrupt strongmen in the province. This illustrates that instrumental legitimacy is short-lived and needs to be constantly maintained if it is not transformed into more substantive legitimacy.

STRONGMEN IN THE KINGDOM OF THE NORTH

We observed a different kind of strongmen governance in Balkh Province. Balkh is located in northern Afghanistan and borders Uzbekistan and Tajikistan. It is famous for its cultural heritage, including the ancient city of Balkh and the Blue Mosque, a shrine in the center of Balkh Province's capital, Mazar-e-Sharif. With an estimated population of around six hundred thousand people, Mazar-e-Sharif is the third-largest city in Afghanistan.[82] It used to host Camp Marmal, where the German military forces were based until June 2021. Ethnically, the province is diverse, with a big Tajik and Pashtun population as well as Uzbeks, Hazaras, Turkmens, Arabs, and Baluchs.[83] In contrast to the complexity and number of strongmen in Nangarhar, the political order of Balkh was simpler, underpinned by a long-standing rivalry between Abdul Rashi Dostum, an Uzbek strongman, and Atta Mohammad Noor, a Tajik strongman, who succeeded in becoming what media the called "king of the north" or "emperor of Balkh."

Mukhopadhyay offers a detailed description of Noor's career. According to her account, he grew up in Balkh and joined the Mujahedin as a teenager, progressing quickly to become a commander of the military arm of the Jamiat-e Islami party in the north.[84] Dostum commanded an even larger group of militias in the 1990s, with estimates ranging between 20,000 and 110,000. Noor and Dostum successfully fought the Taliban in 2001 and recaptured Mazar-e-Sharif with the help of American Special Forces. Then they became rivals for control of Balkh. Noor drew on his commitment to Islamism and his steadfast loyalty to his party to seek support, whereas Dostum, who had shifting loyalties, drew more on his ethnic identity as an Uzbek and a defender of the rights of non-Pashtun minorities.[85]

Noor became the major authority in Balkh by working more closely with the government in Kabul and maintaining his militias, which he claimed were peacekeeping forces, and offering services in the hopes of constructing local legitimacy. In the post-2001 interim governments, members of the Jamiat party were in control of key ministries in the security sector. Noor covered most of Balkh's electricity bill in 2002 and contributed to building a mosque in 2003. But in autumn 2003, Dostum mobilized a large number of fighters from the region, resulting in an increased number of clashes between Noor's and Dostum's militias. Noor was preparing his forces for a battle in Mazar-e-Sharif at a time when observers judged Dostum's forces to be more powerful. But the international community and the Ministry of Interior intervened, forcing Noor and Dostum to establish a joined force and to give up heavy weapons, preventing Dostum from winning. While Dostum behaved with increased aggression, Noor built even closer ties with Kabul and portrayed himself as a politician—a man who had left warlordism behind. In mid-2004, the government in Kabul ruled in favor of Noor, appointing him the governor of Balkh.

In the years that followed, the situation in Balkh was calm. Noor consolidated his power, monopolized force to a high degree, and connected his informal networks with his formal position of authority. He brought his commanders and others who were loyal to him into senior positions of the provincial administration, undermining the government system and allowing him to exercise force through both the formal system and informal militias. With this high degree of monopolized force, he was able to provide stability and security in Balkh. However, according to Mukhopadhyay, Noor also managed to construct local support by advocating for more foreign aid money for Balkh and channeling some of it to his communities. He dropped his jihadi image and transformed himself into a civilian governor in a tailored suit. Part of his transformation was increased engagement in the private sector, using his authority in Balkh and his influence in Kabul to support his companies—for example, to win bids in the construction sector. He ultimately became the most successful businessperson in the province, which gave him an additional incentive to maintain stability and security.

When Noor supported Karzai's opponent Abdullah Abdullah in the 2009 elections, it seemed likely that Karzai, who won reelection, might have preferred to remove Noor. The fact that he didn't suggests that Karzai recognized Noor's hold on power was strong. Noor continued to support Abdullah Abdullah in the 2014 elections, while Dostum supported Ghani as a candidate and was rewarded by being appointed vice president. When Ghani dismissed Noor as the governor of Balkh, he refused to step down. Dostum became increasingly involved in military operations in the north of Afghanistan, and the situation worsened after photos of Dostum were removed from billboards in Mazar-e-Sharif. Uzbek demonstrators took to the streets, blaming Noor for the action, which resulted in clashes between armed supporters on both sides.[86] Even so, Noor managed to remain in control. Finally, in early 2018, Ghani succeeded, and Noor agreed to step down. However, Noor remained an influential person in Balkh and illustrated his power when Ghani dismissed the provincial head of police. Forces loyal to Noor erupted in conflict in 2019 when the new head of police attempted to enter his office in Mazar-e-Sharif. Nonetheless, in the 2019 presidential elections, Noor supported Ghani, to some extent, using the opportunity to elevate his role within Jamiat-e Islami. When the Taliban entered Mazar-e-Sharif on August 14, 2021, the day before Kabul fell, Dostum and Noor escaped to neighboring Uzbekistan together.

"NOTHING HERE HAPPENS WITHOUT HIS PERMISSION": PUBLIC PERCEPTIONS OF ATTA NOOR

Most of my interviews in Balkh took place in three districts: Mazar-e-Sharif, Dehdadi, and Hairatan. Reflecting his power in the province in 2014/2015, most interviewees mentioned Noor without my prompting, and most voiced very positive perceptions of him as the reason Balkh was relatively safe. For example, the farmer Hajji Sultan from Dehdadi District reported, "The security in Dehdadi District and wider Balkh Province is good because of our provincial governor."[87] Farhad, a young mechanic from Mazar-e-Sharif, told me, "We have a good governor, Mohammad Noor, who provides security for us."[88] Some people said that they trusted him. But whether they brought him up or

I asked about him, people emphasized security—they did not mention justice.

People who acknowledged that the province had challenges, including the high and increasing unemployment rate, did not hold Noor responsible. Shopkeeper Hajji Nematullah explained that "everything else depends on living securely."[89] Thus, Noor got credit for supplying it. Nemat in Mazar-e-Sharif, who was unemployed at the time, explained, "Our governor is a good person. But if there is only one good person nothing will change," meaning that Noor alone was not sufficient for satisfying governance in Balkh.[90]

On the other hand, Zahra, a civil society activist, explained that the people either did not understand how Noor benefited from criminality and corruption or were too afraid to talk about it. Indeed, many people I talked to appeared too afraid to talk about problems and criticize Noor. In contrast to the other provinces where I conducted research, several interviewees in Balkh were hesitant, and many interviews were quite brief. This may be explained by the level of monopolization of force in Balkh under Noor. For example, in Nangarhar, the political environment is more fractionalized, possibly resulting in more violence; however, they were also more openly critical in debates. Some who were critical used cautious phrasing, such as Murad, a barber in Mazar-e Sharif, who said, "The powerful people have lots of guns and money. They kill people and take their money. But no one can arrest them."[91] In a similarly diplomatic fashion, the farmer Abdul Majid concluded, "We agree with the government, but they have to finish their tyrannical behavior and land grabbing."[92]

Those who offered more direct criticism were often civil society activists. Darya, a civil society activist from Mazar-e-Sharif, told me, "There are lots of groups creating insecurity. There are people who rape, kill and kidnap. I think that the governor supports them. Because the governor is aware of everything and nothing here happens without his permission." Aliah, a young student and activist, summarized her critique in a similar way: "The governor of Balkh makes the province look secure from the outside. But the outsiders can't look inside."[93] Another vocal critic of Noor was a community leader from Chimtal District. He outlined how Noor accused him and many others from his community of being members of the Taliban movement to justify the use of force against them. He admitted that they were indeed fighting Noor but explained that this was a local uprising resulting from Noor's corrupt mode of governance rather than a Taliban-affiliated insurgency.

Such cracks in the armor suggested at the time that Noor's hold on his people's favor was unstable. Much like Shirzai, it was clear that if he ever lost the authority that was based on force, he would not have the people's confidence. While it is difficult to be sure to what extent people spoke highly of Noor because they feared him, their appreciation of security, which was better in Balkh than most other provinces in the country, seemed genuine. Thus, Noor had gained instrumental legitimacy. The fact that some people referenced "trust" may even indicate some substantive belief in his legitimacy, possibly from people who wanted nothing more than a stable political order and were not threatened by Noor. After all, stability enabled not only a secure income but also predictability for the future. At the time, it appeared as though Noor could have even built a perception of substantive legitimacy over time by providing stability.

While legitimacy certainly played some role in Noor's authority, it remains unclear how honest such descriptions were, as there appeared to be a widespread fear of Noor. The emphasis on Noor's innocence regarding any of the security or economic problems in the province may reflect such fear. It is ironic that Balkh, seemingly the most secure province of Afghanistan at the time I visited, had so many people who were afraid to speak openly. Indeed, his critics argued that Noor was so influential that any violence that occurred must have happened with his consent. Thus, criticizing him was potentially dangerous. Particularly civil society activists, who demanded a more democratic political order in the province, were afraid that if they spoke up too publicly, they would pay the price.

Ultimately, Noor's authority rested solely on force—its control and its application. By monopolizing force, Noor was able to construct instrumental legitimacy through perceived security and stability. But he could also use force to be coercive and create insecurity for people if it was beneficial for him. This made his authority rather authoritarian. Noor seemed to have a personal interest in maintaining stability to construct legitimacy because he benefitted financially. But if individuals or groups got in the way of his personal interests, he could use force that he controlled, including the state's forces, against them. However, his dependency on force as his only source of authority and the absence of other, more lasting, substantive sources of legitimacy made his authority vulnerable. While he looked powerful due to the forces he controlled and the money he had, he could only maintain legitimacy as long he was in control of force in the province.

CONCLUSIONS

Comparing Balkh and Nangarhar provinces, we can see two very different forms of strongmen governance. Strongmen in Nangarhar were part of a competitive political order where multiple individuals and groups were in control. Zahir Qadir himself described it as an "international game," illustrating the usefulness of Bourdieu-inspired conceptualization of political order that has a game-like character.[94] Shirzai and Zahir Qadir claimed substantive legitimacy on the basis of good behavior and family tradition, but strongmen were actually widely perceived as corrupt and criminal, and people did not seem to care much about their family tradition. Conversely, in Balkh, Noor successfully monopolized force for a while, controlling not only informal militias but also the formal government forces, with the exception of some districts, such as Chimtal, where people resisted his efforts. He claimed instrumental legitimacy on the basis of stability and security, and he indeed managed to live up to this expectation.

What Qadir, Shirzai, and Noor have in common and what made them "strongmen" was that they had actual authority as *individuals* in their respective provinces. This authority rested predominantly on the control of armed forces. But in contrast to what strands of the literature on strongmen and warlords suggest, the interviews illustrate that the force of strongmen does not rely on "private" militias only. On the contrary, all three men depended heavily on "public" formal forces, using the state apparatus for their personal gains or formalizing their private forces and outsourcing their salaries by making them part of the state forces while maintaining personal control. But even if strongmen exercise force and influence through the state, they do so as individuals, not as state officials with accountability within a bureaucracy. For example, Zahir Qadir—as the head of the border police in northern Afghanistan—used his forces to stop the government from prosecuting him for alleged drug smuggling. Noor refused to step down from his position even though he was formally dismissed. Beyond using state forces, strongmen were even perceived to be controlling insurgency groups or labeling

some of their militias as insurgents, enabling them to fight political opponents without appearing to be involved.

Resting on the control of armed forces, the authority of Zahir
Qadir, Shirzai, and Noor was of a similar kind. And, indeed,
their authority was also perceived in a similar way by the public. Nonetheless, there also were some differences. In both provinces, people looked at strongmen mainly through the lens of
(in)security rather than conflict resolution. In the case of Balkh,
Noor's control of force and his ability to use it to pursue his own
interests was perceived as coercive and spread fear, particularly
in civil society. However, it also ensured stability and enabled
him to construct instrumental legitimacy, providing a service
people needed. Conversely, Shirzai and Zahir Qadir were seen as
a coercive threat by most people I talked to in Nangarhar. People
described their behavior as corrupt and criminal. Lacking a local
monopoly of force, they couldn't provide stability or security for
a larger group of people. However, they also couldn't spread fear
in a structural way as Noor could, so people felt less afraid to
criticize them. Thus, fewer people spoke positively about them.

None of the strongmen I looked at succeeded in constructing
widespread substantive legitimacy. Some people did say that they
"trust" Noor—possibly because they enjoyed and had become
used to the stability in the province over time or because fear
affected their statements in the interviews. This makes it difficult
to judge to what extent voiced trust actually indicates substantive legitimacy. Overall, then, my case studies seem to suggest
that strongmen have little hope of establishing widespread substantive legitimacy. But lasting authority seems impossible without substantive legitimacy, as already suggested by Weber.

People judged strongmen on the basis of their *actions*. Family
tradition and other personal features did not appear to be relevant for most people I talked to. While Marten proposes that

strongmen co-opt community authorities to gain legitimacy, this strategy does not always appear to be successful.[95] My research indicates that co-option often delegitimizes the community authorities instead of legitimizing strongmen. People were concerned with how strongmen affected their day-to-day lives, how they behaved and how they interacted with them. Even though Murtazashvili suggests that strongmen do not play a role in people's daily lives, the interviews with civilians show that people at least perceive them to be heavily involved.[96] They directly interacted with a large number of people, and their actions, such as land grabs, directly affected people. Furthermore, they were perceived to be in control of state forces and militias, so that how people experienced the behavior of these forces also affected how they perceived the strongmen. On that basis, people drew conclusions about the strongmen's goals. If people had negative experiences and considered the behavior of strongmen and their forces to be exploitative, they perceived them as working for themselves only.

Strongmen's claims about their military strength and legitimacy can be considered to be part of what Malejacq calls "power projection"—trying to appear indispensable to international, national, and local audiences.[97] Drawing on claims of legitimacy and/or military force, all strongmen used their interview with me to project power and emphasize their importance for the future of Afghanistan, possibly trying to shape the international community's view of them. However, the case of Nangarhar illustrates that the strongmen's claims did not matter much for their public perception locally. Shirzai and Zahir Qadir claimed legitimacy on the basis of working for the public and their good behavior with the people. But their recognition of the importance of such perceptions did not prevent them from being seen as self-interested and corrupt. Noor, who made a more instrumental claim of legitimacy, lived up to people's expectations in their day-to-day experiences. But in the absence of widespread substantive legitimacy, the perceptions of strongmen are unstable and can change quickly, as they depend on the extent and ability to which strongmen successfully respond to shared needs.

So, what role do strongmen play in state formation and statebuilding? On the one hand, Shirzai and Qadir in Nangarhar appear to support Marten's work, suggesting that strongmen benefitted from an ongoing war economy and had no incentive to contribute to state formation.[98] On the other hand, the case of Noor in Balkh appears to be in line with Giustozzi's and Mukhopadhyay's more positive views on the issue, as he had monopolized force to a large extent for a while. After all, Noor was called the "king of the north." As Noor aligned his personal interests close to the public interest of stability, he was able to construct a considerable amount of instrumental legitimacy, which made him an effective "stationary bandit"—"who monopolizes and rationalizes theft in the form of taxes."[99]

Perhaps maintaining power and stability could have become a foundation for the construction of more substantive legitimacy—possibly even paralleling the first steps of state formation Elias observed in European history. However, this is unlikely. Even Noor needed the Afghan state. Being close to the state allowed him to push back Dostum. And even after successfully monopolizing force in Balkh, Noor continued to rely on the state to cover the salaries of security forces and officials and provided additional opportunities for revenue generation through corruption. When Noor lost the support of the state, his authority began to fade. While Noor certainly remained influential after being removed from his position as the provincial governor of Balkh in 2018, President Ghani's move nonetheless severely interrupted his attempts to monopolize force. It also substantially weakened the stability of Balkh Province and contributed to a deteriorating security situation. Likely, much of Noor's instrumental legitimacy was lost in the process, and his ability to construct more substantive legitimacy became an even more distant prospect. On the relationship between strongmen and state formation in Afghanistan, Malejacq concludes: "They refuse to accept the existence of a hierarchical superior Weberian state . . . but they do not necessarily want to overthrow the state."[100]

Strongmen in Afghanistan benefitted from having the state. They wanted to use it and, if possible, even control it to further their personal agendas. Nobody depicted the close relationship between strongman and the state more visibly than Dostum, who enjoyed wearing his military uniform and endless decorations at public events—even more so after being promoted to the rank of marshal. However, the growing influence of the Taliban over the years, including in territories controlled by strongmen like Noor, and the Taliban's capture of the state in 2021, which forced most strongmen into exile, suggests that they were not only unable to contribute to state-building in a significant way but that they, ultimately, contributed to its failure.

Generally, the findings of this chapter suggest that strongmen are self-interested individuals who know how to gain external legitimacy and support from the international community and, at the same time, rely on force internally in their provinces, even to construct superficial local support, but they lack more substantive legitimacy. In order to ensure long-term stability as an individual authority, strongmen need to establish a monopoly of the *legitimate* use of force, resting on substantive sources—not just on instrumental ones.

4

THE TALIBAN

"When I went to the governor, he wasn't listening to me. The Taliban were listening to me. So obviously the Taliban are better."

Woman in Ghoryan District, Herat Province, 2019

The pictures of Taliban fighters entering the presidential palace in Kabul on August 15, 2021, went around the world. The Taliban had long been depicted as ideological fighters, religious extremists who wanted to introduce harsh rules in Afghanistan, including the prohibition of music and the suppression of women. Western messaging portrayed the fall of the Taliban government in 2001 as a victory against terrorism and human rights abuses. Now the Taliban were in charge again. Having captured the most symbolic building of the state, they explored the rooms of the palace, posing in front of paintings with Kalashnikov rifles over their shoulders.

The authority of the Taliban had grown steadily after 2001 until their last push for full control of Afghanistan in 2021. It is difficult to imagine such an expansion of control without any legitimacy—relying on coercion alone—even though the latter certainly remained a key source of the Taliban's authority.

Who the Taliban really is has been the subject of a long and often controversial debate, especially as competing narratives were part of the war. For example, the Afghan government pushed the narrative of the Taliban insurgency being highly fragmented, lacking clear command and control structures. Meanwhile, the Taliban tried to show unity. Indeed, their ability to maintain several countrywide ceasefires over the Eid holidays in 2018, 2019 and 2020 helped the Taliban and contributed to the image of a more organized movement.

The Taliban long remained a murky phenomenon, especially for people in cities and other areas in which the movement had little influence. In 2014/2015, many people in Afghanistan referred to all kinds of armed groups—whether they were political or criminal—collectively as "the Taliban." For example, one interviewee from Mazar-e-Sharif, the provincial capital of Balkh Province, told me, "There are people who create insecure situations in the name of Taliban. But we don't know who they are and what they want. We don't know if they actually are Taliban, but everyone calls them Taliban."[1] The sudden emergence of the Islamic State Khorasan (IS-K) in Afghanistan around the same time caused additional confusion.

Meanwhile, groups were also labeled "Taliban" for political reasons. This problem could be seen across Afghanistan. An interviewee from a rural district in Balkh Province complained that the provincial governor, Atta Noor, called the people in his village "Taliban" to justify military actions against them. While the interviewee confirmed that they were indeed fighting the governor, he argued that, at the time, they were not linked to the Taliban movement. Another interviewee from the village confirmed this view stating, "There are no real Taliban here. These people are fighting because they are dissatisfied with the government."[2]

The Taliban were viewed much more clearly as one very real political movement in those areas in which people interacted with it more frequently. By 2019, these areas had expanded significantly, with much of rural Afghanistan being under Taliban control. In these areas, the Taliban had become the de facto government long before capturing the formal state structures, even providing some public services, such as, crucially, justice.

After briefly outlining the history of insurgency and the complexity of the "Taliban" label in Afghanistan from 2001 to 2021, this chapter examines how members of the Taliban movement perceived themselves, why they joined the movement, and on what basis they claimed legitimacy. The interviewees' stated motives to fight with the Taliban ranged from more instrumental ones aimed at personal advantage to more substantive ones that rested on values, such as the fight for justice or the fight against the corrupt government. Most interviewees named a negative experience with the Afghan state as a driving force in their opposition. While the Taliban's official claim of legitimacy rested on the stated goal of reestablishing an Islamic system, most interviewees claimed legitimacy on the basis of fighting against the corrupt and unjust government with its foreign allies, not religion.

The chapter then explores how the general public perceived the Taliban in different parts of Afghanistan during their time as an insurgency. Many people in government-controlled areas viewed the Taliban as a threat to their security. But in urban areas, the Taliban's attacks also undermined the legitimacy of the Afghan state. Meanwhile, the interviews from territories that the Taliban could influence or control show that they successfully constructed a degree of legitimacy. But again, it was often not their "Islamic" idea of authority that appeared to matter and match people's expectations. The people I talked to were far more concerned with how the Taliban behaved and interacted with them on a daily basis. Respondents indicated that conflict resolution was particularly crucial for the Taliban's legitimacy, both in an instrumental and a more substantive way. This became even more apparent in 2019 during additional research in the Taliban-controlled areas of Herat and Faryab provinces. While many people were left without alternative options for conflict resolution in the contexts of growing Taliban influence and coercive capacity, the interviewees also praised the Taliban's procedures as rapid, affordable, and fairer than those of other authorities, particularly those of the Afghan state.

Comparing self-perceptions with public perceptions shows that instead of drawing on the Taliban's official claims of legitimacy, the personal claims of members and supporters were often aligned with what many people were hoping for—a less corrupt political order. This claim did not remain abstract but, to a certain extent, was realized in some of the areas the Taliban could access, offering what was perceived to be fairer conflict resolution procedures than other authorities. This enabled them to construct a degree of substantive legitimacy successfully. It was the daily interaction between authority and the people—the "how" an authority behaved—that shaped opinions on it.

Most people did not expect much more than to be treated like human beings—with respect. Even though this finding does not come as a surprise, it has not often been applied in the Afghan context, where people's lives have been dominated by corruption and violence. Denying people respectful and fair treatment not only drove many people toward the Taliban but also provided the Taliban with a powerful claim of legitimacy and justification to fight the state. However, after having gained control of the state themselves in 2021, the Taliban's potential focus on implementing a more ideological idea of authority, which was not a key source of their legitimacy as an insurgency, risks establishing another system that denies people, especially women, the dignity that they demand.

THE TALIBAN IN AFGHANISTAN

The Taliban have their roots in the chaos that ensued when the Mujahedin groups turned against each other in 1992 after the fall of the pro-Soviet government. Afghanistan quickly disintegrated into multiple regions controlled by strongmen who fought each other and frequently changed their alliances. Displacement, sexual violence, and robbery were rampant; various groups demanded tolls of all passers-by on the highways.[3]

Two narratives on the rise of the Taliban have surfaced. Rashid describes a group of Mujahedin who had ceased fighting after the fall of Najibullah and returned to study at *madrassas* (religious schools) in Quetta and Kandahar. They elected Mullah Omar as their leader and formed a group they called Taliban—the "students" or those "seeking knowledge." They sought to institute Sharia law, peace, and disarmament.[4] Barfield disputes this account and argues that the Taliban formed because Pakistan shifted its support from Hekmatyar and promoted its formation to fight the Rabbani government in Kabul.[5] Even though both narratives are likely true to some extent, the Taliban successfully portrayed themselves as Robin Hood figures who opposed the Kandahari strongmen who had committed many human rights violations in the province.[6] Their popularity grew steadily in the early 1990s, and the Taliban controlled Kandahar by December 1994 and took control of Kabul on September 26, 1996.[7]

While the Taliban successfully expanded their influence further north, they introduced a new political order for the territory they controlled. They called this territory the Islamic Emirate of Afghanistan and proclaimed Mullah Omar Amir ul-Mumineen (commander of the faithful). He governed Taliban territory with a small *shura* (council) of chosen people.[8] They taxed the population, asking all people to pay *zakat* (a form of income tax) and making farmers pay *ushr* (Islamic tithe) of ten percent of their products.[9] While they claimed to be implementing (*Salafi*) Islam, the Taliban often enforced rural customs. Their governance included many elements of the Pashtun's cultural code, the Pashtunwali. In some ways, it also reflected local customs in each locality. Yet, the Taliban also violated certain local customs. Sufism and the veneration of saints and shrines had long been established in the country, and Taliban law was hostile to both.[10] Banning music and exclusion of women from public life also violated local customs in many urban areas like Kabul and Mazar-e Sharif, which impeded their legitimacy in those places. While the Taliban's claim of legitimacy was powerful—presenting religious ideology as a way of uniting the divided country—many non-Pashtuns and urban populations perceived them as a Pashtun group trying to impose a Pashtun ideology. Hence, even though many people in the rural Pashtun areas of southern Afghanistan had positive views on the new order, Taliban rule was perceived to be oppressive in many non-Pashtun regions and more urban areas such as Kabul.[11]

After their government fell in 2001, the Taliban reorganized in the Afghan-Pakistani border area and began fighting again as an insurgency around 2004, supported by the Pakistani intelligence agency ISI. Violence escalated in 2006 when the Taliban tripled their rate of attacks compared to the previous year. The U.S. surge in 2009 further escalated the conflict, and the following U.S. troop drawdown enabled the Taliban to expand their influence further.[12] In 2020, the Taliban were assumed to control more than 50 percent of Afghanistan's territory, predominantly rural areas. Despite the ongoing international support for the Afghan government, the influence of the Taliban continuously grew as they took over district after district. In addition, the Taliban controlled, or at least frequently interrupted, many of the major roads in the country and increasingly asserted their influence in urban areas, including through attacks, assassinations, and full-fledged offensive operations, often at a high cost for civilian populations. UNAMA estimates that the Taliban were responsible for almost 700 civilian deaths and more than 1,350 injuries just between January and June 2021.[13]

The Taliban, who continued calling themselves the Islamic Emirate during their insurgency, claimed legitimacy by portraying themselves as "jihadists," fighting against the "occupying" U.S. forces and "infidel" government forces.[14] This rhetoric underpinned most of the Taliban's public statements on their *al-emarah* websites, which was used to justify attacks and announce the beginning of the annual "fighting season" in spring. For instance, in April 2016, the Taliban declared on its website: "The Islamic Emirate's armed Jihad against the American invasion has completed fourteen years and is now in its fifteenth year. Jihad against the aggressive and usurping infidel army is a holy obligation upon our necks and our only recourse for re-establishing an Islamic system and regaining our independence."

When the United States announced the withdrawal of its troops from Afghanistan, the Taliban justified their continued fighting by focusing on their goal of reestablishing a "pure" Islamic system in their public messaging.

In order to build authority, the Taliban used both threats and claims of legitimacy in their messaging toward local populations. According to Johnson, the Taliban tried to "reinforce easy-to-understand grievances, promote anti-Western sentiments, delegitimize the Afghan government and attempt to sow fear among the local neutral/undecided population."[15] To achieve this, the Taliban applied different communications strategies for different audiences, having distinct messages for local people who supported them, those who were undecided, and those who opposed the Taliban.[16] However, after the Doha Agreement was signed in 2020, which promised the withdrawal of international troops, the language of the Taliban shifted to criticizing the Afghan government, which they referred to as the "Kabul administration."

Until their capture of the Afghan state, the Taliban leadership remained in Pakistan, mainly in the cities Quetta and Peshawar. Prominent leader Mullah Omar died in 2013, but the Taliban kept his death secret for two years. In 2016, Haibatullah Akhundzada became the emir after his predecessor Mohammad Mansur had been killed in a drone strike. At the time, the emir had two deputies, Mullah Yaqub, who is Mullah Omar's son, and Sirajuddin Haqqani, the son of the influential commander Jalaluddin Haqqani.[17] In addition, a leadership council called Rahbari Shura, which included many of the key Taliban figures, advised the emir. The leadership structure was complemented by military and civilian ministry-like commissions—not only the prominent political commission with its representation in Doha but also other commissions covering topics like education and health. Within the commissions, responsibility was often divided between Quetta and Peshawar. The two shuras had long been opposing poles of power within the movement, even coexisting and competing in parts of the country, such as in the eastern and central regions.[18] However, reportedly, following the financial difficulties of the Quetta Shura around 2011/2012, the local commanders had to accept the authority of the Peshawar Shura. In the following years, the Quetta Shura covered the south, southwest, west, and northwest of Afghanistan. Meanwhile, the Peshawar Shura covered the east, northeast, southeast, and central regions of Afghanistan.[19]

The military commission and many civilian commissions had provincial and even district-level representatives within

Afghanistan, such as, most prominently, shadow provincial and district governors. Meanwhile, the military structure was in a dominating role, as the shadow governors reported to the military commission. On the local level, the Taliban consisted of small fighting units, the so-called *mahaz*, that followed individual commanders. Traditionally, these mahaz were fairly independent actors with localized agendas. However, the Taliban leadership tried to strengthen its own role and exert more influence over the mahaz from 2014 onward, for instance, through the creation of special forces, the Taliban's so-called Red Unit, which reported directly to the shadow provincial governor.[20]

The Taliban's governance structure at that time is best understood as decentralized, with local commanders maintaining some independent authority. Jackson and Amiri describe the complexity of how decisions on policies were made within the Taliban. Being both top-down and bottom-up, the leadership and local commanders and fighters shaped the rules of the movement. The complexity of decision making and the need to balance ideology and local practical concerns resulted in a "patchwork" of policies across Afghanistan. Following the leadership's attempts to centralize decision making, certain high-level decisions were respected by most commanders. For example, when the Taliban leadership announced a three-day ceasefire during Eid in June 2018, most forces across the country obeyed. However, Jackson and Amiri conclude that "although the rules may be set at the top, local variance, negotiation, and adaptation is still considerable."[21]

In addition, there were some Taliban groups that acted entirely independently. Most prominently, Mohammad Rasoul, who fought the Soviets with Mullah Omar, declared war against the Quetta Shura in 2015, as he opposed the appointment of Mohammad Mansur as the successor of Mullah Omar.[22]

He established his own Taliban movement called the High Council of the Islamic Emirate of Afghanistan. The United States and the Afghan National Directorate of Security (NDS) supported such fragmentation, including Rasoul's group, trying to use them as proxies for their fight against the Taliban. For example, in Herat Province, it was an open secret that Mullah Manan Niazi, the leader of the Rasoul group in west Afghanistan who was reportedly killed in May 2021, received support from the NDS.

In 2015, another insurgency group appeared that acted quite clearly outside of Afghanistan's "Taliban cosmos." A group of people, presumably members of the Pakistani Taliban group TTP (Tehrik-i-Taliban Pakistan), pledged allegiance to the Islamic State Khorasan (IS-K). People in Afghanistan widely referred to them as "Daesh." Osman provides a detailed analysis of how the IS-K evolved in Afghanistan.[23] He describes how groups of militants had been arriving from Pakistan in Nangarhar Province since 2010, claiming to be refugees fleeing from Pakistani military operations, then turning increasingly repressive over time. In May 2015, the militias officially changed flags from TTP to IS-K. The tensions between what now was called IS-K and the Taliban quickly started to grow, with both groups vying for control of the same territory, resulting in both groups declaring jihad against each other.[24] In July 2015, the Afghan government also joined the fight against IS-K. While the IS-K's control of territory in Afghanistan still appears to be limited to certain districts in Nangarhar Province, they repeatedly claimed attacks with high numbers of casualties against civilian targets, such as a hospital in Kabul in March 2017.

While IS-K quickly established a reputation for violence and imposing harsh rules on communities,[25] the Taliban's interpretations of Islamic governance at the time, to some extent, resembled those of conservatives in Islamist political parties in Pakistan and Egypt.[26] Amiri and Jackson show how the Taliban's approach to education evolved considerably between 2001 and 2021. After opposing education for years, the Taliban later started allowing government schools to operate and enforced the attendance of teachers more thoroughly while taking credit for providing education. However, there continued to be considerable variation with regard to the Taliban's education policies in practice. This was especially apparent with regard to female education that was often, but not always, allowed until the age of twelve. Communities had agency and often played a role in shaping its implementation the implementation of education policies.[27]

Similarly, the Taliban justice system developed fast. Reportedly, mobile Taliban courts emerged around 2007 in southern and eastern Afghanistan.[28] From 2009 onward, more permanent courts were established in areas under firm Taliban control, while the use of mobile courts was extended to other areas the Taliban could influence. The U.S. surge made it more difficult for the Taliban to have fixed courts. However, following the U.S. drawdown in 2014, the influence of Taliban courts expanded again. By 2019, when I was doing interviews on justice in Taliban-controlled areas, the Taliban had established a fairly sophisticated parallel justice system across most rural areas of Afghanistan. It mirrored the state system, with primary courts on the district level, appeals court on the provincial level, and a national high court. These organized courts—consisting of a judge, a mufti providing religious advice, and a secretary—met at locally known spots on certain days of the week. In principle, anyone could take their case to the Taliban. Taliban judges were instructed to use the Ottoman Empire's codification of Hanafi jurisprudence, the Majallat al-Ahkam al-Adliyya, for guidance on civil disputes. The courts provided templates that needed to be filled in by both claimants and defendants, and once a decision had been made, which could take several weeks and many hearings of witnesses in more complex cases, both conflict parties received a copy of the decision.[29] However, criminal cases were often known to be dealt with harshly.

In parallel to their expansion of territorial control and the provision of public service, such as justice, the Taliban also reestablished and expanded their taxation practices, adding to their control of populations. The Taliban demanded *ushr* from farmers (in theory, 10 percent of the produce; in practice, often a negotiated fee based on the size of the land and type of produce), but they also taxed businesses and shopkeepers, trucks and other transportation operators, and mineral extraction. Additionally, they taxed development projects, often taking a cut of around 10 percent, especially when involving construction, and projects on the community level, such as the Citizens' Charter (chapter 5).[30]

Compared to their rule before 2001, the Taliban were more concerned about their local legitimacy until 2021. In his detailed analysis of Garmser in Helmand Province, Malkasian illustrates how, upon their return to the district in 2006, the Taliban made a considerable effort to win over the population by being more inclusive and less oppressive than before, drawing especially on the support of the poor and landless populations.[31] However, we know surprisingly little about the Taliban's legitimacy, how local communities viewed the movement, and on what basis Taliban members claimed legitimacy. Especially with their growing influence, perception data on them became increasingly unreliable, as data collection was often limited to areas that were considered safe. Hence, the voices from urban populations from government-controlled areas dominated studies on Afghanistan, while the perspectives of people from Taliban-controlled areas were less understood and represented in national surveys.[32]

Some of the sources of legitimacy that scholars attribute to the Afghan state may also apply to the Taliban as an insurgency. In particular, "tradition" in the form of the Pashtunwali could have played a key role, as it influenced how the Taliban governed as well as people's expectations in the Pashtun areas of Afghanistan.[33] On the other hand, Rangelov and Theros suggest that dissatisfaction with the abuse, injustice, and corruption of the Afghan state drove support for the Taliban, who weaponized these objections.[34] But service delivery may have also provided the Taliban with some legitimacy. For instance, Giustozzi argues that the provision of justice was central.[35] Building on these ideas, this chapter compares the Taliban's claims to legitimacy with the reasons why members of the Taliban and the public perceived them to be legitimate—or not.

THREE PERSPECTIVES ON JOINING AND DESERTING THE TALIBAN

In late October 2014, I was conducting an interview with a former Taliban commander in Herat City. Another person walked in and interrupted the interview, introducing himself as Mohammad, the former deputy shadow governor of west Afghanistan, and launched into a summary of his biography.[36] He spoke rapidly, enthusiastically. He told the other interviewee and me all about his past as a Mujahedin commander of the Mahaz-e Milli-ye Islami-ye Afghanistan (National Islamic Front of Afghanistan) in the 1980s and early 1990s. I came to see that the life histories of active and former Taliban interviewees were a vital way to distinguish claims of legitimacy from genuine views in relation to their understanding of the goals of their fight and why they personally felt it was legitimate.

According to his account, Mohammad spent five years fighting the opposing Jamiat-e Islami, with its key figure, the later governor of Herat, Ismail Khan. He emphasized that when the Taliban gained power in the 1990s, he did not join them. Nevertheless, he spoke admiringly of what they had achieved. His account emphasized security; as he said, "The Taliban were able to provide security with very few people. People were able to travel across the country without being in danger." He was also one of the few interviewees praising their interpretation of religion: "In addition, the Taliban believed in the Quran. They based their lives on the orders of the Quran and were dying for the Quran and Allah's sake. If a woman committed adultery, she was hanged to death, right in front of people while the current government is using the name of democracy to make women liberal, which is totally against our culture and beliefs."

But he also emphasized equality under the law (for men), "One of the Taliban's achievements was that the law was the same for everybody across the country. . . . If criminals are caught today they only need to pay enough money and will be released within minutes. In the times of the Islamic Emirate this didn't exist at all. . . . During the Taliban regime we had a council, which consisted of religious elders—and their decision was based on justice."

Despite these perceived advantages, Mohammad only joined the Taliban after the international intervention of 2001. He explained that the idea of taking revenge for bad treatment experienced by Ismail Khan's people had driven him: "I was not a Taliban supporter when the Taliban were in power. Actually, I didn't like their behaviour at all as they always carried a stick and hit people without any reason. I constantly told them to stop this. But then the Mujahedin along with US forces entered the country. One of Ismail Khan's commanders . . . robbed an entire truck filled with my carpets, my 480 cows, my [Toyota] Surf vehicle and [Toyota] Corolla as well as 470,000 Pakistani Rupees [circa $3,000]. They even took the dry meat of the people, which they had stored for winter."

Later he would emphasize the greed of the governor's operation, saying: "Ismail Khan is the only one who causes insecurity in Herat. His commanders own dozens of buildings, public baths, hundreds of trucks, more than 2,000 hectares of land and huge companies."

This incident where he lost his fortune because of one of Ismail Khan's commanders had been pivotal, however. "They also wanted to arrest me and accused me of being a Talib. I told them that I didn't even share a single a cup of tea with the Taliban throughout the seven years they governed the country. At that point, with a single pistol in my hand, I joined the Taliban and started my fight against this government. Soon I became the deputy of the [Taliban] West Zone Governor."

Mohammad would not tell me what he actually did as the shadow west zone governor. But he emphasized, still using the present tense, that "our main concern is not the implementation of Islamic laws . . . but the absence of justice and the corruption of the government." From Mohammad's point of view, it was not ideology or ethnicity but marginalization that drove people to the Taliban: "The war is not between the two big ethnicities— the Tajiks and Pashtun. The war continues because rights are violated."

Mohammad decided to leave the Taliban for financial reasons. He was promised rewards for joining the peace process, an initiative of the government's High Peace Council that offered financial and other rewards for Taliban fighters willing to lay down their arms. However, he found the government just as extractive as ever. He explained:

A few nerveless and coward[ly] men of my tribe sold me to this government. They promised me financial help and then took me to the police headquarters where they introduced me to the [provincial] governor Mr. Nooristani. I would have preferred a wolf attack to joining the government. They made lots of promises but didn't keep any. They cheated on us by promising us paradise on earth before joining but then treated us badly. . . . I handed over one RPG-7, one RPG-9, one AK47 along with 3,150 bullets, 27 rockets and my three personal vehicles. But I haven't received three Afs in exchange.

Mohammad responded to the betrayal by calling the members of the tribes that he considered to be marginalized to "continue their fight against the government so that they die or that their rights are respected." I had not had an opportunity to ask most of my questions, but Mohammad was done. He left me with the parting words that this book started with, a warning meant for the state that unless his demands were met, he and his men would take "decisive action."

The interview does illustrate what motivated him to fight the government—or at least what he wanted other people to think about why he took up arms—and why he considered this fight to be legitimate. Mohammad framed the legitimacy of the historical Taliban regime with reference to their interpretation of Islam, which underpinned their idea of authority and served as the foundation for their practices. Nevertheless, this was not sufficient for him to join the Taliban, as he was unhappy with their routine use of violence against civilians. It was also the perception of unjust behavior—this time directed against him by individuals associated with the new government after 2001— rather than the Taliban's idea of authority that made him join the movement. Mohammad's motivation to join the Taliban was based on grievances that resulted from a personal experience of perceived unjust behavior of Ismail Khan's commanders, whom he associated with the government.

Mohammad claimed that the Taliban's fight and his own role in it were legitimate as they fought for justice against an unjust and corrupt government that marginalized entire groups of people. As people associated with the government treated him badly, he could easily frame his own fight as one of the marginalized and disadvantaged for the general "good" against the "bad" government. This generalization might not have been propaganda, but his actual perception of the legitimacy of fighting the government. In addition, aligning with the Taliban was often the only way of fighting individuals linked to the government. The fact that he left the Taliban for financial reasons illustrates that, ultimately, his support for them was based primarily on personal motives. Mohammad was much richer and more influential than most in Afghanistan, but his actions suggest how personal, instrumental intentions may have played a role in the motivations of supporting a certain authority. In addition, the case shows how personal frustrations and experiences translate into politics and justify a fight against "the government." Finally, the case illustrates that when people perceived the behavior of individuals associated with the Afghan state as "unjust," they could join the insurgency, which provided a platform to fight the entire government system that allowed the perceived injustice to happen.

The second of the three Taliban members whose backgrounds I will explore in this chapter is Abdul, who was much further down the hierarchy than Mohammad.[37] I met him, a young man in his early thirties, on one of my trips to Nangarhar Province in June 2015 on the opposite side of Afghanistan. He had spent some years fighting with the Taliban in Nuristan Province, north of Nangarhar. Like Mohammad, he was unusual among the Taliban members I interviewed in being eager to share his perspective with me, though he wasn't quite as pushy.

Abdul grew up as a refugee in Pakistan. He attended school in Peshawar up to tenth grade when his family decided to move back to Afghanistan. Abdul's family settled in Nuristan Province, where he got a job as a nurse at a clinic run by a European NGO located near the U.S. base in Kalagush.[38] One day, around 2006/2007, some American soldiers came to the clinic and wanted to speak to him:

> They invited me to their base where they asked me why I was treating insurgents. I told them that I was treating all human beings. The Americans responded that they wanted to clear the area of the Taliban. . . . They asked me not to treat members of the Taliban anymore. So I told the Taliban that I couldn't help them anymore as I relied on my salary from the clinic. . . . They still came, however, only when they had serious injuries. I treated them outside of the clinic. They didn't force me to do it. But they are human beings. I felt obliged to help them.

Some months later, the tipping point came when, according to Abdul's account, a number of U.S. helicopters killed around twenty-five workers living in tents close to the construction site where they were building a road. Abdul came to collect the remains of the people killed. "My motivation to join the Taliban resulted from this very personal experience of civilian casualties," he explained. "I felt so hurt that I decided to join the Taliban to fight the Americans and the government of America."

He gave me the details of his involvement in the insurgency. He joined the Peshawar Shura branch of the Taliban

and became a radio operations commander, supervising a group
of up to fifty people and reporting to the shadow district governor. They conducted "missions" against the American forces
and the Afghan government, which he believed to be an ally
of the Americans. They were also interacting with local communities on a daily basis. He explained, "We were not governing communities. But people often contacted us when they
were facing problems. Back then we were a small group, trying
to support communities. So we often got involved in conflict
resolution. We were a small, idealist group." They applied their
interpretation of Sharia law to resolve conflicts. Most people in
his community praised his decision to join the Taliban, he said,
although he also noted that some were concerned that their village might get bombed in response. But Abdul said he was firm
in his decision because the United States "came as occupiers
not as guests, not behaving like guests doing construction, but
targeting innocent people."

Abdul nonetheless left the Taliban in September 2009. One
reason was that he felt the growing influence of the Quetta Taliban Shura undermined the idealism of their group. "Members of
the Emirates joined our group, doing intelligence on our activities.
So, the trust among the members of our group was lost. . . . I used
to pay for the fighting out of my own pocket. But people started to
fight about positions and were not idealistic anymore." He felt the
rival Taliban faction was greedy. For example, he explained, "The
Emirates wanted to destroy a bridge connecting two districts to
prevent the government accessing mines, so they could keep the
revenue for themselves." He also objected to a decision to blow
up a government-run school, suggesting to preserve it by turning
it into a madrassa [religious school]. He lamented, "There was no
transparency and accountability anymore."

Abdul also felt that commanders were being bribed by the
government, such as one who did not conduct a mission planned

to prevent the transportation of ballot boxes during the 2009 presidential elections, notwithstanding the commander's claim that he was at a party at the time. But other less idealistic reasons also contributed to Abdul's decision to leave the Taliban. The fact that the U.S. base in Kalagush was given over to the Afghan forces took some of the urgency away from the fight for Abdul. In addition, some of his relatives started to work for the government, turning family members into potential targets. "I didn't want to fight relatives. That would have caused family problems." In the end, his father and community convinced him to lay down his arms to avoid such issues.

Abdul decided to join the government's peace and reintegration process, which promised him "food, clothes, counselling, and safe accommodation" and wanted to enable his further education. But he experienced a different reality:

> When I joined the peace process . . . it got a lot of media attention as the governor of Nuristan was attending the ceremony. But none of the promises were kept. I started to work for a construction company and then moved to Jalalabad to study. I fulfilled my wish. But it was not due to the help of the Americans or the government. The Taliban continued to call me and asked me to return. They threatened me. I had to change my phone number to sever contact with them. At some point the director of the Peace Council in Nuristan invited me to a hotel in Jalalabad and promised me a salary. And indeed, I received 250 USD per month for a year. Then I was invited by the NDS and got another 30,000 Afghanis for a year. So, I got some help.

He concluded: "Today I am happy, but jobless." Toward the end of our meeting, I asked Abdul about his relationship with the Taliban today, at the time of the interview, and if he had plans of returning in the future. He responded:

I am trying to find a job. It is not the right time to return. I don't want to go back because the leadership has been arrested or killed. That creates problems though. I recently graduated from college. My father wants me to celebrate in our village. But the ANA had asked me to help them as the Taliban were burning their fuel trucks. So, I released a statement that got broadcast asking the Taliban to join the Peace Council. And I actually persuaded a group, and that was also broadcast. Now the Peshawar Shura is saying that "Abdul is convincing people to join the peace process." Friends delivered the message to me and a member of the [Peshawar] Shura called me.

When I asked Abdul whether it was worth the fight, he did not answer me directly. He said, "There is no reason to fight anymore. We want peace. We respect guests like you and want to give them the best hospitality. You have to respect every religion. Islam is a religion of peace. We were fighting because the Americans were fighting humanity, not because of Islam. They treated people in a way not even animals deserve to be treated."

Abdul was clearly religious, but whereas Mohammad listed Islam as a reason he fought with the Taliban, Abdul made no mention of this factor. Both men had come to the Taliban because of a personal experience with injustice—in Abdul's case, U.S. forces, and in Mohammad's, the Afghan government. Abdul framed his motivation in far more humanist and idealist terms than Mohammad, who was primarily driven by personal grievances. Even though Abdul left the Taliban primarily because of family pressure, his idealist way of thinking was also reflected in his voiced frustration when other insurgency groups became involved. In Abdul's case, therefore, the reason for joining the Taliban and the reason why the Taliban's fight was legitimate were identical. His main concern appeared to be about inhuman and cruel behavior.

My colleague and I met Nassir at a group interview I performed just outside Herat City's security belt in west Afghanistan. We parked the car at an inconspicuous single-story office building. Previously, the Taliban had risked meeting me in government-controlled areas, even in the city centers, and I did not feel I could give them less trust than they had given me. A muscular man in a white *shalwar kameez* (traditional clothes) came to the car and welcomed us. He guided us to the door of the office, which was packed with men sitting on sofas and the floor, drinking tea and chatting. All heads turned to the door, and the conversations died down when we took off our shoes and walked in. I walked from person to person rattling off greeting phrases. After politely declining several times to sit on a sofa that was cleared for us, we sat down on the floor at the end of the room and accepted cups of tea. My colleague introduced us, explaining the reasons for our visit. A man on the sofa interrupted him, pointing at me as he spoke. Everyone looked at me, and the room was filled with laughter and giggles. He had jokingly made an offer to buy me from my colleague to make money with the ransom. Fortunately enough, my colleague declined.

Some of the people in the room had formally left the movement, although, unlike Mohammad and Abdul, they often winked as they said it. Others said they were still active members. Nassir was one of the ones who winked. He had been a low-ranking commander of a local Taliban group in Herat Province.[39] We began the interview by talking about his background. He told me that he used to work as a teacher in a rural district of the province. But when the influence of the Taliban in the district started to grow in Herat, he and some others from his village decided to join. When I asked him why, he explained how the government failed him. "Because the government was not supporting us or paying any attention to us," he said. "We could not fight against them. So we joined the Taliban instead to be equal to them. . . . We joined the Taliban to ensure our security as the government wasn't doing anything for us. . . . The government was very corrupt. We wanted to fight them. . . . When we joined the Taliban, they didn't promise us anything. They didn't have to convince us. We wanted to join them to fight against the corrupt government."

Unlike Mohammad and Abdul, Nassir did not describe a pivotal moment that led him to join the Taliban. This may be related to the fact that he joined with a group from his village. However, like them, direct experience of the Afghan state had made the Taliban seem enticing. He also joined the Taliban because he thought there was no alternative—no other way of resisting them.

Nassir described his daily work in his local Taliban group, outlining how it gave him a sense of invincibility despite the risks:

> When our leaders commanded us we would get ready for our operations. . . . We had coordination with the other groups of the Taliban and every group had separate work to do in separate places. This way we would not get into each other's way. When we wanted to have an operation in any area we would join forces with other groups. We then made plans together and decided what to do. . . . We had no worries because we could do anything and we had the ability to fight against anyone. But sometimes we were hit by rockets or bomb blasts from the government and the foreigners.

Nassir outlined what his daily routine looked like: "Every morning at 8:00 a.m. we used to find a place where [the cellular] network works and then we used to call every group to ask about their condition. If there was an order from the head, the commander or the commission for us we would then get ready to execute it. Otherwise, we would have a normal day."

His personal motives for joining the Taliban were not entirely aligned with what he described as his claim of legitimacy: "Our goal was the jihad against the foreigners and to bring peace to our area." However, apart from fighting, he explained, a big part of his work was conflict resolution:

> There were local *shuras*, but they were very weak and were not able to solve people's problems. And we joined the Taliban because even the government was not able to solve our problems. Our behaviour was good with the local people and most of the time we tried to solve their problems and people were happy with us. . . . When people asked us to solve their conflict we tried to help them. They accepted our decisions and obeyed us because of our good attitude and behavior. Our attitude is also what made people agree to us taking over their area [from the government].

But, he admitted, sometimes they also were coercive. "We used force for our work. This way we were able to do what we wanted or to take the place we wanted—and we did."

While his group opposed foreign intervention, they were friendly to some NGOs if they were building schools or roads or providing supports to students. Others, which they perceived as threatening to their agenda, they opposed: "If there was an NGO that wanted to bring change by spreading awareness and manipulating people's minds according to their plans, we would receive a report and we would stop them."

To finance their activities, Nassir said that his group "taxed" local communities: "We used to collect ushr and zakat for our monthly salaries, to buy weapons and so on." He explained that he and his colleagues received a fixed monthly salary and bonuses on top when their missions were successful, often paid in Pakistani rupees. Other interviewees in the room claimed that Pakistan played an important role in their fight, despite the fact that it was in the Western part of Afghanistan, far from the Pakistani border.[40]

Nassir explained that he decided to leave the Taliban for pragmatic, instrumental reasons: "because most foreigners left our area . . . and the government made lots of promises. Especially . . . the members of the Peace Council promised us that the government would give us jobs, they would support students and teachers, release the prisoners and much more. Then we accepted. The government encouraged us and welcomed us in a very friendly way at the beginning. We were so happy."

However, Nassir's hopes were soon dashed. And his disappointment in the government had a value-based substantive component, to be treated unfairly and without respect, in a way that could also be described as symbolic violence: "But then we slowly started to realise that we had lost everything, because of their lies. Now I am unemployed and we are a total of nineteen family members with no income. . . . The government hasn't done much to fulfill its promises. They only gave some of our group members jobs, only those who are really poor and were able to be convinced to collect garbage to earn some money for the family. Once we were in command and now we have to collect garbage and clean the roads."

He concluded: "We have begun to live peacefully. But if the situation gets worse then we will again buy weapons and join our group."

THE LEGITIMACY OF THE TALIBAN FROM THE INSIDERS' POINTS OF VIEW

The interviews with former and active Taliban members illustrate that there can be differences among people's motives and purpose for fighting with the Taliban, their personal claims of legitimacy, the Taliban's public claim of legitimacy, and their assumed sources of local legitimacy.

Looking at the *personal motives* of why the interviewees fought with the Taliban, three different factors emerged. On the one hand, some people joined the movement for *instrumental purposes*— because it was useful for them and allowed them to achieve personal advantages. This might have been driven, among other factors, by opportunism, revenge, greed, or sheer survival. By joining the Taliban, they could fight for what they thought they had lost, deserved, or wanted. Instrumental reasons seemed to be paramount for Mohammad, who fought with the Taliban to take revenge and regain his wealth. On the other hand, Abdul was more of an idealist who joined the movement for *substantive purposes*. Notably, he and the other Taliban fighters I spoke to were more concerned about (in)humane behavior by the government than Islam. They joined the Taliban because they opposed the state's practices rather than the idea of authority propagated by the state and its foreign allies. Others were *followers*, like Nassir, who joined because friends convinced them or because the local society considered it to be normal or even demanded it. In some parts of eastern Afghanistan, there appeared to be a strong public discourse portraying the U.S. forces as cruel occupiers. For instance, an interviewee in Nangarhar told me that he joined the Taliban "because everybody was saying that we had to fight them," meaning the U.S. forces.[41]

Notably though, neither Mohammad nor anyone else seemed to be motivated to fight with the Taliban only out of greed or other purely instrumental reasons. Indeed, almost every interviewee offered at least one substantive reason when explaining their decision to join the Taliban—the perceived *corruption*, *injustice*, or *bad behavior* of the Afghan state or international forces. In Mohammad's case, perceived unfair or unjust behavior of an individual associated with the government or the international forces triggered his decision to join. Most interviewees reported *negative personal experiences* of that kind. For example, another former Taliban fighter from Herat told me, "My main concern was the bad behaviour and the manner of government officials towards local people. The district administrator and police commander were particularly cruel. For example, once the police came and said that the people in the village were hiding weapons. But we actually didn't have any. So they made us pay them the price of weapons instead. It was frustrating. So I decided to join the Taliban."[42]

Local and personal experiences of perceived injustice motivated people to fight the entire Afghan state. A few interviewees had not had direct personal experiences of the injustice or cruelty of the government and international forces. Rather, they joined on the basis of reports of such behavior. Interviewees told me that the Taliban used videos of cruel behavior by U.S. forces as part of their recruitment strategy to trigger emotions and convince people to fight for "Islamic ideals," which, in this case, expressed not much more than basic human values and rights. For instance, a former Taliban fighter in Nangarhar explained to me: "The Taliban told us that jihad against occupiers is necessary. . . . Look at the cruel activities of Americans in Laghman. They are killing innocent people, even children. . . . If you see the videos of the bombardments, everybody wants to join the Taliban."[43]

While people's motives to actively support the Taliban were mixed, with varying degrees of instrumental and substantive reasons, all interviewees emphasized the substantive aspects in their *claims of legitimacy*. Surprisingly, however, few interviewees justified their fight in religious terms along the lines of the Taliban's official claim. While some interviewees, like Mohammad, appreciated the Taliban's interpretation of Islam or, like Nassir, used the word "jihad," few said that they wanted to "reestablish an Islamic system." When asked about the goal of their fight, most interviewees usually instead referred to general human values rather than specific Islamic values and nations and claimed to be fighting for a better society, against unfair treatment, marginalization, injustice, and the corrupt state or the cruel foreign forces. Indeed, most interviewees also thought that their *good behavior* and *attitude* or their fight against corruption and injustice would explain their *local legitimacy*. Hence, their claims fit with what they thought local people expected from them. In addition, the claims responded to their negative personal experiences with individuals who were part of the Afghan state, which were projected to a societal level and provided a powerful justification for their fight against the Afghan state.

It can be concluded that the Taliban's legitimacy, through the eyes of its members, was not purely instrumental. People not only joined the movement because it was beneficial for them, but they also joined for substantive reasons. However, the fight of many people appeared to be significantly more against what they perceived to be wrong on the basis of basic human values in relation to the daily behavior of the Afghan state than for what they believed to be right. Thus, the Taliban's legitimacy rested substantially on the perceived *illegitimacy of the state*. And regardless of a person's individual motives for joining the Taliban or another armed group, ultimately, such authorities provided their members with a platform to achieve their goals—whether they were personal or societal, instrumental or substantive—both with coercion and legitimacy. The Taliban enabled its members to fight individuals associated with the state and its armed forces.

The following sections will discuss public perceptions of the Taliban. As Mohammad's account of his changing perceptions of the Taliban over the decades suggests, its characteristics varied spatially and changed over time. To do justice to this fluidity and variety and to identify patterns, I examine a number of different cases—urban and rural areas of Kabul and Nangarhar provinces, some being controlled by the government and others by the Taliban. To cover changes over time, I also draw on interviews conducted in 2019, five years after my initial round of interviews, with people living under Taliban control in Herat and Faryab provinces.[44]

KABUL: SUICIDE ATTACKERS AND CRIMINALS

The people of Kabul already experienced several years of actual Taliban governance before 2021, as the Taliban controlled the city throughout the time of the Islamic Emirate of Afghanistan from 1996 to 2001. Interviewees still had strong opinions, regardless of the extent of their personal experience. In particular, people had positive memories of the security situation and non-corrupt justice. For example, the security guard Jawid, who was only eight years old in 2001, said his family was more "secure" at that time than they had been since, even though they were poor.[45] Mohammad Hanif, two years younger than Jawid, was also positive: "During the time of the Taliban regime there was no corruption in the formal conflict resolution mechanisms. We still have the same conflicts resolution procedures but now they are very corrupt."[46] Navida was older, but she was living in

Pakistan when the Taliban were in power. In contrast to Jawid and Mohammad Hanif, she described the period as a time when "there was no democracy and it was not safe for people, especially not for women."[47] The fact that opinions in Kabul about the Taliban had little to do with direct experience gives their views a particular relationship to the question of legitimacy and indicates that there were competing narratives in the public discourse about how the historical Taliban government should be assessed.

In 2014/2015, however, people in Kabul City felt insecure, with almost everyone I talked to voicing concerns about security and most people agreeing that the Taliban were the cause. For instance, shopkeeper Fazal called the Taliban "the biggest reason for insecurity in the area."[48] People blamed the Taliban for the many attacks and explosions that had happened in the city in recent years, as well as activities like kidnappings and robberies. Most claimed that Pakistan controlled the Taliban because it wished to destabilize Afghanistan. However, few people in Kabul had personally encountered the Taliban in the previous years. Consequently, most people's perceptions were based on experienced insecurity, especially large-scale violent attacks, combined with media reporting, rumors, and second- or third-hand information from relatives and friends living in other parts of the country. Most interviewees in Kabul did not distinguish among the various armed groups and considered all of them to be "Taliban" and a threat to stability and security.

In addition, another group suddenly emerged as a perceived source of insecurity in my interviews in 2015—Daesh—or IS-K. Not one interviewee in Kabul City had mentioned this group to me in late 2014, but a few months later, people were concerned about IS-K's growing influence in Afghanistan. While, at that time, no incidents in Kabul City had been linked to IS-K, rumors and reports had been increasing about their growing influence in the eastern province of Nangarhar. This changed over the following years when IS-K claimed responsibility for often particularly violent attacks killing large numbers of civilians in Kabul City, frequently targeting not only Hazara neighborhoods but also and other minorities, such as the Sikh community. Meanwhile, many people in Kabul City continued viewing IS-K and the Taliban as a closely connected threat.

The negative view of the Taliban, as well as IS-K, also dominated the perceptions in the rural districts of the Kabul provinces of Char Asiab in the south and Farza in the north. However, people felt safer in those districts than in Kabul City, and the Taliban did not play a big role in most people's lives. In Char Asiab, almost all the interviewees told me that they felt relatively secure. Despite this, a high proportion of people also said that they were concerned about growing insecurity. Others refused to talk about the security situation, possibly indicating a certain level of fear. But, in contrast to the people in Kabul City, the interviewees in Char Asiab described the fear of growing insecurity as a more recent phenomenon. For instance, the shopkeeper Zaqaria stated, "Char Asiab used to be a very secure district in the past 14 years. But now insecurity is growing."[49] Like the people in Kabul City, those who openly expressed worries about growing insecurity blamed the Taliban for attacks and other crimes. Even though people still felt secure, they thought that the influence of the Taliban was growing, with negative implications for their security.[50]

In the similarly rural district of Farza, people were even more satisfied with the security situation because the Taliban did not appear to be playing any role in their area at the time. Most had negative memories of the Taliban's behavior during the civil war. Looking back, Hajji Jahfar, the headmaster of a school, told me, "The people were dishonoured, the houses were robbed, the gardens were burned and the values of humanity were called into question."[51] However, about the present day, he said, "Now things have taken a positive turn. The people's rights are observed, their property is secure and they live in a peaceful environment."[52] Similarly, shopkeeper Auzoballah expressed his satisfaction in April 2015: "Our security is totally reinforced on the district level. There are no threats for us." While some people raised concerns about criminal activities in the district, almost everyone felt they were basically secure.

Throughout Kabul Province, people looked at the Taliban mainly as a threat to security. The Taliban did not control territory in the three analyzed parts of Kabul Province at the time, and people saw them as intrusive outsiders without any legitimacy. Particularly in Kabul City, with its high number of government and foreign institutions, which were a symbolic and attractive target for attacks that often killed mainly civilians; a comparatively high level of education; and, in small pockets, a more liberal lifestyle, people feared the Taliban and their mode of governance. In addition, the Taliban were viewed as driving crime in the city—even though there was little evidence that they were responsible for many of the kidnappings and robberies, which were more likely to be conducted by criminal networks that often draw on good contacts to state authorities.[53]

In keeping with this negative perception, even those who saw the Taliban regime of 1996–2001 in a positive light did not perceive the Taliban positively in 2014/2015. The Taliban's legitimacy—or the lack thereof—in Kabul Province appeared to be based mainly on the people's perception of their activities at the time. This perception was based mainly on attacks in the city, which were associated with the Taliban or IS-K.

JALALABAD: A COMPLEX THREAT

The city of Jalalabad, the capital of Nangarhar Province, is only a three-hour car ride from Kabul. The road follows the Kabul River and twists 1,300 meters down through the mountains. The views are stunning, but I often felt a little uneasy on the way, glimpsing patches of new asphalt on the roads, reminders of the fuel trucks that caught fire after someone shot at them. Surobi District, one of the eastern districts of Kabul Province, was particularly well known for frequent attacks on the ANSF. Leaving the mountains of Kabul province behind, the road reaches the plains of eastern Afghanistan, first Laghman Province—where many people stopped to take selfies with an old Soviet tank lying next to the road—and finally Jalalabad in Nangarhar Province. The terrain is much flatter and the temperature much higher than in Kabul. In this part of the country, it hardly ever rains and the heat is often unbearable in summer. But because of the pleasant temperatures in winter, Jalalabad was a popular seasonal home for many Afghan kings over the centuries. With about 300,000 inhabitants, it is one of the biggest cities in Afghanistan.[54] From here, it is barely 80 kilometers to the Pakistani border. Indeed, the main currency used in this part of Afghanistan is the Pakistani rupee.

Like Kabul, the predominantly Pashtun province of Nangarhar was controlled by the Taliban from 1996 to 2001. Already at the time of my interviews in 2014/2015, the Taliban had regained control of many parts of the province. As in Kabul Province, IS-K entered the ring in 2015 and began to conduct violent attacks and control small territories in the province, which further increased the complexity of the armed opposition in Nangarhar. However, Jalalabad remained under government control, with some surrounding districts being "grey" areas, technically controlled by the government but influenced by the Taliban. Although the visible presence of the Taliban in Jalalabad was low, there was an atmosphere of fear driven by suicide attacks, kidnappings, and robberies.

Even though the Afghan state was in control of Jalalabad at the time of my research, the Taliban frequently arose as a topic of conversation in the interviews, as both a historical and a contemporary phenomenon. Most interviewees in Nangarhar had positive memories of Taliban control, particularly in terms of security. Rahmanullah, a mechanic, stated, "During the Taliban regime there were no kidnappings or other crimes in our province."[55] A few were more equivocal, such as Taher, a farmer who recalled that under the Taliban the security situation was better but that his economic situation was worse.[56]

At the time, Nangarhar Province had several armed groups with different interests and alliances. Some were linked to strongmen or the government, while others claimed to be "Taliban," and still others were only labeled "Taliban" by others. The armed groups that were mentioned most frequently in my interviews were Hekymatyar's Hezb-e Islami,[57] also known as the Islamic Political Party, the forces controlled by the Islamic Emirate, and the militias of the various strongmen. Mohammad Ibrahim, a civil society activist, explained the structure of the armed groups in Nangarhar:

> There are two main opposition groups here. It's the Islamic Party and the Taliban. The Islamic Party usually only attacks foreigners, not the ANA or the ANP. The Taliban attack foreign *and* government forces. The Taliban also collect *ushr* and *zakat*, which the Islamic Party isn't doing. The Taliban are much stronger and consist of different factions. The government is linked to these groups as it has some of its people within the Taliban. In addition,

strongmen—who often are part of the government too—hire militias to achieve their personal interests. Every strongman, every political party and every group has its own armed force. Most people just call all of these armed groups Taliban.[58]

Most of the people I interviewed in Jalalabad had strong negative views of the Taliban. As in Kabul, positive memories from the past rarely translated into contemporary perception. For example, university student Gulagha told me, "Taliban means 'the one who is seeking knowledge.' But now it is nothing more than the name of an illegally armed group, which is destroying the country with bombs and suicide attacks."[59] Similarly, Rohullah, also a student, stated, "Taliban for me means murderers. Especially city people hate them."[60] Very negative perceptions were particularly prominent in spring 2015, which followed closely on an attack on Kabul Bank in Jalalabad, killing and injuring dozens of people. Like people in Kabul, interviewees in Jalalabad also blamed the Taliban for crime in the city. Kidnappings by unknown groups were frequently happening at the time of the interviews, which many people attributed to the Taliban even though they appeared to be carried out only for ransom money. Nonetheless, people perceived the Taliban as a political actor—albeit one not necessarily fighting for ideological reasons but as a tool of foreign intervention, driven by what was often viewed as Pakistan's desire for insecurity in the country.[61] For example, Jamil explained his view to me: "In case the Taliban managed to stop the infiltration of their organisation through foreigners they might be accepted. But our nasty neighbour Pakistan causes insecurity through the Taliban."[62]

In contrast to the people in Kabul, many people in Jalalabad also had recent personal experiences with the Taliban, who at the time of the interviews controlled parts of Nangarhar Province.

Based on these experiences, people in Jalalabad not only perceived the Taliban to be an armed opposition group with links to
Pakistan, but they also saw connections to the Afghan state. For
instance, Mohammad Ibrahim, the civil society activist, told me:

> My son was kidnapped and I was asked to provide [the kidnap-
> pers] with ten AK47s. . . . Fortunately, my son was released again.
> But I still think that the police cooperate with [the kidnappers].
> When I was walking out of the police station after filing my case
> I got a call from the Taliban telling me that the police couldn't
> help me. About six months ago I was attacked in front of a police
> station. And after filing my case they arrested a number of police
> officers. They called me to identify their faces, but I was too afraid
> to do so. In fact, the police commanders cooperate closely with
> the illegally armed groups. Whenever these people notice that
> their interests are in danger they will take advantage of their links
> with the insurgents and call on them for help.[63]

The civil society activist was particularly open about his experiences, however, other interviewees also complained about the
links they saw between the police and the Taliban.[64]

On the other hand, Mohammad Ibrahim also explained that
the support for the Taliban in other parts of the province was
understandable, highlighting the role of Taliban conflict resolution procedures:

> For instance, if there is a conflict about money and people take it
> to the government courts it's going to take at least five months.
> They will try to make a criminal case out of this simple legal issue.
> This way both sides will have to spend an even bigger amount
> [on bribes] than what their case is actually about. Therefore,
> people prefer taking their case to the Taliban. They will call the

other party of the conflict and guarantee him that he will be safe. They will ask him if he really owes the other person money. If he says "yes," the Taliban give him a few months to pay back the full amount. And after a few months the amount will actually have been paid back.[65]

People in Jalalabad differed from those in Kabul Province in that such recent personal experiences with the Taliban were much more common, and they came to their negative conclusions on that basis. While the people in Kabul often describe "the Taliban" as a uniform group, in Jalalabad, people saw it as more complex, consisting of various interconnected groups. As in Kabul, violent behavior delegitimized the Taliban in the eyes of the people. But the Taliban's attacks in Jalalabad also illustrated that the Afghan state was incapable of providing security for its citizens, even in major urban areas. Hence, people became dissatisfied with the Afghan state, making the attacks a successful delegitimization strategy for the Taliban.

BEHSOD AND SURKH ROD: A SPORADIC PHENOMENON

People in the districts of Surkh Rod and Behsod, also in Nangarhar Province, saw the Taliban in an overwhelmingly negative light. However, in contrast to those in Jalalabad, most people were confident about the security situation.[66] Their contact with the Taliban, they explained, was sporadic. In contrast to Jalalabad, the experience of insecurity was based less on attacks and more on the Taliban's attempts to extract money. For instance, Haiatullah, a farmer, reported: "There are no Taliban in our village. But they sometimes show up in Samarkhel village close by."[67] Similarly, NGO employee Subhanullah told me, "Every now and then the Taliban come from Khogyani and Chaparhar districts and ask us for tithes. And when they come we feel insecure."[68] But another interviewee, teacher Mohammad Yusuf, said that the Taliban recruited successfully in Behsod. "Many people from our district go and join the Taliban because of poverty and unemployment."[69] The same was true in Surkh Rod, and high unemployment in both areas aided recruitment.[70]

Only one of the people I talked to in Behsod had an openly positive perception of the Taliban, and here again, conflict resolution played the deciding role. Wais, a village elder in Behsod, told me that he liked the Taliban because they were helping to solve conflicts at the community level: "Here in our village two brothers had a conflict on land rights. They went to the government to solve the conflict but nothing happened for a month. Then one brother went to the Taliban instead. They solved the conflict very quickly. And the result was acceptable for both brothers." As he was unsatisfied with the government's conflict resolution procedure and the growing insecurity, he expressed hope that in the future, the Taliban would regain control, at least of Behsod. He praised the Taliban's "mobile courts"—judges that come to the village by motorcycle when requested that were common at the time—which had made it easier for his acquaintances to access conflict resolution services. Like others, he decried the influence of neighboring countries in Afghanistan. He said, "I don't like Iran and Pakistan because they cause insecurity in our country," but he did not see the Taliban as their instrument. Meanwhile, he complained that the United States and government forces sometimes accused people from his village of being members of the Taliban. "A month ago international forces and ANA soldiers came and accused our mullah of being a Talib. They looted his house and burned his motorcycle even though he is innocent."[71] According to Wais, this reinforced the perception in his village that the government was a threat and that only the Taliban could provide security.

Nader, a teacher, told me that the Taliban were only present and a concern in the Kakrak area of Surkh Rod.[72] However, as in the other districts, others used the label "Taliban" more broadly, and any criminal activity, especially if it was violent, might be attributed to them. For instance, Mohammad, a member of a local council, reported, "In general, security is enforced and there is no threat from insurgents. But there are criminal activities. . . . The Taliban use weapons to kidnap, rob, ambush and threaten people."[73] Samar Gul, the head of a civil society organization, further explained that many people and groups described themselves as Taliban: "A great number of people are only fighting for their personal interests. But they do so using the Taliban label."[74] Many interviewees concluded that the violence in the country was not a consequence of opposing ideologies but was purely about economic interests.

In Surkh Rod and Behsod, as in Kabul and Jalalabad, the state authorities dominated the political order. However, in the rural districts, many people experienced the Taliban's attempts to extract money from them. Hence, the Taliban were an actual authority in the districts but one that relied on coercion rather than legitimacy. Wais was a rare instance of someone in Behsod and Surkh Rod who saw the Taliban as legitimate. He did so on the basis of the state's failures and on his personal observations of the impacts of their conflict resolution procedures, which he considered to be prompt and fair. Like the Taliban fighters I spoke to, he did not reference ideological considerations, such as a preference for a certain code of law (e.g., state law or Islamic law) or a preference for a certain defined procedure of how an authority should be gaining power (e.g., democracy or theocracy).

KHOGYANI AND SHERZAD: FAST AND FAIR JUSTICE

In the interviews, Khogyani and Sherzad districts were often described as the Taliban's "bases" for driving insecurity in Nangarhar. However, interviewees from these districts often had a very different view.

For example, shopkeeper Obid and unemployed engineer Khalid described the situation in Khogyani District. Based on the comments of people elsewhere about the situation in the district, I expected them to have the most negative view possible of the Taliban. Indeed, they said that security was very poor. "Five years ago at least the main roads were safe. Today not even these roads are safe anymore, as the number of bombings and kidnappings has increased dramatically." However, they argued that collaboration between government forces and other armed groups was the cause. "The security is both enforced and sabotaged by the government, as the government cooperates with insurgency groups." They also stated that the political landscape of insurgency groups was complex: "There are . . . the Islamic Political Party, the Islamic Emirate's Mahaz, a new group called Karwan Fidaye as well as ordinary criminals. Karwan Fidaye is particularly active in Khogyani.[75] Once they get you, escaping from them is very challenging. The members of this group cover their faces with black masks and people say that most of them are from Punjab in Pakistan. This group fights both the Taliban and the government."[76]

They felt most threatened by the government, but they also criticized the various groups for demanding levies. Meanwhile, they thought that the Taliban were at least providing good conflict resolution. Khalid explained, "My father-in-law spent $90,000 to 100,000 on building a house in the Ahmad Khail area of Khogyani. Now the head of the Afghan Local Police, Malik [name], has taken the house. He refuses to leave the house and doesn't even pay rent. The Taliban started to attack him and as a result the house got partly destroyed. A suicide bomber even blew himself up inside the house." His family had not received satisfaction from the police. They had brought their complaint there but were not even admitted because the head of the district police had connections to the Malik. Therefore, said Khalid, "The next time I am involved in a conflict I will go to the Taliban first. They solve conflicts quickly. The government isn't solving my problems, it's making them bigger."[77]

Similarly, Obid praised the Taliban's conflict resolution procedures. He said:

> I had a fight with my brother regarding our inheritance. I was insisting that my sisters' rights need to be observed as well. But my brother denied it. We took the case to the government courts and it took two years—without any result. Then they referred the case to the local council. They did not solve it either, because they were scared of my brother whom they thought was a militant. The local council simply asked each of us to pay 10,000 USD as Machalgha. We didn't want to accept that. Then we took the case to the Taliban. They instantly called the local elders to return the money they had taken from us as well as an AK47 they had also taken from me. They also made a decision about our case. On the basis of Islamic Law they decided that my sisters as well as my mom had inheritance rights.[78]

The case illustrates that de facto rules applied by the Taliban in Nangarhar had been changing. Several other interviewees reported that the Taliban enforced women's rights to inherit land. Others pointed out the Taliban had changed their approach to education in parts of Nangarhar, not only accepting schools for girls but even enforcing their attendance and visiting families if their children did not attend on a regular basis. However, some people objected to this, preferring to decide for themselves whether their daughters attended school.

In Jalalabad, I also met Wasiullah, a young man from Sherzad District. He said that the Taliban essentially controlled his district, and he felt this was a good thing. "I think it is much better in Sherzad than in Jalalabad. Because in Jalalabad there are two governments in one city [meaning the Afghan state and the Taliban]; in Sherzad it is only the Taliban. And all people in Sherzad are happy with the Taliban." He distinguished swift and impartial conflict resolution. "When a person has a problem he goes to the Taliban. The Taliban then refer the conflict to their Hoquqe Department and courts.[79] Their conflict resolution procedure is much simpler than the formal justice mechanisms. The decisions are made on the basis of Islamic law, and they are fast. They sometimes ask for a small bribe to cover the expenses of their motorcycle. But apart from that there are no costs for the involved parties.[80]

Wasiullah also described Sherzad as having strong security due to Taliban control. When I asked him about the use of force by the Taliban, he said that they would "use force if necessary. But they are not corrupt. So people prefer the Taliban's conflict resolution."[81] He expressed his hope that the Taliban would be governing the country again soon.

It seems unlikely that all people in Sherzad were happy with the Taliban. But his case suggests that some people were and that those people likely approved of the Taliban because of their day-to-day experiences.

FIVE YEARS LATER: TALIBAN JUSTICE IN HERAT AND FARYAB PROVINCES

Over the years following my research in 2014/2015, Taliban influence and control spread further across Afghanistan, even in areas that were previously considered to be strongholds of the state, such as Herat Province. Building on the findings that the provision of justice in a way that responded to people's expectations was an important source of legitimacy for the Taliban, we conducted more than two hundred additional interviews with people living under Taliban control in 2019 in western Afghanistan, in Herat and Faryab provinces, to gain a more detailed understanding of their view on Taliban justice.[82] Taliban justice had developed considerably since 2014/2015, becoming much more widespread and organized. This was also reflected in public perceptions.

Interviewees emphasized the accessibility of Taliban justice. By 2019, for many people in rural areas, Taliban courts had become the most accessible ones. For example, as discussed in chapter 2, facing Taliban pressure, the government had withdrawn its courts from most districts in Faryab Province and moved them to the provincial capital Maimana, making them de facto inaccessible for the wider population. Meanwhile, Taliban courts were easily accessible on the district level, which many people appreciated in the interviews. But while they appeared to be genuinely happy with the accessibility of Taliban courts, the Taliban applied coercion to discourage the use of alternatives. For example, a man from Pashtunkot District in Faryab explained, "As the area is controlled by the Taliban, we have no other option than taking our case or problem to the Taliban courts."[83] Another interviewee further stated, "We would be killed, if the Taliban got to know that we contacted the government."[84] The Taliban had de facto monopolized justice in many parts of Faryab, also discouraging elders and other more traditional authorities from offering conflict resolution.

Relatedly, the interviewees emphasized that the Taliban were able to enforce the decisions of their courts. When living under Taliban control or wanting to take a person from a Taliban-controlled area to court, only Taliban courts were a viable option that ensured that the result was actually enforced, as the government courts could not enforce decisions in areas under Taliban control. Meanwhile, the Taliban did have a reputation for being able to enforce decisions—and even attendance in their courts— far beyond their areas of control. For instance, Mohammad Zarif from government-controlled Herat City reported: "I had borrowed 25,000 Afs [about $375] from somebody, but couldn't pay the money back on time. He came often and asked for the money back. But I couldn't pay. The other party submitted a complaint to the Taliban. They then sent me a letter and asked me to appear in court. I didn't go. They sent a second letter and said that if you don't come, we will send a car with Taliban fighters to pick you up. And you will have to pay 10,000 Afs [about $150] for the vehicle. So I went."[85]

In addition, as in Khogyani and Sherzad, people praised the speed of Taliban justice. An interviewee from Almar District in Faryab Province told us, "The Taliban make decisions quickly. The Afghan government is distinguishing between the rich and the poor if someone is rich or high profile, they will get released. If it's a poor person, no one will ask about him. The Taliban government is not like this. Both rich and poor are equal. For everyone. And, also, their decisions are sharp and fast."[86]

Contrary to a popular notion, though, Taliban justice was not always as fast as commonly assumed, and it varied considerably depending on the type of case. While debt cases were usually resolved quickly, on average taking nine days, land disputes and inheritance cases on average took about three months—in some cases, it took over a year.

Reinforcing the initial impressions gained in Nangarhar in 2014/2015, more substantially, a key reason people used Taliban justice was its perceived fairness, particularly in comparison to the government courts that were viewed as corrupt. A man from Kohistan District in Faryab Province explained, "We took the case to the Taliban for two main reasons: First, for having justice and fairness when handling cases and, second, the lack of existence and access to the government courts and the wide-spread corruption there."[87] Most interviewees thought that the Taliban's approach to conflict resolution was conducted in a consistent and predictable way, treating people more equally, regardless of social status and influence. While some interviewees also voiced complaints about corruption in Taliban courts, such cases were the exception. Some people in Faryab, but almost none in Herat, also stated that they used Taliban courts because they viewed them in line with their religious values. In particular, women appreciated the Taliban's references to Islam, as they thought court decisions made in their favor gave them more standing in their communities.

Perhaps surprisingly, many female interviewees had a positive perception of Taliban justice.[88] They explained that while the Taliban courts were not treating men and women equally, their system was better than the other available options. In inheritance cases, women often pointed out that traditional authorities and, in some cases, even government courts, would not give them any land, while the Taliban would at least give them 50 percent of the share of men. For instance, a woman from Gurziwan District in Faryab Province explained, "When my father died three years ago, only me and my brother remained. I asked my brother to divide the heritage, but he didn't accept it and didn't give me my part. The case was referred to the government's courts many times, but they couldn't solve it. We then used tradition authorities and elders, but we didn't get any result from them either. When our area fell under control of the Taliban, I went to Taliban with my husband. They decided to give me 4 acres of land, half an acre of garden and a 200-meter yard as per Sharia law."[89]

In several cases, women also filed divorce cases in a Taliban court. Many had tried traditional authorities and the government system before unsuccessfully. While according to Taliban justice, divorces are only possible in specific cases, most interviewed women in Herat and Faryab provinces who tried to get divorced were successful, arguing that they had been married against their will or that their husband was not taking care of them, providing food, or was being violent towards them. For example, a woman from Khusk-e-Khona in Herat Province told us about her case:

> One day my husband beat me a lot because he wanted me to give him money, but I refused. I worked as a tailor and had earned some money. He also kept me hungry and was not giving me food. . . .
> I thought a lot about my life and finally I decided to fight for my right by myself. So in 2017 I made my brother share the issue with the mullah. . . . My brother understood me, and he went to the mullah of the village. . . . But the mullah told my brother that divorce is a shameful issue and that it should not even be discussed. Instead, we were asked to find a peaceful solution. But that didn't work. . . . I heard from people that the Taliban observe justice very seriously. So we discussed the issue among our family members and my mother asked my brothers to refer the problem to the Taliban. My brother took me to the Taliban court and wrote everything on an application to the Taliban. After explanation of

my problem to the Taliban they told us that next week along with your husband should come to the court. . . . After explaining my problem and delivering our evidence, which was witnesses, to the court, the court obligated me to pay the bride price back my husband. We accepted the decision and my brother paid 200,000 Afs [about $3,000] to my husband and he divorced me.[90]

The findings show that the Taliban's expansion of the provision of justice also enabled them to enhance their legitimacy. To construct public support, they did not have to offer an outstanding system. Instead, they had to be less corrupt than the available alternatives, allowing people to claim their rights—even if these rights were more limited than in the state justice system particularly for women. As the more extensive rights that existed on paper in the state system could not actually be claimed successfully by most people, they preferred the perhaps more limited but more accessible system of the Taliban that allowed them to solve pressing conflicts in a predictable way. However, the Taliban's authority in Herat and Faryab provinces certainly did not rest on legitimacy only. Coercion continued to play an important role. Many people only used Taliban courts because they could not access other conflict resolution mechanisms anymore, with the Taliban threatening people not to use government courts while also trying to reduce the influence of community authorities.

CONCLUSIONS

The overall assessment of the Taliban appeared to be *pragmatic*, predominantly based on the *day-to-day experience* of their *actions*, particularly the *interaction* with them rather than their history or idea of authority. Two conflicting images of the

Taliban were prominent in my research. While people in many parts of the government-controlled territories I went to looked at them through the lens of "insecurity," some people in Taliban-controlled territories viewed the Taliban more favorably, focusing on their role in "conflict resolution" or "justice." These views were closely aligned with the two different roles the Taliban played in Afghanistan, governing some parts or offering services that were associated with governing authorities while fighting or conducting attacks in others.

On the one hand, most people I talked to in the government-controlled areas perceived the Taliban as a coercive authority or simply a threat to their security. There was no sign that the Taliban were even trying to construct actual authority in Kabul or Jalalabad at the time of my research. Rather, they were focusing on undermining the legitimacy of the state by illustrating that it could not protect its citizens. Beyond the physical impact of their violence, the Taliban benefited from its symbolic effects. In Kabul City, with its high symbolic value due to being the capital of Afghanistan, the number of attacks people experienced was particularly high.[91] But, apart from witnessing or becoming victim of such attacks, people had rarely personally experienced the Taliban, so that media reporting and second-hand information played an important additional role in shaping their perceptions. Similarly, in Jalalabad, people experienced attacks and criminality, for which many blamed the Taliban. However, in contrast to Kabul, more people had recent personal experiences with the Taliban, which directly shaped their perceptions.

At the time of my interviews, the rural districts of Kabul Province, Char Asiab and Farza, were under government control and in some distance from the insurgents' targets in the city and fighting in other rural parts of the country. People in those districts perceived the Taliban as more of a remote security threat.

The Taliban were merely potential authorities at the time of the research, lacking any ability to have a direct impact. However, in Behsod and Surkh Rod, which were in close proximity to insurgency-controlled territories, people frequently experienced the Taliban. Here, they were not only seen as an abstract threat but also as an actual authority, using coercion to exercise social control. Meanwhile, people in Nangarhar had a more complex understanding of the Taliban, who they saw as linked to the government and strongmen. And despite the widespread rejection of the Taliban, some people from these areas decided to join the Taliban to make a living—a signal of instrumental legitimacy if nothing else.

On the other hand, many residents from Taliban-controlled areas and territories that were technically government-controlled but accessible for the Taliban had more positive opinions. This was most prominently the case in many rural areas of Herat and Faryab provinces in 2019, but I also came across such positive views earlier in Khogyani District and Sherzad District in Nangarhar Province and elsewhere. For example, the university student Hamidullah told me about the positive role the Taliban played in providing security in Wardak: "We don't like the Afghan security forces such as the ANP at the district level because they are incapable of providing security for us. I think that the Taliban are doing a much better job in Wardak."[92] These people described the Taliban as their preferred authority—which indicates a degree of legitimacy. In terms of the Taliban's role in security provision, this legitimacy appears to be instrumental. People viewed the Taliban as the best security provider for pragmatic reasons, not because of values and beliefs. For instance, some considered the Taliban to be threatening but thought the state was even worse. Or they simply preferred to have a monopoly of force over the ongoing violent competition.

But the Taliban's role in security provision was a marginal point for most who saw it in a positive light. Those people focused on the Taliban's positive role in conflict resolution, supporting Giustozzi's conviction that justice plays a key role in the Taliban's legitimacy.[93] Supplementing Giustozzi's work, my findings indicate that the Taliban applied this strategy not only in territories where they had a local monopoly of force but also in territories that were government-controlled but which they could access, attracting people for conflict resolution and building legitimacy. The Taliban's conflict resolution procedures provided a substantive dimension to the Taliban's legitimacy in this context since most interviewees preferred the Taliban because of the *fairness and predictability* of these procedures. The fact that the Taliban's interpretation of the Islamic code of law appeared to adjust to match people's expectations, being more favorable to women in some cases than assumed, also supports this view.[94] But the people's main concern seemed to be the rule of any law, regardless of its ideological sources, to counter the perceived high level of corruption and arbitrariness. Only if the procedures are clearly defined and implemented accordingly do people have a certain degree of predictability. And only if people have the feeling that everybody is treated the same way, regardless of money or influence, do they consider the procedures to be fair. By living up to these very basic expectations and making people feel like subjects who are equal to their authority—not necessarily perfect but at least better than the state—the Taliban constructed substantive legitimacy.

My research indicates that the Taliban was often successful in areas that it could access and where it actually wanted to construct legitimacy. However, it would be wrong to conclude that everyone living under the control of the Taliban at the time viewed it as legitimate. The Taliban's authority was not just based on legitimacy—it also drew on coercion. This is particularly illustrated by the fact that people in Taliban-controlled areas were often afraid of using government courts. Taliban governance might be even more oppressive in other districts and provinces, and in the areas analyzed in this book. Especially the experience and perspective of women requires further investigation. In addition, many people questioned their sources of legitimacy, not just in cities. Qari, a university student from Loya Paktia, complained, "The Taliban's conflict resolution mechanisms is the most corrupt one."[95] While Qari did not consider the Taliban's justice system to be fair, his perspective supports the view that people care more about fair procedures than on which code of law or ideology it is based. Anecdotal evidence from southern Afghanistan, where the Taliban established courts much earlier, suggests that court cases were taking longer and longer due to a growing number of cases and that an increasing number of people thought that Taliban courts were becoming more corrupt over time.

Meanwhile, people actively supported the Taliban to achieve different purposes. Some people joined to gain personal advantages or goals—driven by opportunism, revenge, greed, or simply the need to make enough money to survive. Others were more humanist or idealist and fought for a "better" society, possibly defined in a religious way, but, in most of my interviews, described in terms of general human values with regard to the authorities' practices. Then there were followers who joined the Taliban, willingly or unwillingly, because of social pressure. The Taliban provided all of these people with a better platform from which to fight against the state and its foreign allies.

Some people undoubtedly used the insurgency for their personal interests, but almost everyone I talked to, regardless of their goals, had experienced a *behavior* of the government or foreign forces that they considered to be deeply unfair—even if they only witnessed it on video. Hence, while the Taliban's legitimacy bestowed by its active supporters was instrumental in some cases, it also had a substantive component, which was linked to *basic human values regarding interaction.* Though there certainly are ideological supporters of the Taliban, most active and former Taliban members I talked to presented a similar claim of legitimacy framed in terms of fighting a corrupt government or the cruel foreign forces for a just and humane society. This behavior on the side of the Afghan state—and not the Taliban's idea of authority, based on Islam or some other ideology—legitimized the Taliban from its supporters' points of view.

While the claim of legitimacy by the Taliban in Afghanistan is quite consistent, the local perceptions were much more multifaceted. People had different and often contrary perceptions of the Taliban, and, in some cases, it was difficult to define who the Taliban actually were. Nonetheless, there are some common patterns. People judged the Taliban *pragmatically* on the basis of what it actually did and considered it to be legitimate or illegitimate depending on its actions, in particular its *day-to-day behavior* and *procedures of interaction.* In the government-controlled areas, its behavior was perceived to be threatening and illegitimate by most interviewees. The main concern of the people was not religious extremism but the attacks the Taliban launched and the instability it caused. But, in territories under Taliban control—also in some territories that were government-controlled but they could access—some people considered the Taliban to be legitimate, specifically because they felt that it was treating them better than other authorities, particularly the Afghan state.

Indeed, negative experiences with the Afghan state and its high level of corruption were crucial for the legitimacy of the Taliban, as, for instance, the repeated references to conflict resolution procedures suggest. In the massively corrupt and volatile political order of Afghanistan at the time, people wanted to be treated equally, with respect, showing little concern for which code of law was actually applied. In some cases, the Taliban seemed to be responding to these local demands much better than the government. Thus, the Taliban not only built instrumental but also substantive legitimacy, responding to people's value-based expectations of authority's behavior and the interaction with them.

The public perception illustrates that the Taliban's official claim of authority did not matter much in relation to its legitimacy on the local level. People did not care much about "jihad" or the "reestablishment of an Islamic system." But the Taliban's personal claims of legitimacy, the fight against injustice and corruption, responded well to people's concerns. As Rangelov and Theros[96] and Johnson[97] argue, the Taliban successfully mobilized support through a discourse of injustice, abuse, and grievances. This discourse matched people's personal experiences, and many joined the Taliban because of the grievances and frustration they had with the Afghan state. More importantly, the Taliban's claim of legitimacy in this regard did not remain a claim only. The interviews indicate that the Taliban, in some cases, did a better job of living up to expectations than other authorities. The provision of conflict resolution played a particularly key role in legitimizing the Taliban. But even beyond conflict resolution, the Taliban appeared to be more pragmatic than often assumed and adjusted its practices to suit people's expectations, as illustrated by the example of enforced schooling for girls in Nangarhar. The Taliban's legitimacy, whether bestowed by active supporters and members or by those living under its rule, was in both cases usually based on the same sources. While instrumental factors and personal advantages certainly matter, the Taliban also had substantive legitimacy, grounded in behaviors and procedures that were perceived to be fairer than those of other authorities—particularly those of the Afghan state.

5

COMMUNITY AUTHORITIES

"Local councils only treat the symptoms, like painkillers."
Head of village in Kushk Robat Sangi District, Herat Province, 2014

Policy makers have generally agreed that community authorities, such as elders, councils, and mullahs are more legitimate than other actors in Afghanistan, either because of their traditional character, grounded in local customs such as the Pashtunwali, or because of their participatory structure, which grants them a kind of democratic legitimacy. As a consequence, many interventions by the state and the international community targeted the local level and community authorities in an effort to benefit from their legitimacy. For example, the World Bank launched the Citizen's Charter program to enhance the legitimacy of the Afghan state by empowering and constructing new community structures and linking them to the state.

Afghanistan has different traditions and forms of community governance. Scholars and policy makers often explain these variations through an ethnic lens, emphasizing the particularities of and differences among the Pashtun, Uzbek, Tajik, Nuristani, and Hazara populations of the country. For example, the Pashtunwali is an element of the culture of the Pashtun population, dominant in southern and eastern Afghanistan. It is a system of rules and recommendations for behavior (*narkh*) such as the importance of hospitality (*melmastia*), equality (*seyal*), social network (*qawm*), and forgiveness (*nanawati*), as well as the design of political order that includes a hierarchical system of councils.[1] However, geography, more than ethnicity, often creates communities and therefore norms and traditions.[2]

Pristine, independent community governance has long ceased to exist. Noelle-Karimi aptly points out that what is "traditional" "by no means [implies] timelessness or immutability."[3] Migration and exogenous factors, such as conflict in the country and military intervention, can change traditions. Interventions at the community level by the international community and the state have an impact as well. Nonetheless, perhaps because of such external factors, most communities have local authorities of similar character, which have been described by scholars such as Nixon[4] and Murtazashvili.[5] These include collective decision-making bodies—councils, such as shuras and jirgas—and individuals with authority—such as maliks, arbabs, khans, and mullahs.

This chapter sets out to gain a better understanding of these community authorities and their legitimacy between 2001 and 2021. It shows that community authorities, particularly councils, village leaders, and elders, played an important role in conflict resolution. Procedures of interaction and other practices gave them both instrumental and substantive legitimacy in this area. Other aspects of their authority, such as how they came into power and if they were elected, mattered considerably less, according to the comments of interviewees. Community authorities were often simply closer and easier to access than the state, and the process of conflict resolution was cheaper and faster. In addition, their procedures were often considered fairer and less corrupt and, hence, also more predictable than the state's, giving community authorities a substantive, values-based legitimacy. Equal treatment rather than, for instance, specific local traditions was the basis of fairness. But most interviewees hoped that the state would take over the perceived responsibility of conflict resolution again in the future. In a way, the legitimacy of community authority seemed to result from a perceived insufficiency in the state's practices.

COLLECTIVE ACTORS: COMMUNITY COUNCILS

A prominent community authority in Afghan villages is councils. *Jirgas*, groups of people, usually men, who gather to resolve disputes and make decisions for villages, are a central element of local governance in rural Pashtun villages.[6] Similar bodies are usually called *shuras* (councils) in non-Pashtun areas.[7] Members are referred to as "elders" or "white beards," regardless of their age.[8] Some villages have a fairly static group assigned to this function, while others assemble people who are best equipped or motivated to deal with a certain problem or conflict.[9] In some cases, the qualification for members has to do with conduct and behavior as well as means to host guests and travel to government offices or to dispute sites.[10]

Different councils in different parts of the country have different customs and apply different rules for conflict resolution. But certain shared characteristics exist, such as a strong focus on mediation instead of conviction and punishment.[11] According to Saltmarshe and Medhi, conflict resolution in councils "seeks to take into account everyone's right . . . while at the same time maintaining village stability."[12] The Asia Foundation's survey data suggests that 64 percent of the people had confidence in community councils in 2015,[13] and 43 percent of those who required conflict resolution turned to local councils.[14]

Community councils have a long-standing tradition in many parts of the country. However, outside forces have shaped this "tradition" for decades.[15] In the 1980s and 1990s, NGOs established "development shuras" to channel aid through councils, under the assumption that they had legitimacy that would serve the NGOs' goals.[16] Other actors, such as Mujahedin fighters, established their own councils. Over time, people began to conflate "traditional" structures with the newer ones.[17] After 2001, the Afghan state and the international community sponsored the creation of new community councils—for example, through the National Solidarity Programme (NSP), a project of Ashraf Ghani, Afghanistan's minister of finance and later president of Afghanistan under the impetus of the World Bank.

Specifically understood as building on the concept of "traditional" jirgas and shuras,[18] NSP promised "to improve the access of rural villagers to basic services and to create a foundation of village governance based on democratic processes and female participation."[19] Under the program, the state set up thirty-two thousand community development councils (CDCs) in 361 districts in all of Afghanistan's provinces by 2013 with the help of "facilitating partners," international and national NGOs. The members were supposed to be elected by the community, and a certain number of seats were designated for women. In many parts of the country, the representatives of multiple CDCs formed an additional district development assembly, bridging the decision-making structures at the local and provincial levels.[20] Communities received block grants of up to $60,000 to implement development projects at the village level. The total budget for the three phases from 2003 to 2016 was $2.7 billion.[21]

Until 2021, CDCs looked set to continue to play an important role in Afghanistan. In September 2016, the Afghan government launched the Citizens' Charter, a program that was supposed to link CDCs more closely to the state to improve public perception of them. The Asia Foundation found that 61 percent of the people had confidence in CDCs in 2015, which was almost as high as their more traditional counterparts, but it dropped to only 53 percent in 2016, remaining stable on a low level.[22] However, we do not know what underpinned this confidence and whether support of CDCs could translate into state legitimacy.

The provincial councils (PCs) were even more closely linked to the state than the councils at the community and district levels. PCs were established in 2005 to increase the local accountability of the state to increase its legitimacy. The size of PCs ranged between nine and twenty-nine members, again with seats reserved for women, who were elected every four years. But the PCs' mandate was unspecific and contested. Members of the PCs suggested they should have authoritative oversight over the provincial government, while Parliament wanted the PCs to be advisory bodies.[23] The National Democratic Institute, which worked with PCs, describes them as "the only elected representatives [most Afghans] are likely to meet, making them the face of government for most citizens."[24] However, Larson and Coburn point out that some PCs were captured by local elites and describe the connection they made between local communities and the state as "shaky."[25] Similarly, Miakhel and Coburn find that many councils did not represent the people much as they were corrupt and had been co-opted by government officials, militias, or criminals.[26]

The cases of the NSP, the Citizens' Charter, and the PCs illustrate the assumption, which underpinned many national and international interventions at the local level, that "community councils" were legitimate authorities, either because of their tradition, their democratic or participatory character, and/ or their proximity to the people. The hope was that if public services were channeled through such structures, the Afghan state could also gain legitimacy. However, Bhatia and coauthors' research on the NSP in Wardak Province suggests that the program achieved certain development goals but did not affect the relationship between state and society much.[27] Even though councils are certainly close to the people, scholars question the extent to which their traditional and democratic structures make them legitimate. For instance, Lister points out that councils that were set up by the state could not have traditional legitimacy.[28] Wardak's analysis of jirgas in the Pashtun parts of Afghanistan concludes that arriving at a decision "fairly and in accordance with the tenets of Pashtunwali" gives it legitimacy rather than a "traditional" institutional structure as international organizations suggested.[29] Meanwhile, other scholars doubt whether councils are as democratic as presumed and argue that they often did not actually represent their communities.[30]

INDIVIDUAL ACTORS: REPRESENTATIVES, LANDOWNERS, COMMANDERS

In addition to the Afghan state and the Taliban, individual strongmen were also trying to shape community governance to their advantage. Gul Agha Shirzai, who was interviewed in chapter 3, sought to consolidate his power after he was appointed governor of Nangarhar in 2005 by co-opting maliks, strengthening their role, and replacing those he could not co-opt. Also called *arbab* or *qaryadar*,[31] the malik is often described as the "village leader," although Murtazashvili finds that the people in the village often considered them to be "first among equals."[32] While many communities elect their maliks, in some villages, it is an inherited role.[33] Not all villages have them, and their functions differ. Just like with councils, conflict resolution is a common role, and, in many villages, the malik is the main interlocutor between the state and the village, representing the community toward the state and other outside actors.[34]

The maliks' role as "community representative" is rooted in their history, which is closely linked to the state. During the monarchy, the king selected the maliks, who functioned as local powerbrokers and were given power over the daily functioning of rural communities.[35] Maliks held a certificate of authority (*wasiqa*), and some of their responsibilities were encoded in national law, including tax collection and local registration. The link between the state and maliks and the practice of the state formally legitimizing the maliks' authority continues to exist in some parts of the country, though based on tradition, not laws.[36]Murtazashvili concludes that the local legitimacy of maliks became founded in tradition and no longer required the state.[37] Meanwhile, Mielke suggests that the role of elders as brokers, managing "the interface between the rural populace and outsiders" and allocating goods to their people, continue to be key for their legitimacy.[38]

Other individuals who may have power in Afghan communities are the *khans*. While the term can be a synonym for malik, it also can refer to wealthy landowners.[39] With a large portion of a community often working on land belonging to a few individuals, the khans have a lot of authority. Khans are often members of councils, if not maliks, although many villages that used to confer power on khans no longer do, mainly because new authorities have gained importance in some villages. After the Saur Revolution in 1978, the government turned against "traditional" community authorities, murdering many elders, maliks, and other local elites. Many survivors joined the armed resistance.[40] More militarized commanders (*qumandan*) arose in their place in some villages, and they monopolized power and resources.[41] Their authority rests mainly on coercion, making them a local form of the strongmen discussed before. Nonetheless, Wilde and Mielke argue that because they behave according to the expectations people have of elders, such as hosting guests, settling disputes, and coordinating with the government, they have some degree of legitimacy.[42]

Finally, another type of important actor at the community level is the religious authorities, commonly termed *mullahs*. In contrast to the formally trained *imam*, mullahs are low-level religious authorities with no formal training.[43] Their main responsibility is to lead prayers. However, they can also play an important role in community life beyond that, particularly in the context of conflict resolution.[44] Most are poor and depend on the community to provide them with food and money.[45] However, because of their influence, the mullah has always been another focal point for the interventions of the Afghan state at the local level. The Durrani empire tried to co-opt the mullahs; later, the PDPA prosecuted them; then the Taliban tried to turn the mullah into the central community authority and to sideline, and in some cases even kill, maliks and elders. Instead, the Taliban charged mullahs with collecting taxes and implementing their code of law. While their formal role diminished again after 2001, Murtazashvili concludes that mullahs continued to play an important role because of their religious legitimacy and the services they delivered to the community.[46]

With the growing influence of the Taliban, the configuration of community governance in Afghanistan changed once more. While elders and local councils played a key role in conflict resolution at the community level in the districts I researched in 2014/2015, the Taliban proceeded to monopolize justice provision in some areas under their control in the following years. The Taliban often treated community authorities as key witnesses, however, actively discouraged them from providing conflict resolution unless the area was too remote for Taliban courts to reach.

While the authority of khans seems to rest primarily on wealth, the commanders' on force, and the mullahs' on religion, the sources of the legitimacy of community councils, elders, and maliks appears to be more difficult to pinpoint. The community councils' legitimacy may rest on tradition, its participatory or democratic character, and/or its membership if its members had gained legitimacy over time by behaving according to the community's expectations. Maliks may have legitimacy for traditional reasons, because they were elected, because they helped community members to solve their conflicts, and/or because of their links to the state. But looking at different types of community authorities in different parts of Afghanistan shows that there are strong similarities in terms of why people consider certain community authorities to be legitimate.

THE RURAL EAST—SURKH ROD, NANGARHAR PROVINCE

Despite its close proximity to Jalalabad, the urban center of eastern Afghanistan, Surkh Rod District is predominantly rural. Most people consider themselves to be Pashtun; Pashto is also the dominant language. The literature indicates that in rural

Pashtun areas, community authorities play a particularly important role. And, indeed, the list of community authorities the interviewees referenced was long. Importantly, there were elders, whom people often also referred to as "maliks"—in contrast to the literature, where maliks are described as the heads of a village or village leaders. These elders formed "malik councils" at the village level and a superior one at the district level.

Additionally, many villages had development councils that consisted of elected members. Groups of ten development councils were organized as clusters. At the district level, the 145 development councils of Surkh Rod were represented by a district development assembly. This structure was a more recent phenomenon and was established in the course of the NSP. Most villages had mullahs, and some had youth councils and tribal councils as well. Structures often overlapped considerably. For instance, elders were also elected members of the development councils.

Malik Shukrullah, the head of a village, and Mohammad Ibrahim, a member of the community development council in the same village, spoke to me in a joint interview.[47] They explained to me how they perceived their responsibilities as members of different councils and how they collaborated closely. "The elders' council's responsibility is conflict resolution, while the development councils organise development projects. Typically, we meet every two days. But in addition, we also meet for special occasions. To solve conflicts, we often have joint meetings of both councils too."

They explained that most conflicts relate to inheritance and land rights, particularly women's inheritance rights. They described a succession of authorities people approach in their village: "If people face a problem, they usually go to the head of the village or the elders first. The second choice are local councils, youth councils, and civil society organisations. The third choice are development councils and the governor's office. If after that the conflict still hasn't been solved, people would go to the government [courts]. . . . But often the government [court] returns the cases to the local councils and asks us to solve them."

Asked about why people preferred them over the state for conflict resolution, they responded, "Unfortunately, the government is not serious about providing fair justice."

Hajji Batel was the head of a different village.[48] He described conflict resolution as his main responsibility, but he also coordinated between the government and the community with regard to security-related issues. Like Malik Aziz Mohammadi and Mohammad Ibrahim, he noted that criminal cases went to the government first, but for other kinds of disputes, the people's first choice for conflict resolution was community authorities: "If people face a problem they would go to the local elders first." He said that they used either "customary law" or "Islamic law" and that the state provided the books for the council to record its decisions.

Hajji Batel noted that local elders' decisions were not revocable and that they asked "both sides for guarantees so that the conflict does not erupt again." He claimed that "people trust all elders." He attributed people's assumed preference for community authorities for conflict resolution to this trust as well as to speed and the fact that elders do not demand money. Hence, he hoped that community authorities would maintain their role in the future: "It is much better if conflict resolution continues to be done through local councils, it saves times and money."

Members of the public in Surkh Rod confirmed that community authorities played an important role in the context of conflict resolution and that inheritance and land disputes, including access to water for irrigation, were common. They said that criminal

cases usually went to the state. In addition, several interviewees argued that women often "caused" disputes. For instance, the
laborer Mohammad Nasim explained, "Women escaping [their
marriages], sexual harassment, and such things often result in
small conflicts that get big very fast."[49] The teacher Ismail noted
that marriages and marriage proposals also resulted in conflicts
between families.[50]

To solve such conflicts, most interviewees in Surkh Rod told
me that they would approach local elders or the council of elders
and the development councils, not mentioning other councils
or mullahs. A few interviewees said they would consider taking their cases to one of the strongmen, such as Hajji Qadir.[51]
Mohammad Nasim told me, "The preferred option for conflict-
resolution is the local councils and the second is the government."[52] Similarly, Ismail said, "I would take my cases to the local
council. . . . For instance, all land conflicts are solved by local
councils. Only criminal cases are taken to the government."[53]

In Surkh Rod, there was no standard code of law at the local
level. Different communities and community authorities relied
to different extents on customary law or Islamic law.[54] A number
of interviewees explained that community authorities' interpretations of Islamic law were usually more liberal than customary
law—for example, in terms of women's rights. The knowledge of
the two bodies of law was passed on from generation to generation. Halim, a tailor, described the situation in his village: "Here,
conflicts are still solved like they were solved ten years ago. On
the basis of customary laws."[55] Conversely, Nader, a teacher from
Surkh Rod, noted, "In family-related conflicts, customary law is
used. But in other cases, such as in inheritance disputes, Islamic
law is applied."[56] But while the interpretation of religious rules
had not changed much over time, the traditional body of law was
adapted constantly.

Furthermore, customary law can be different in different communities. For example, as discussed in more detail in chapter 2, *Machalgha* is a practice of solving conflicts according to which both parties pay a deposit to the community authority. This money is only returned after a few years when the conflict has not erupted again. School principal Hajji Muhebullah explained that communities further from the city were far more likely to use this approach than those closer to Jalalabad.[57]

When I asked the interviewees why they preferred local elders and councils for conflict resolution, people did not reference "tradition." Instead, they pointed to the selfish attitude of government authorities and the flaws of the state system, making local elders a "cheaper" and "fairer" alternative. Samar Gul outlined: "Local elders take a lot of time to solve people's conflicts without expecting money in exchange from any side. They do this work voluntarily. The government's formal justice mechanism is very corrupt and solving conflicts there takes a lot of time. . . . Local elders are closely linked to our daily social life. They are visible. And they deal with the problems the government can't take care of."[58]

The tailor Halim, like most other interviewees, supported this claim and stated that the main reason why people rely on community authorities are the bribes in the state system.[59] The teacher Ismail concluded, "I trust the local elders. Their conflict resolution is based on justice."[60]

There were a few people in Surkh Rod who preferred the state's courts for conflict resolution. For example, the shopkeeper Najibullah said that he would go to the government with any conflict he couldn't solve within his family.[61] Others in Surkh Rod preferred to go to the Taliban to get their conflicts solved, as they perceive the local elders as driven by self-interest. Najibullah explained, "Local elders try to maintain their social status and earn money. Only a small number of them work hard to solve the people's problems without any demands."[62] And two others argued, "The local elders are not honest. They make a living by being a member of the council. For instance, they took 100,000 Afs [about $1,500] from us and an AK47."[63]

Some of those preferring community authorities were critical. For example, the laborer Mohammad Nasim said that some of the elders are corrupt and that others are "totally uneducated," meaning that they are illiterate and have no formal education, and therefore do not provide effective resolutions.[64] Civil society activist Samar Gul complained, "Local elders try to satisfy both sides of the conflict. Their conflict resolution is not based on justice. It only works temporarily, like a painkiller."[65] Ismail also claimed that some elders were corrupt. School principal Hajji Muhebullah complained, "Only 20 percent of decisions made by local councils are based on justice and equality. Usually they do favours to some people or are driven by their own interests. . . . For example, they sometimes only return a part of the money they took, keeping money to host a reception to celebrate the reconciliation between the conflict parties."[66] Hence, even though community authorities were the preferred option for conflict resolution for many in Surkh Rod, in some cases, this was simply because it was viewed as the least corrupt authority available.

When asked about the future of conflict resolution in Surkh Rod, all members of the public interviewed argued that the state should be in charge, in contrast to the village leader Hajji Batel's view of a future in which community authorities would retain this role. Samar Gul told me, "In the future the government has to solve the people's problems, on the basis of the law."[67] Shopkeeper Najibullah said, "In the future, the government has to take responsibility again and solve people's conflicts."[68]

In the context of security provision, no one I talked to brought up any community authority as a relevant actor. When asked to name key security providers, the interviewees in Surkh Rod mainly pointed toward state actors and the Taliban. Leaving my thematic lenses behind and asking people about their views on a number of other potential authorities on the community level, most argued that they were not playing an important role.

Not one interviewee in Surkh Rod thought that the mullah was a relevant actor at the community level. When I specifically addressed CDCs, some people said they were important for conflict resolution, much like the elders' councils. However, there were also more critical voices and complaints about CDC members implementing development projects for their own advantage. Asking people about their views on the provincial council, several people acknowledged that they were indeed influential, and some interviewees stated that provincial councils were helping them. For example, the laborer Mohammad Nasim remembered that a provincial councilor had given him help with some unspecified issue on one occasion.[69] But most people maintained they had never met a provincial councilor and assumed they were only working out of personal interest. For instance, the teacher Nader stated, "Provincial councillors don't play any role in my life, because they are busy with their personal business."[70] And the tailor Halim told me, "Nobody has ever met a provincial councillor. They never come to our village."[71]

In the case of Surkh Rod, community authorities—mainly elders and councils—played an important role at the local level. While their authority appeared to be extensive, it also seemed to be limited to the context of conflict resolution. The reason for people's decision to choose community authorities for conflict resolution, and hence their legitimacy in this sector, rested on a perception of them being faster, cheaper, and less corrupt than the state. This perception of the public resonates with the self-perception of interviewed community authorities, who claimed legitimacy and assumed that people chose them for conflict resolution for the same reasons. Only if the case was "big" and the involvement of the state could not be avoided did people tend to take their case to the police or the courts.

Both those who spoke positively about community authorities in Surkh Rod and those who spoke negatively illustrated the fact that avoiding corruption was paramount. Complaints about the corruption of community authorities largely related to the provincial council, which, like MPs, did not play a visible role or make a visible contribution at the community level. But others considered elders and local councils to be corrupt and, therefore, preferred other actors like the Taliban for conflict resolution. This could have resulted from a difference in perception of what constitutes a fair or corrupt procedure—for instance, with some people viewing Machalgha as legitimate for traditional reasons and others considering it to be a form of corruption—or it could have stemmed from different community authorities behaving differently in different villages. The interviews point to the latter. There appeared to be general broad-based support for traditional procedures like Machalgha as long as the amount was reasonable and as long as the full amount of money was repaid. But perceived fairness quickly tipped into perceived corruption once community authorities did not return the full amount to the conflict parties. This indicates that traditions like Machalgha are no blank check for legitimacy per se, but their legitimacy depends on how traditions are applied, particularly with regard to whether the full amount of money is repaid. Depending on the scale of corruption and personal experience with community authorities, some people consequently used other authorities for conflict resolution.

At the same time, supposedly "informal" conflict resolution at the local level in Surkh Rod was linked to the state. At the institutional level, the state asked community authorities, such as Malik Aziz Mohammadi, to keep an official record of their work. This illustrates Nixon's (2008) analysis that, historically, maliks have been local powerbrokers of the state. But the importance of the state was also prevalent at the level of perceptions. People chose to use community authorities to solve conflicts because they considered them to be better than the state, often emphasizing the failures of the state more than the advantages of community authorities. Even the interviewed community, authorities themselves claimed legitimacy by comparing themselves to the state. Thus, what legitimacy the community authorities had really stemmed from the failures of the state with respect to speed, expense, and fairness. And, while the community authorities I talked to wished to continue to be the main providers of conflict resolution, all members of the public I interviewed ultimately viewed conflict resolution as a responsibility of the state. They invariably hope to be able to rely on the state again in the future, once it lives up to the expectation of fair procedures.

THE RURAL WEST—KHUSHK ROBAT SANGI, HERAT PROVINCE

To see if the views on community authorities in the districts in Nangarhar were an isolated phenomenon or more widely shared, I decided to compare them with perceptions in Herat Province, in the far west of Afghanistan. Herat Province is predominantly rural, with about 77 percent of its population living outside Herat City. While historically Herat City had been a

Tajik stronghold in a Pashtun-dominated province, the city has became more ethnically mixed over time.[72] The most remote part of Herat Province where I conducted research in 2014/2015 was Kushk Robat Sangi District, which is located north of Herat City, borders Turkmenistan, and is also in close proximity to Iran. When I returned to Herat Province in 2019, the Taliban had gained control of most of the district.

Five years before, my colleagues and I took a car from Herat City up north to Kushk Robat Sangi, the district in which we had selected a village to conduct interviews. The village was remote but nonetheless accessible.[73] Even though we were fairly confident about the security on the road, the atmosphere in the car that day was more tense than usual, as we were passing through "grey" areas where the border of government and Taliban control was not clear. I was dressed in traditional Afghan clothes, as I usually did for trips to rural parts of the country. But despite the hat I was wearing, I had the feeling that anyone in the barren landscape could have spotted my blond hair from miles away. We started telling each other jokes, and this helped. The ride only took about ninety minutes, but everybody looked relieved once the gates closed behind the car at the house of one of my colleague's friends. To avoid further attention, we decided to conduct all interviews in this house instead of visiting the people in their homes. We only spoke to a small number of people, all of who were community authorities.

Mahmood was the head of the village and a previous member of the peacebuilding council. He had studied social sciences and was also a medical doctor.[74] According to him, the Taliban were very active in the district, using IEDs, conducting suicide attacks, and blocking the highway. This had eroded the "widespread public support" for the government. Regarding his own role in providing security as the head of the village, he said, "I am

trying to contribute to an improved security situation . . . by calling for unity and trying to keep peace between the people. We
have always advised people not to listen to the promises of insurgents and not to support them, as they are not legitimate and do
not care about the people or the country. They come, attack their
targets and leave again."

According to Mahmood, the village had NSP-created CDCs
and two sets of conflict resolution councils that an NGO had
established in 1995—one for men and one specifically for women.
He said it was "fortunate" that the conflict resolution councils
still existed, even though the conditions in the village were very
"fragile," referring to the security issues we had all sensed on our
way in. He explained that councils did not have a long-standing
local tradition; however, they now played an important role in
community governance:

> After the NSP was launched and development councils were set
> up, people started to become increasingly used to councils. . . .
> In the years after 2001, the transitional government established
> peacebuilding councils. They used to be quite active. But when
> the NSP's development councils were set up, the peacebuilding
> councils' role started to fade. In addition to these councils, there
> are elders and religious leaders in each village, who are involved in
> conflict resolution. They either do so as members of a council or
> independently. And as people trust them, they are often invited to
> participate in conflict resolution meetings. And even those elders
> who prefer working independently of the councils usually have
> good relations with them.

Mahmood made conflict resolution his focus. He told me that
conflicts often evolved in the community, often within families.
"We live in a very traditional society with a high percentage of

illiteracy. . . . Fortunately, the number of organisations working on human rights, especially women's rights, has increased and they are teaching women about their rights. But the understanding of their rights in rural areas is still not widespread. And it's not only women's rights. Many men are not aware of their rights either. So, conflicts between men and women often evolve, for instance, if a woman isn't doing household work and the man reacts in a harsh way."

I asked him what he did in such cases. He explained, "In the case of such a family conflict, we would call both sides and talk to them to find out about what causes the problem. Furthermore, we sit down individually with the man and the woman to give some advice and reconcile them."

In his view, people in state-controlled territories relied on local councils for conflict resolution. Elsewhere the Taliban offer attracted many people to their procedures. By contrast, "People do not take their cases to the government as the government is unreliable and delays the process. Even tiny conflicts are sometimes not solved by the government for months." In addition, he explained that many people could not afford to travel to the courts and are therefore dependent on the local councils for conflict resolution. However, he admitted that people also made their choice on the basis of whom they knew and where they expected better chances of winning a case. "It is all about knowing someone in the government or the local councils. Sometimes people are very keen to take a case to the government as they might know someone there who can help them."

Like many interviewees in Surkh Rod, Mahmood hoped that one day the state would take over conflict resolution. He seemed to look at it as an inevitability. "Of course, as soon as the government becomes stable, they have to strengthen formal justice mechanisms so that people go there and solve their conflicts formally. Local councils only treat the symptoms, like painkillers."

Fahima provided another intimate view of the local authorities. She was a teacher and member of both the district women's council and the district development council. She described the monthly meetings she attends, along with two men, on behalf of the cluster of approximately fifteen villages she represented, where council members discussed challenges and shared their experiences. She also mentioned that the district had a conflict resolution commission of fifteen women and thirty men that discussed the cases that had been solved.

Like Mahmood, Fahima considered conflict resolution to be the main responsibility of community authorities. She explained to me how the local councils dealt with conflicts:

> Within local councils, conflicts are usually solved by reaching an agreement, based on guarantee letters from both sides. . . . If one party rejects the decision of the council we ask other elders, who have more direct influence on the involved parties, to assist. For instance, I recently dealt with the case of a woman who was the victim of a family conflict. She was beaten by her mother-in-law [and two other relatives], because she had punished one of her children for something he had done. . . . After this incident, she left the house, fled to her mother's place and complained about her in-laws. She stayed at her mother's place for several months. Finally, she took the case to the head of the district development council. He called me and asked me to take over the case. So, I had several meetings with both sides, and managed to solve the conflict in the end. She returned to her husband's house in exchange for strong guarantee letters by her in-laws. I am still in regular contact with her on the phone as we used to be close friends in school.

With respect to why people choose local authorities, Fahima said that people would rather not take family conflicts to the government because they find it shameful, and that local authorities were an easier route. Like Mahmood, she mentioned the Taliban as an alternative. "There are rural villages in which people prefer taking their conflicts to the Taliban. For instance, one of my uncles was involved in a conflict on land rights. He took it to the government first. But it hadn't been solved after a year. Hence, he took the case to the Taliban instead. Although they haven't dealt with it yet, they have promised to do so soon." The state courts were so slow that even an unenforceable promise from the Taliban to provide better speed was worth something. Nonetheless, like Mahmood, Fahima felt that the state should provide conflict resolution in the future.

Beyond conflict resolution, Fahima also thought that community authorities could play a positive role in security provision. She shared Mahmood's view on growing insecurity in the district, stating that "the security situation has become worse over the past ten years." She said that the influence of the Taliban and their extractive practices had been growing. She recounted that the Taliban had kidnapped one of her uncles and threatened to take him to Pakistan if his family didn't pay a ransom. However, the local elders, who often maintained contact with all sides, intervened and secured his release after two days.

Nonetheless, Fahima also blamed the government for the insecurity in the district. She pointed out that it was not only insurgents who threatened people and demanded money since it was easy to obtain a gun in her area. She added that community authorities also had to play a role in security provision: "We live in a very traditional society. Therefore, people trust local elders and want them to be involved in providing security."

Mahmood and Fahima's narratives illustrate how connected their roles as community authorities were with the state and sometimes the Taliban as well. Both saw the role of community authorities in security provision more as a bridge between the state and the people. While they were actively involved in conflict resolution, both Mahmood and Fahima preferred the state take responsibility in the future. Mahmood, like an interviewee from Surkh Rod, described conflict resolution at the community level as a "painkiller," not a lasting solution. Nonetheless, they viewed conflict resolution at the community level to be better than what the state offered, thinking that they, as community authorities, had local legitimacy and were preferred by people for conflict resolution over the state with its practices. Even though they, as members of councils, worked closely with the state and saw the Taliban as a threat and source of insecurity, they understood people who preferred the Taliban's conflict resolution mechanisms to those offered by the state.

Five years later, much of Surkh Rod had been taken by the Taliban. An arbab, whom I interviewed in February 2019, explained how this had affected his own role. He said, "I am an arbab and used to solve local conflicts. Ten or 15 big cases have been solved by me. But no more. It changed when the Taliban gained influence. But if the Taliban can't solve a case easily, they ask for my advice."[75] Similarly, members of the community reported that the Taliban had replaced justice by community authorities to a large extent. Nonetheless, community authorities continued playing an important in the Taliban court system, helping people to make contact and acting as key witnesses or guarantors. However, the growing influence of the Taliban also resulted in new responsibilities for community authorities, such as mediation between the state and the Taliban. Another arbab explained, "If something happens between the ANA and the Taliban we are mediating. For example, if an ANA soldier is killed and the body is with the Taliban, we will go to get the body and vice versa."[76]

This view on the new role of community authorities was shared by ordinary people. For example, a farmer from Robat Sangi described the important role of community authorities in maintaining stability, saying, "There are connections between Taliban and government, such as the elders and the arbabs."[77] He detailed an incident in a bazaar area, where community authorities had secured a very localized ceasefire. After two ANA soldiers were killed by the Taliban, the government closed the bazar and did not allow a reopening without a guarantee by the Taliban that ensured their safety. "The government asked for a letter by the Taliban that government officials are safe in the bazaar. If they want to fight, they can do it at the checkpoints, but not at the bazaar." While the Taliban initially rejected such an agreement, community authorities were ultimately successful in securing an agreement that allowed for the bazar to be reopened. This agreement even held through more difficult times. The interviewee detailed the situation: "In the mentioned bazar area they have a security guy. He got killed at night. The government came and found people [perpetrators]. But they couldn't arrest all of them, only two out of three. So, they asked the Taliban. But the Taliban didn't arrest him. Then the local people gathered and complained to the Taliban. They arrested the guy [themselves] and handed him to the Taliban in Robat Sangi. They [the Taliban] now keep him in their own jail."

The development in Robat Sangi shows that the Taliban were aware of the potential of justice for the construction of legitimacy on the local level, as we already discussed in chapter 4. Even more so, the case also illustrates the fluidity of community governance that did not limit the role of local authorities to conflict resolution and the Bourdieusian dynamic nature of political order in Afghanistan, with constantly changing relationships among the various types of authorities. At least in some cases, community authorities in Robat Sangi quickly adapted to the changing political circumstances, maintaining authority and legitimacy by taking on new roles that were needed locally, mediating between the two parties at conflict to enable community life to continue.

THE URBAN WEST—HERAT CITY, HERAT PROVINCE

Herat City, the provincial center with an estimated population of around seven hundred thousand people, is the second-largest city in Afghanistan, after Kabul.[78] Like other urban areas in the country, the city has grown considerably in recent decades due to migration and displacement.[79] Strolling through the buzzing streets of the city, despite growing criminality, I always felt far away from rural and less secure places like Kushk Robat Sangi. As the Taliban did not have much influence in Herat in 2014/2015, one could imagine the state to be the only authority here. Indeed, Herat City does not have a longstanding tradition of councils solving conflict. Instead, people used to rely on the conflict resolution mechanisms offered by the state. In contrast to rural areas, the state's courts in Herat City were physically close and easy to reach. However, due to frustration with these mechanisms, which were also considered slow and corrupt, people started to adapt rural structures and create local councils or elect street representatives. "Traditional" community authorities offering "traditional" conflict resolution began to evolve in

Herat City, even though there was no local tradition of such mechanisms.

According to the interviewees, many conflicts in Herat City were about land rights. Civil society activist Ahmad pointed out that some of these conflicts dated back to the civil war.[80] During the war, many people fled and left their land and houses behind. When they returned, often years later, others had claimed their land. Abdul Karim said that strongmen often made illegal claims to land and that in the absence of the rule of law and widespread corruption in the government, people had little means to resist.[81] But conflicts also evolved in families and between neighbors. For instance, inheritance disputes, conflicts about the access and use of water, and conflicts resulting from divorces were common.

Surprisingly, in Herat City, as elsewhere, many interviewees used community authorities to solve conflicts. In some parts of the city, people elected street representatives to deal with small conflicts in the neighborhood. For example, the shopkeeper Farid told me, "If I am involved in any kind of conflict, I would go to the street representatives."[82] Similarly, laborer Nassir Ahmad said, "In the case of a conflict I would first approach my neighbours."[83] In other parts of the city, as in some rural parts of the country, people relied on elders or local councils to deal with conflicts. Many people, including high school student Zalmai, stated, "To solve a conflict I would go the local council. And if they are not able to help me, I would take some members of the council along and approach the government."[84] As in Surkh Rod, interviewees did not see religious leaders as playing significant roles in conflict resolution. Zalmai commented on this directly, saying that the clergy's role "is to teach and guide the children."[85]

According to the people I interviewed, most elders and community councils use "traditional" or "customary" law to solve conflicts. Schoolteacher Abdul Wahab reported, "The conflict resolution of local councils is totally based on customary law."[86] In some cases, however, people also applied Islamic law. Zalmai said, "Local elders . . . try to solve the conflict on the basis of traditional law. The only exceptions are inheritance conflicts, which are solved on the basis of Islamic law."[87] But using community authorities for conflict resolution was a recent phenomenon, at least in some parts of Herat City. Shoaib pointed out that, as an urban society, they had traditionally relied on state authorities to solve conflicts.[88] Similarly, Ahmad stated that "in Afghanistan's urban societies, people usually use the formal conflict resolution mechanisms, such as the courts."[89] Indeed, Parwiz, who worked as a cook, explained that there were no community councils in Herat City in 2005, with everybody using the state's court system.[90] So, while community authorities such as councils and elders applied a traditional code of law, these authorities did not necessarily have a longstanding tradition in Herat City.

As in Nangarhar and rural Herat, most people viewed community authorities as faster and fairer than those the state offered and believed they treated people more equally and did not demand bribes. For example, laborer Nassir Ahmad said, "Local elders make decisions quickly and base them on justice."[91] As to why, Masoud, who worked in social media at the time, offered the following analysis:

> Having the choice between the informal and the formal system of conflict resolution, the shura and the court, the people in our area usually choose the informal one. There are two reasons for this. The first reason is that there is no equality [of the conflict parties] in the formal system. The second reason is the high level of corruption. So instead of going to the courts people take their cases to the local shura or an elder. They solve conflicts in a traditional

way and ensure equality when dealing with a conflict, treating everyone the same way. There is no corruption either. They solve conflicts in a fair way.[92]

The shopkeeper Aminullah told me this about his local elder: "He is a really good person and serves everyone equally. And if anyone faces a problem, he will try hard to help without expecting anything in return."[93] Similarly, civil society activist Mujibullah concluded, "We usually try to solve problems ourselves, with the help of elders and local councils, because we don't trust the government and don't like to take cases to the government. They take lots of bribes and we have simply become fed up with dealing with them."[94] Laborer Nassir Ahmad was the only person who mentioned selection processes; he declared that he also had more trust in community authorities, as he was involved in selecting them.[95] Nonetheless, as in Nangarhar's Surkh Rod, most people told me that they would approach the state, not community authorities, for criminal matters.

I did talk to some people in Herat City who preferred state authorities for civil issues as well, such as Naimullah, who was unemployed. "In case I am involved in any conflict, I would take the case directly to the government," he said. He did not believe that local elders were treating people fairly. "They stand on the side of the rich."[96] Mujibullah believed community authorities to be corrupt as well. "They sometimes are as corrupt as the government," he said.[97] Thus, he would go to the Taliban if he needed help resolving a problem. By 2019, people traveled to Taliban-controlled areas from Herat City to use their courts. Some did so voluntarily to seek less corrupt justice and others went out of fear, such as Mohammad Zarif who reported how the Taliban threatened him on the phone to appear in court, ultimately convincing him to travel to an area under their control against his will.

Some people in Herat City, like Nassir, thought that community authorities should continue to provide conflict resolution. However, the majority of people agreed with interviewees in other places that the state should be the only authority to provide justice. Mujibullah outlined this vision: "In the future, the government should take on its responsibility for solving conflicts. But it needs to ensure justice. The courts and lawyers have to follow the laws. The state has to follow the rules it has created. Then people will also agree to the force it applies."[98]

In contrast to those in rural areas, some people in Herat City did think that provincial councils were relevant and positive actors. For example, Abdul Khalil said, "Provincial councillors play a positive role in my life as they work honestly."[99] For the most part, however, such approval was tempered with a degree of dissatisfaction. The civil society activist Ahmad said that provincial councilors should be more active in bringing jobs to the city, especially for women.[100]

CONCLUSIONS

Without a doubt, different kinds of community authorities are a central ingredient of Afghanistan's political order, especially given their role in conflict resolution. And even though many community authorities were closely connected to the state, for instance, through NSP, people categorized them as a different type of authority. The case studies illustrate the differences and similarities in the political order of communities in Afghanistan with regard to conflict resolution. They support Barfield's argument that the difference in community governance is not among ethnic groups but among geographic areas, particularly between urban and rural ones.[101] For example, Surkh Rod in Nangarhar and Kushk Robat Sangi in Herat, which are on opposite sides of the country, had similar structures. At the same time, a city like Herat was increasingly adopting rural traditions.

Community authorities were clearly the first choice for conflict resolution for most interviewees. They maintained that they would prefer to take their cases to the elders, the local council, village leaders, or, rarely, to the local mullah. Only where these authorities were not able to solve the conflict or if they were not satisfied with the result would they take the case to "the government"— namely to state institutions such as the police or the courts. A notable exception was in the case of severe criminal matters like murder, where many conceded that they "couldn't avoid" involving the state directly. In addition, as discussed in chapter 4, the Taliban expanded their influence through their courts and became the main providers of justice in many rural areas, not accepting the use of alternative systems. While in 2014/2015 the presence of Taliban courts was still limited to remote districts, their justice system had reached Herat City by 2019.

That people chose councils, village leaders, or elders over other actors for conflict resolution illustrates that they had authority. That people chose them *voluntarily* and followed their decisions shows that their authority rested on a degree of legitimacy – even though in some cases their authority was certainly also supported by an ability to direct social pressure within a community. Both instrumental and more substantive sources underpinned this legitimacy. In line with the policy literature on legitimacy, many interviewees emphasized the usefulness and accessibility of community authorities. For many people, *proximity* was a key consideration, as they could not afford the trip to the district or provincial capital. But, in contrast to what are widely assumed to be community authorities' substantive sources of legitimacy, tradition, or their participatory structures, few interviewees mentioned either of these aspects, and the adoption of these structures in Herat City belies the idea that they rely on tradition. Many pointed out that they preferred community authorities because of the relative *fairness* of the conflict resolution procedures. And, even though most people agreed that community authorities were not flawless, they considered them at least to be less corrupt than the state. Some people indicated the *serving* character of community authorities and emphasized that they were volunteering for the community without payment.

Looking more closely at the sources of legitimacy and distinguishing the beliefs from the aspects of authority they relate to show that neither the institution "community authority" per se, as a *concept or an idea*, nor a certain type of community authority seems to have had much legitimacy in this context. Rather, most people hoped the state would play the role of resolving conflicts in the future. Also, the *history* of how an actor gained authority— whether it happened democratically through rational-legal structures, because of tradition, or through "self-appointment"— was not brought up by many interviewees as a reason for their support or preference of authority. A decidedly small number of people mentioned a democratic selection process.

Instead, people judged the *attitudes* of community authorities, appreciating unpaid service to the community. And, while not being particularly interested in the history of how an actor gained power, the referent object of people's concern was the "output" side of authority—the *authorities' actions*. To begin with, it was quite naturally the actual output, the result of authorities' actions, that mattered. People wanted to get their conflicts solved and looked for authorities that were close, fast, and cheap. In addition, they may have preferred an authority for conflict resolution where they had the chance of getting the best result, for instance, through personal contacts. However, it was not just the result that mattered. People also cared about the process of getting there, the way the *interaction* between authority and subject was designed. In this regard, people had quite substantive, value-based concerns.

The examples suggest that what was central to the community authorities' legitimacy in the context of conflict resolution was the extent to which these interactions were perceived to be *fair or corrupt*. Communities applied customary and Islamic law to different extents, and, as indicated by Barfield, what customary law looked like was different in different communities and changed over time.[102] That the rule of law was more important than the underpinning code of law shows that people did not have very ideological expectations. I got the impression that, for most, a "bad" law that was applied rigorously was still better than a "good" law that only applied to those who could afford it. The interviews indicate that people wanted predictability and hoped to be treated equally. When approaching community authorities, they knew what to expect, and they had a degree of predictability. In addition, in many cases, the procedures were perceived as fairer than those of the state. Corruption and the perception that people could influence the decision-making process with money were looked down on and undermined legitimacy.

Even those who preferred the state or the Taliban to community authorities did so for the same reasons that others preferred community authorities: less corruption, speed, accessibility, and fairness. Some interviewees also argued that they considered the state or the Taliban to be less corrupt than community authorities. This illustrates that not all community authorities were necessarily perceived to be less corrupt than the state, and the behavior of community authorities could vary from village to village.

Tradition certainly mattered, and interviewees did often mention the "traditional character" of society, especially in rural areas. But, crucially, what is traditional is not necessarily legitimate, and what is not traditional can still be legitimate. For instance, many described Machalgha to be a legitimate tradition of solving conflicts. This indicates that what is perceived as "traditional" can play an important role in the legitimacy of conflict resolution procedures, contributing to an understanding of what is "fair." However, a number of interviewees were wary of the practice and its potential for abuse. Hence, framing practices as traditional does not ensure that people consider them to be fair, and perceived corruption undermines the legitimacy of traditions. Conversely, new traditions may evolve to counter perceived corruption, as in the case of Herat City. My findings support scholarship on the transmutability of norms and tradition.[103] As Pain points out, communities do not exist in isolation. Traditions from other geographic areas might be copied, becoming legitimate traditions without being a local traditions.[104]

While traditions may differ and change, the expectations of people with regard to conflict resolution across the country were very similar. The frequent references to Machalgha in Pashtun areas appear to support Wardak's argument that to achieve legitimacy in such places, the decision-making process of community authorities has to be in accord with the Pashtunwali.[105] But this seemed a minor detail in relation to the overall sameness of people's desires for equal treatment. Ultimately, the people I talked to across the country had similar understandings regarding what they expected conflict resolution procedures essentially to be like, without distinct differences between Pashtun and other areas. They considered the equal treatment of all people to be "fairness," constituting the basis of the legitimacy of many community authorities. Conversely, the behavior of authorities considered to be driven by greed or self-interest was considered to be "corrupt" and undermined their legitimacy.

There is an obvious tension between people's interest in winning their cases and choosing an authority they can influence, if necessary, through bribes, on the one hand, and their belief in and hope for fair procedures on the other hand. Further research is required to investigate how people balance these dimensions and their understandings of fairness and corruption. My own observation is that paying bribes in conflict resolution in Afghanistan had become so normal that people felt compelled to try to influence authorities through bribes, as they knew that the other conflict party would be doing the same. Furthermore, it created a temptation to pay even more to outperform the other conflict party, possibly win the case, and settle the conflict quickly. Nonetheless, most people were unsatisfied with this way of solving conflict. They hoped for a system in which paying bribes was not a necessity or even a possibility. Hence, they chose authorities for conflict resolution that they expected to be the least corrupt and that treated people in the most equal way possible.

With conflict resolution, community authorities also mattered for security provision in some cases. Most members of the public I talked to in 2014/2015 thought their role was not significant in this sector. But some interviewed community authorities pointed out that they were helping to "coordinate" security by being a "bridge" to the outside world. So, while they were not visibly fighting or policing, as village representatives, they would speak to the state's security forces or to the Taliban. Hence, as Mielke suggests, elders continued playing an important role in managing the interface between communities and "the outside."[106] Beyond negotiating access to goods, in some communities, elders also contributed to stability, if necessary, by brokering localized agreements between the Taliban and security forces. Perhaps because of the increasing need to mediate between warring parties to ensure stability on the community level, considerably more people acknowledged the role of community authority in maintaining security in 2019, such as in the case of Khushk Robat Sangi.

Overall, the case studies contribute to a better understanding of what legitimizes community councils, village leaders, and elders. Contrary to our understanding of community governance in Afghanistan, interviewees often did not distinguish much between community councils, village leaders, and elders, looking at them through the same lens, even when directly asked about their views on specific community authorities. While certainly different authorities were more or less influential in different communities, instead of distinguishing between individual and collective authorities on the community level, people essentially considered them to be the same type of authority. However, the interviews indicate, in support of Murtazashvili's work, that the legitimacy of community authorities is centered around conflict resolution, being at the core of what people expect from authorities at the local level.[107] Even when asking people specifically about each of the other potential community authorities, few people thought these actors had any significance in their community. For example, while some people considered mullahs to be a second or third option for conflict resolution, few thought they had much authority beyond their religious duties.

The little attention people appeared to pay to CDCs casts doubt as to whether they were a promising method for the construction of state legitimacy, as intended by the NSP and later the Citizens' Charter. People were often not aware of the existence of CDCs nor did they see much of a difference between CDCs and other local councils, describing them as one of the community authorities offering conflict resolution. Only a few people had distinct views on CDCs, for instance, seeing them

270 COMMUNITY AUTHORITIES

as responsible for conflicts in the community due to unfair distribution of aid money or projects. The case of CDCs further shows that the legitimacy of community authorities is closely linked to conflict resolution. Hence, a newly established authority is not "automatically" considered to be legitimate in a substantive way, simply because it is a local actor, because councils are a local tradition, because its members are elected, or because it provides services.

Many people had strong views on provincial councils, albeit mainly negative ones. The low confidence in PCs appeared to be driven by the perception of them to be working only for their personal interests rather than serving the public. As scholars such as Larson and Coburn have pointed out, people in Afghanistan seemed to think of a PC seat being nothing more than a valuable commodity.[108] In addition, the fact that people who held these seats were not visible at the community level played a role. Some people in Herat City, but not elsewhere, had met provincial councilors, and they were the only ones who saw them in a positive light. This indicates that in the absence of proximity and personal interaction, authorities easily lose legitimacy unless it is balanced with other measures, such as positive media reporting. In addition, it further supports the findings on perceptions of MPs that even though PCs, like MPs, were elected, this potential "input" legitimacy alone was not sufficient without being linked to "output" through a rational-legal system that ensured fairness in a structural way. In the absence of an accountable system on the macro level, people looked for accountability on the micro level in their day-to-day interactions with authorities. Being part of the community, even "self-appointed" corrupt community authorities were likely to be more accountable, fairer, or at least less corrupt than authorities that are external to and distant from the community, even when elected.

We can conclude that the proximity, predictability, and perceived fairness of their conflict-resolution procedures were particularly important sources of legitimacy for many community authorities. Community authorities were not legitimate simply because they were traditionally influential. Nevertheless, traditions can matter in an indirect way, influencing what kinds of procedures are viewed as fair. How community authorities gained power and whether they were democratically elected matters even less. Hence, my research redirects the focus of attention from the "input" side to the "output" side—the actions and interactions of authorities. But that does not mean that authorities simply have to provide more public services to construct legitimacy. There were many authorities people could turn to for conflict resolution in Afghanistan at the time. What mattered was *how* it was done, whether the process was considered to be fair—or corrupt.

6

WAITING FOR DIGNITY

"The state has to follow the rules it created. Then people will also agree to the force it applies."

Civil society activist in Herat City, 2014

This book explores how people in Afghanistan attributed legitimacy to various authorities and how these authorities perceived themselves. Building on conceptual propositions and empirical analysis, we can draw some theoretical conclusions on political order and the mechanisms of legitimacy. The findings show that *interactive dignity* played a primary role in establishing—or failing to establish—substantive legitimacy in Afghanistan.

But what does interactive dignity entail, and what are its limits? Why do some people consider a particular authority legitimate while others do not? And how do authorities perceive themselves? What does this book tell us about the failure of state-building in Afghanistan? What does it tell us about the Taliban's future?

Afghanistan's Political Order

Throughout my research in Afghanistan, political order and legitimacy were in the process of constant change and transformation. Nonetheless, in several respects, a picture of this political order evolved.

First, despite its complexity, Afghanistan's political order from 2001 to 2021 consisted of distinct authorities. Following Weber, people distinguished clearly among the various types of authorities discussed in the book. This enables us to talk about different state actors, the Taliban, and various strongmen, despite them often being fuzzy categories.

Second, authorities in Afghanistan were multifaceted and interconnected. Following Bourdieu, the interviewed population viewed the country's political order as dynamic and fluid, a field of power in which various actors with different types of capital interacted and competed. For instance, many authorities—the state, strongmen, and the Taliban—tried co-opting community authorities to increase their influence. However, community authorities also actively used their ties with other authorities to advance their own agendas. Often, different forms of interaction among the same authorities existed in parallel, with many people seeing links between state authorities and the Taliban despite the ongoing fighting. Modes of interaction could change quickly, with alliances turning competitive and competitors joining forces.

Third, authorities in Afghanistan's political order did not have defined functions and were incredibly adaptable, rendering functional definitions of the state and authority unsuitable. Malejacq illustrates how warlords in Afghanistan managed to survive in changing political environments.[1] His findings also apply to many other authorities in Afghanistan. By filling in gaps left by other authorities and taking on new roles that were locally needed, community authorities demonstrated incredible adaptability that, in many cases, allowed them to maintain authority and remain influential in changing environments. For example, community authorities quickly stepped in when the state was unable to provide conflict resolution and justice in remote areas. When the Taliban started threatening the influence of community authorities in this domain again, community authorities took on new responsibilities, such as brokering agreements between the Taliban and the state on the local level.

Fourth, in addition to the low level of monopolization of the legitimate use of physical force also the legitimate use of symbolic violence—the "gentle invisible form of violence" that Bourdieu describes—lacked monopolization in Afghanistan.[2] In conflict zones, where visible physical violence remains widespread, often less attention is paid to symbolic violence. However, in Afghanistan, competing authorities also tried to impose institutions and classifications that reflected their respective ideologies and preferred social hierarchies on the population— for instance, through different codes of laws. For example, the practices of the state supported the domination of a class with access to education and the globalized world, putting especially people from rural areas at a disadvantage. Meanwhile, other forms of symbolic violence were consistent despite the low level of monopolization and ongoing armed conflict, ultimately constituting what Galtung would call "structural violence."[3] For example, to varying degrees across all types of authorities, symbolic violence in the form of norms, institutions, and standardized practices contributed to the oppression of women.

Fifth, there was a remarkable lack of uniformity in terms of whom people considered to be legitimate. Even the Afghan state itself was not viewed as one entity, but people viewed its branches and their legitimacy independently. Some people even considered competing authorities to be legitimate in different sectors, such as viewing the Afghan army as a legitimate authority providing security and the Taliban or community authorities as legitimate authorities providing justice. It does indicate that all authorities in Afghanistan enjoyed a certain degree of legitimacy, at least among a certain stratum of the population.

Public Perceptions of Legitimacy

Regardless of who people considered to be legitimate, the reasons underpinning their conflicting views are strikingly similar. There are distinct patterns in terms of why people considered authorities to be legitimate—or not. Based on these patterns, we can draw some more general conclusions about the mechanisms that link aspects of authority to people's needs and beliefs and root legitimacy and authority in Afghanistan.

To begin with, the *visibility* of an authority, or the visibility of its actions—whether it be negative ones, such as attacks and other forms of violence, or positive ones, such as services provided—had an impact on people's perceptions. Not surprisingly, the people I talked to tended to have stronger views, positive or negative, on those authorities that were more visible to them. Violence committed by authorities in a particularly visible way—such as large-scale attacks in Kabul City—had a considerable symbolic effect, shaping the perceptions of those even not directly affected. Conversely, people often did not care much about authorities that were invisible to them—even those that had an impact on their lives. Afghanistan had an active media landscape, and yet, people had little to say about the legitimacy of actors they only heard about on the radio. This was particularly evident in discussions of security forces in that people only had strong views of those branches of the ANSF that operated visibly in their own localities.

Beyond visibility, *accessibility* enables people to not only see an authority but also experience it by having a direct interaction, changing the basis on which they formed their views and resulting in even stronger perceptions.[4] Accessibility appears to be an important aspect of authority for the construction of instrumental legitimacy. In the context of conflict resolution, it is a necessary condition, as conflict resolution only functions when people can access it. Being more accessible than another authority can also be a comparative advantage, increasing instrumental legitimacy. Similarly, people expected security providers to be close enough to provide security. MPs and members of provincial councils had little local legitimacy, despite having been elected, because many were perceived as inaccessible and distant.

The *actions* of an authority and how they are perceived played an important role in its legitimacy as well, both in instrumental and in substantive terms. People in Afghanistan had general expectations with regard to the authorities' services. Security was the most crucial one, but they also wanted justice, education, and healthcare. At first glance, this observation is in line with the literature on output legitimacy and state-building, which emphasizes the importance of providing public services in order to construct legitimacy. However, the picture that evolved from my research shifts the focus from the output or result of an action to *modes of interaction*. This is in line with findings in psychology literature, especially the work by Tyler on democratic policing, and supports recent studies on state legitimacy suggesting that people care more about how services are delivered than what services are delivered.[5] Supplementing their findings, this book illustrates that this mechanism does not only apply to the state, but it is also of a more general nature, applying to all types of authorities.

Because most public services, regardless of the authority providing them, are set around an interaction between the authority and the public, the output is closely linked to the preceding process. For instance, to what extent a public hospital can provide "health" for people depends on the interaction between the patient and healthcare providers. And, indeed, people's expectations toward authorities focused on modes of interaction, such as *processes, procedures,* and the authorities' *day-to-day behaviors,* not the formal results. Even an encounter with a police officer or a Taliban fighter at a checkpoint had a process of interaction. Modes of interaction are vital both for instrumental and substantive legitimacy. The interactions that people experienced had to live up to their needs-based expectations, such as *costs, predictability,* and *convenience.* But people also have value-based expectations with regard to interaction, which are concerned with basic *human dignity,* such as *fairness* and *respect,* founded on the hope of being treated as equal citizens.

Conversely, the *history of how an actor gained authority* does not appear to be a particularly important aspect of the construction of legitimacy. The interviewees did not usually care if the way an actor had gained authority was in line with democratic, Islamic, or traditional procedures. While negative experiences certainly undermined legitimacy, as suggested by Arendt, who emphasized the destructive role of violence, even those who violently grabbed power might be viewed as legitimate by some people who were far removed from this violence.[6] This finding illustrates that "input" alone does not construct legitimacy but needs to be linked in people's minds to "output." In the absence of rational-legal structures connecting input and output legitimacy and translating people's values into an authority's actions,

278 80 WAITING FOR DIGNITY

people have little concern for the input side. Thus, despite the former state's official claims of legitimacy resting on it, people had little interest in elections or even *loya jirgas* as a means of establishing legitimacy. However, they also had little interest in the implications of other ways of gaining authority. The general pattern of considering community authorities legitimate did not respond to whether they were elected, self-appointed, or had inherited their positions, and whether this process was traditional in an interviewee's locality or not. The historical behavior of an authority also mattered little. Even though some people said that they were happy with the Taliban government before 2001, this view did not lead them to perceive the Taliban as legitimate later on. Some people had opinions about how actors should gain authority, but it was a subordinate concern that in itself was not a sufficient source of legitimacy. The output side of authority was the focus of their feelings about its legitimacy.

People still expected accountability, however. Instead of focusing on accountability on the macrolevel, as suggested by Scharpf,[7] the findings of this book suggest that people are more concerned with the accountability of authorities at the microlevel in their day-to-day lives, particularly when interacting with them. What matters for them is the *process* of getting to the "output." As people could not rely on formalized institutions, they closely observed the behavior of the various authorities around them and judged to what extent each was useful and fair. Scholars in psychology working on police legitimacy in rational-legal contexts have emphasized the importance of procedures of interaction for the construction of legitimacy.[8] The findings of this book suggest that such interactions are equally if not more important in political orders without functioning rational-legal structures.

Another important aspect of authority for the construction of substantive legitimacy is the perceived *attitude* of an authority. In fact, this might be the most crucial aspect. The judgment of an authority's attitude is firmly rooted in the subjects' values. In Afghanistan, people had strong expectations with regard to an authority's attitude. They expected them to be *serving the public*, the country, the nation, and the people. This expectation was sometimes underpinned by nationalism; however, it was usually linked less specifically to the public. For example, many interviewees emphasized how the army or community authorities were serving the people. Such a perceived attitude is a form of symbolic capital, which is instantly recognized as legitimate. Conversely, people were heavily critical if they perceived an authority to be driven by self-interest or foreign interests. This was present in their praise of the army for serving the nation. But it was also present in their criticism of police officers for apparently working only for their own economic benefit and the Taliban for being Pakistan's henchmen. Because attitude as such is invisible, people drew their conclusions on proxies of what they could see or even feel, such as, most importantly, the interactions they had with authorities. Again, people's assessments rested on the extent to which authorities could live up to their value-based expectations, such as being treated with dignity.

How people experience interactions with an authority and the extent to which they match their expectations affect the perception of the authority's legitimacy directly. But people also draw wider conclusions on the basis of the perceived procedures and behavior with regard to an authority's attitude, judging if it actually serves the public or if it is only driven by greed and self-interest. Thus, while different aspects of authority matter for how people perceive its legitimacy, they all seem to be linked to modes of interaction between authorities and subjects.

Examples: Justice and Security

Discussions of conflict resolution and justice show that, first of all, people wanted *fast and predictable* procedures so that they could estimate when a conflict was going to be solved and what the result was likely to be. In Afghanistan's "coping economy," where many people struggled daily, and some lived on the edge of survival, solving conflicts fast and being able to predict what result was likely was essential.[9] By living up to these expectations, authorities could construct instrumental legitimacy, and people would choose it for conflict resolution as long as no other authority did so on a closer or cheaper basis. Authorities had to match people's expectations of *fair* procedures to construct more substantive and, hence, long-lasting legitimacy. If people perceived the procedures as fair, they assumed that the authority was working in the public interest. If, however, people perceived an authority as *corrupt*, they assumed it was driven by greed. Only if people thought that an authority worked in the public interest did they believe in its right to exercise social control. By living up to the basic expectation of fairness, an authority could construct legitimacy founded on a belief.

What fairness and corruption mean may be established through discourse over time, in line with Habermas's theory of communicative action,[10] resulting in meanings with different nuances in different communities across the country. Future, more ethnographic, research needs to explore such meanings. However, as Barfield and Nojumi suggest, perceptions of fairness seem to be very similar across Afghanistan, not linked to geography or specific ethnic groups.[11] The notion of fairness appears to be underpinned by the notion of equality. In contrast to the theory of adaptive preferences, people had not given up on such basic values in the course of the conflict. On the contrary, they felt deprived of them and demanded them. People wanted conflict resolution procedures in which everyone was treated the same way—regardless of income, influence, gender, or social status. Which code of law authorities applied and what ideology underpinned the procedures was of lesser significance.

Similarly, to construct substantive legitimacy by providing security, authorities had to respond to the expectation of *coordination*. Communities did not just want to be passively viewed as areas where security needed to be provided, but they also wanted to be actively included in the process. It shows that even the process of using physical force can contribute to building legitimacy. Coordinated security can be seen as a form of input legitimacy, enabling the participation of the subjects. But beyond that, like the expectation of fair conflict resolution procedures, the expectation of a coordinated security provision appeared to be closely linked to expectations regarding general ways of behaving. People want to be treated with respect, as equal citizens, not as recipients of a superior authority. If security forces interacted respectfully and inclusively with communities, addressing their concerns, they could enhance the perceived level of security. Beyond that, respectful behavior by an authority could construct a belief that it served the public, resulting in a perception that it had the right to exercise authority. Conversely, people in the interviews rejected those authorities whose procedures they perceived as corrupt and whose behavior they experienced as extractive.

Going Beyond Interactions

This book further shows that the perceived legitimacy of one authority often rests on the perceived illegitimacy of another authority. For example, many interviewees did not support the Taliban because they were in favor of the Taliban but because they were *against* the Afghan state's practices. The Taliban provided them with support and allies with which to fight the state or people associated with the state. The perceived illegitimacy of authority often rests on experiences that are perceived as *unjust*, such as, in the case of the Afghan state, the experiences of expropriation or unfair treatment. Obviously, not everyone decides to fight an authority after an experience of perceived injustice. But in less extreme cases—for instance after perceived corruption in conflict resolution—people preferred other authorities and, if available, were likely to choose another body for conflict resolution in the future. Even in the urban center of Herat, where there was no history or tradition of community authority, such authorities quickly gained legitimacy as an alternative to the corrupt state. It shows that behavior and procedures of authorities that were perceived to be unfair or unjust, or else negative on the basis of basic values of dignity, had far-reaching consequences. In a way, behavior that is seen as negative appears to have more extensive implications than positive behavior, delegitimizing an authority and, thereby, legitimizing another authority.

The army and, to a lesser degree, the intelligence agency NDS seemed to garner legitimacy without such interactions. This legitimacy related to people's perceptions of the entities' attitudes. The army especially managed to construct an image of being servants of the people who were fighting for the nation. In the absence of interaction, there was a fairly high level of visibility, which symbolized security and safety. However, beyond that, my research suggests that their legitimacy also resulted from a perception of these agencies *not being coercive* and not using force to extract money from people while having the perceived ability to do so. Hence, their legitimacy again was based on their behavior, resisting the temptation to easily supplement their income. This indicated to people that the army was carrying weapons to fulfill their duty, not to extract money. This form of legitimacy could also be described as rational-legal, with people believing that the army was acting according to the rules of the state. In addition, in the absence of personal interaction, media reporting was likely particularly important and could influence public perceptions more easily, reinforcing the agencies' public image. Conversely, other authorities, which lacked the perceived ability to be coercive, such as most MPs, were perceived more negatively if they did not do anything visible for the people and did not interact with them.

The Idea of the State

In contrast to an authority's attitude and modes of interaction, the *idea of authority*, or what an authority stood for in terms of official narrative or communicated ideology, appeared to be of as little relevance for constructing legitimacy as the history of how authority was gained. This finding contradicts a commonly stated view on Afghanistan, which explains legitimacy with references to competing "big" ideologies. Few interviewees explained their support for an authority with reference to what authorities stood for or their institutions' formal aspects, such as the Afghan state's democratic and liberal constitution, the traditional character of community authorities, or the Taliban's jihad. It is hardly surprising that people did not care about what an authority stood for unless it determined the authority's practices and affected them. But even if ideas of authority did translate into actions, with interactive dignity being essential, they were not a primary concern. For instance, which code of law was applied and whether it was derived from the Taliban's interpretation of Islam or based on the community's traditions was often a secondary or of no concern at all for interviewees in choosing an authority for conflict resolution.

On the other hand, most people I talked to expressed hope that the Afghan state would assume responsibility again and provide conflict resolution, for instance. This shows that there is a deep-rooted belief in the *idea of the state* as a *concept*. Regardless of whether people supported the state at the time of the interviews or even different authorities in different sectors, in the long term, most people hoped for one state to govern and considered the state, not other authorities, to be *responsible* for governance. This indicates that people believed in the ideal-typical Weberian state, characterized by a monopoly of the legitimate use of force and possibly by rational-legal structures. Conversely, the more specific features of the state, such as its liberal and democratic constitution, did not seem to be legitimizing the state to any extent. Meanwhile, people were certainly not opposed to the democratic ideology advocated by the state. For example, while there are many good reasons to be skeptical of the official numbers,[12] the claimed voter turnout in the first round of the 2014 presidential elections was 58 percent, which, to some extent, indicates a belief in the democratic system. But the character of the state's formal institutions appeared to have been of little relevance because it did not translate into the state's practices and, ultimately, did not greatly affect people's experience of the state. Furthermore, people appeared to be more concerned with having rules that ensured predictability, thus making the ideology that underpinned the rules a secondary concern.

As long as the state did not satisfy people's more immediate expectation of interactive dignity, people supported and considered alternative authorities to be more legitimate. While the idea of the state had substantive legitimacy, it did not translate into legitimacy of the post-2001 Afghan state. Nonetheless, the finding indicates that the Afghan state was in a stronger position than any other authority to construct legitimacy. People only considered other authorities to be legitimate as long as the state was not a viable alternative. Therefore, the widespread assumption that Afghans rejected the state and considered it to be illegitimate has to be viewed in a more nuanced way. While most people were indeed disappointed with the state as it was, and many did not even consider it to be legitimate, they did believe in the concept of the state. If the state had met more basic expectations—particularly with regard to procedures and behavior—it would, in theory, have been able to construct a stable political order based on substantive legitimacy.

Authorities' Self-Perception of Legitimacy

Comparing the view of the public to the self-perceptions of authorities shows that authorities were aware of people's expectations and addressed them rhetorically but failed to satisfy them in practice. As I have illustrated, the official claims of legitimacy, which were linked to the idea of authority, did not meet people's expectations because they had more immediate concerns of interactive dignity. But people who were authorities themselves, such as strongmen and community authorities, or who were associated with an authority, such as the state or the Taliban, were clearly aware of the importance that people placed on their behaviors and procedures as well as the expectations people had with regard to their attitude. This is reflected both in their *assumptions about what legitimized them* locally and their *personal claims of legitimacy*. For instance, police officers pointed out how their corrupt behavior undermined the trust of the people, and community authorities appeared to be well aware that their legitimacy rested primarily on conflict resolution mechanisms, which were faster and less corrupt than what was offered by the state. Similarly, the personal claims of legitimacy were in line with the expectations of the public. For example, insurgents pointed to the importance of fighting the corrupt state, and the strongmen I talked to emphasized behaving and talking to people in the right ways and stressed their work for the nation and the people. Conversely, an authority's official claims of legitimacy rarely translate into personal claims of legitimacy. For instance, apart from MPs, government officials barely ever mentioned elections and democratic values, and surprisingly few Taliban fighters relied on religion as a claim of legitimacy.

However, while these personal claims matched public expectations, they did not always match public perceptions. The mismatch was particularly striking in the case of strongmen, who, regardless of their claims, were usually seen as corrupt and criminal. In contrast, most of the employees of the state I interviewed, such as police officers, did not even try to claim legitimacy. They were more openly reflective than strongmen and MPs, acknowledging the high level of corruption in their institution. This indicates that they saw less of a need to try to claim legitimacy and openly state their views, while strongmen and MPs tried to construct legitimacy discursively in their interviews.

Looking at the *personal motives* of why people joined and actively supported an authority further illustrates the importance of interactive dignity. Some interviewees, notably several MPs, seemed to be genuinely driven by the idea of serving the country. Other interviewees also explained their decision with reference to substantive reasons linked to values of humane behavior, bringing up personal experiences, including violent ones, that contradicted their expectation of being treated with dignity. This became particularly visible in the case of the Taliban, with members explaining that they joined the group after experiencing perceived injustice. Meanwhile, the ability to fight back and exercise force against the perceived injustice also mattered, further linking violence and legitimacy. But, more commonly, interviewees simply joined or became an authority for instrumental reasons, to earn an income, for instance, particularly those who joined the ANP.

Interactive Dignity and its Limits

Weber proposes rational-legality, tradition, and charisma as sources of legitimate authority. This book suggests that we consider an additional source: *interactive dignity*. In the absence of a monopoly of force, people's primary concern is their day-to-day experience of authority. How an authority gained power and whether it happened democratically, traditionally, or violently, and what idea an authority stands for and if it claims authority on the basis of Islam, tradition, or Western values matter less. No specific ideology drives the values that underpin people's expectations about interactions. Rather, these are basic values linked to human dignity. At the time of my research, people were tired of the corruption they faced daily and expected authorities to serve the public and treat people with respect, ensuring that conflict resolution was fair and that security provision was coordinated. By satisfying these expectations, any authority could have constructed legitimacy. But while authorities seemed to be well aware of this, they kept failing to meet people's expectations.

The theory of interactive dignity is certainly not all-encompassing, however, and has several limitations. Most importantly, the theory is limited by its conceptual underpinning and the methods applied. The use of "big" and rather abstract categories for empirical research comes with inherent limitations. Indisputably, for instance, it can be difficult to categorize perceptions of authority as "legitimate" and "coercive" in the context of empirical research. Furthermore, the conceptual divide between coercion and legitimacy as sources of authority makes it difficult to identify phenomena that do not easily fit into the categories, such as social pressures and the role of discourse. As the theory draws on Weber and Bourdieu and is inspired by their understandings of political order, authority, and legitimacy, it has similar blind spots. For instance, the theory does not consider the role of language. In the specific context of Afghanistan, much more research needs to be done on specific words, such as "corruption," in Dari and Pashto that are used to describe notions of legitimacy and illegitimacy, their meanings, and how different meanings have been constructed. For example, women, who were underrepresented in my research, may have different views from men on what authorities are "fair" and "respectful." Similarly, the role of media reporting and other drivers of the discourse needs further investigation.

More specifically, the applied methods have shaped the findings of this book and the resulting theory. The findings are limited to what interviewees were willing to share and what they were aware of themselves. For example, an intangible phenomenon like charisma may not always translate into interview answers, even in life stories, if interviewees attempt to rationalize their views. Similarly, gaining a comprehensive understanding of symbolic violence requires a more thorough investigation through analyses that go beyond perceptions due to its rather invisible character. Additional research, especially in conflict-torn spaces other than Afghanistan, could help to further develop our understanding of interactive dignity.

The Failure of Statebuilding and the Persistence of the Legitimacy Challenge

The conclusions on interactive dignity, while certainly not all-encompassing, do have significant implications for how to build legitimate authority in Afghanistan and, perhaps, other conflict-torn spaces.

The question of what kind of authority and governance arrangement people consider to be legitimate is crucial for any authority and future government in Afghanistan. Despite the despairing situation, in many ways, the findings of this book indicate that peace, stability, and legitimate governance in Afghanistan are possible. People crave security and justice. Particularly encouraging is how little people ultimately care about the ideologies that are used by different authorities to claim legitimacy. This finding should be used to think about peace and future governance arrangements in more constructive ways, focusing on the experienced reality of ordinary people—which all authorities claimed to have in mind. Rather than getting caught up with ideology, to ensure lasting peace, the governance arrangement needs to ensure interactive dignity for ordinary people across the country.

Ultimately, state-building in Afghanistan failed because the authority that was constructed failed to treat its citizens with dignity. This book shows that neither imposing a Weberian state "top-down" nor enhancing what is local from the "bottom-up" necessarily ensure legitimacy, despite large sums of international aid. The U.S. priority of fighting the war on terror further undermined attempts of building legitimacy in Afghanistan, confirming Arendt's argument of violence destroying, not creating, power.[13]

Building state legitimacy will be at least as challenging for the Taliban as it was for the governments in power from 2001 to 2021. The state the Taliban controls continues to face the same legitimacy challenges as in the years before—not being able to govern in a way that ensures interactive dignity for all Afghans. Just like before, the Taliban have to deal with increasing corruption and a slowing bureaucracy. Before the Taliban took control of the state, people had already been complaining about slow proceedings and growing corruption in Taliban courts, illustrating that the Taliban are not exempted from such challenges once their structures become more institutionalized. Living up to people's expectations and ensuring fairness in day-to-day interactions throughout an entire state and over time is an even bigger challenge.

The Taliban increased its influence in Afghanistan slowly, often first expanding governance into areas of state control and attempting to build legitimacy before pushing forward militarily. But when the Taliban rapidly expanded control in the summer of 2021, capturing all provincial capitals within ten days, it had not been able to create legitimacy in advance. On the contrary, it was suddenly facing a population that had long perceived the Taliban as mainly a threat to their security and viewed it as illegitimate and coercive. In these often more urban areas, many people had personally experienced attacks committed by the Taliban, losing friends and relatives. Here in particular, many were associated with the former state, didn't trust the Taliban, feared revenge, and were concerned about setbacks on issues such as access to education and work for women, and the rights of the non-Pashtun population, including the Hazara people. Changing public perception and building legitimacy in places like Kabul is challenging for the Taliban but necessary for maintaining authority.

As it transitions from an insurgency to being fully responsible for governance in Afghanistan, the Taliban cannot gain legitimacy in a relational way vis-à-vis the state anymore—simply offering conflict resolution that is less corrupt than the state's isn't an option. Instead, the Taliban not only have to offer a state that lives up to people's expectations to maintain legitimacy in areas that it had long controlled, but it also must establish legitimacy in the areas that it captured in 2021. Meanwhile, the state's monopoly of force is still being challenged, including by IS-K, which continues to claim large-scale attacks with many civilian casualties. If the Taliban fails to build more widespread legitimacy, more widespread violent resistance is likely to evolve. Reports of arbitrary arrests following the Taliban's capture of the state, including members of the former state's security forces who were promised amnesty, indicate that the Taliban is repeating the mistakes of previous governments, including the 2001–2021 ones, which hunted down suspected supporters of the Taliban. Failing to treat people with dignity while trying to consolidate their authority as the state, the Taliban will ultimately undermine its own legitimacy and create new enemies.

The Taliban will have to rely more on what it stands for rather than what it is against. The Taliban were fairly united in its fight against the state; however, the movement comprises different views of what a state under Taliban control should look like. As the Taliban's idea of authority does not translate into a clear vision of statehood, and faced with the need of ensuring cohesion within the movement but having only slow consensus-building mechanisms, the Taliban might increasingly focus on implementing its official rhetoric of a "pure" Islamic system in an authoritarian way. Its interpretation would potentially threaten women's rights, minorities, civil society, and freedom of the press in the country. For example, the Taliban could attempt limiting women's access to education and work as well as women's general freedom of movement. Such a move would ignore that few people supported or even joined the movement because of the Taliban's idea of authority. It would further undermine its legitimacy not only in those areas that enjoyed such freedoms and rights before but also among supporters. Meanwhile, the enforcement of rules such as a ban on music or a certain dress code for women could undermine the Taliban's legitimacy in day-to-day interactions. Furthermore, prioritizing internal cohesion over the inclusion of the wider political spectrum in Afghanistan could further drive armed resistance in the long run—just as the Taliban reemerged after not being incorporated in the Afghan state in 2001.

Nonetheless, legitimate statehood in Afghanistan is possible. While people in Afghanistan differ on which authorities are legitimate, they all believe in the idea of a state as a concept and hope for one with rational-legal features to take over in the long term. Thus, the findings of this book, to a limited extent, support the conclusions of traditional state-building literature, which advocates for the construction of Weberian states in conflict-torn spaces. But the book also shows that people's more immediate concerns have to be addressed first—or, at least, they should not be neglected. For instance, elections do not help to construct legitimacy if people see that their "input" does not affect the "output" they experience and the reality they live in. Such a perception ultimately legitimizes alternative systems and authorities. But it is also not sufficient to simply respond to people's needs—providing aid and building roads on the "output" side. As the case of strongman Atta Noor illustrates, instrumental legitimacy can help to ensure a degree of stability, but without substantive legitimacy that authority may quickly fade again.

Constructing substantive legitimacy requires addressing people's value-based expectations of interactive dignity. This certainly is a complex and challenging task. To enhance the legitimacy of the state in Afghanistan, structural measures need to link the self-interest of the individual to the public interest. There are different ways of achieving this. Changes in the governance arrangement itself could help boost the legitimacy of the state to some extent. For example, a less centralized system, which makes accountability more localized, could help. More importantly, regardless of what the future political order of Afghanistan looks like, more specific measures can contribute to enhancing interactive dignity. For example, civil servants need to be vetted and thoroughly trained on how to interact with people. "Good" behavior needs to be institutionalized, "fair" processes need to be turned into procedures, and civil servants need to be paid salaries that do not make them dependent on bribes.

The courts need to be enabled to address people's concerns in a fair manner. This is particularly important for the widespread and often long-lasting conflicts over land and property, which directly affect people's livelihoods. Also the role of the police is particularly crucial, as many people experience "the state" in their daily lives primarily through them. Instead of fighting, they need to be trained to do ordinary policing, tackle criminality, and ensure the safety of the people. Physical force must be used for the construction rather than the destruction of legitimate authority. In order to achieve this, it needs to serve the public instead of catering to the interests of individuals or specific groups and making all people feel equal and protected, especially when interacting with the security forces. Finally, the impunity needs to stop. Those responsible for human rights violations and large-scale corruption in Afghanistan need to be prosecuted, regardless of what side they were on, nationality and country of residence. This would help to build trust in the state as well as the international community, illustrating that accountability can also exist on the macro level, not only on the level of daily interactions.

Such measures can help to construct an image of a state that works in the interest of the people. However, implementing them requires the state, international community, and neighboring countries to put the concerns of ordinary Afghans first, prioritizing long-term stability in Afghanistan over short-term interests and influence. The United States, in particular, needs to ensure that its counterterrorism objectives do not put the safety—and dignity—of Afghan civilians at risk.

By viewing people as citizens who provide legitimacy, not as subjects to exploit, authorities can change how they are perceived and, ultimately, construct legitimacy. For many authorities, focusing more on the procedures of *how* outputs and results are achieved, particularly in terms of interactions with the people, would already be a positive change. Matching people's expectations in Afghanistan does not necessarily depend on a certain ideology, but it requires treating people with dignity. People often have to choose the lesser of many evils, but they hope for an Afghanistan with better choices. They are waiting, demanding and fighting to be treated with dignity. Ordinary people hold the power to provide the legitimacy that authorities want, claim to have, and, indeed, require.

NOTES

ACKNOWLEDGMENTS

1. Grant numbers ES/J500070/1 and ES/S010858/1.

INTRODUCTION

1. Interview with Taliban commander, Herat City, Herat Province, October 2014.
2. Crawford and Lutz 2021.
3. George W. Bush, "Address to a Joint Session of Congress and the American People," September 20, 2001, https://georgewbush-whitehouse.archives.gov/news/releases/2001/09/20010920-8.html.
4. In this book I use the terms "violence" and "physical force" interchangeably. For example, in the context of Weber's work translated from German, I use the term "force," while I use the word "violence" in reference to Bourdieu's work translated from French.
5. Friedrichs and Kratochwil, 2009.
6. Jackson and Weigand 2020.
7. Berger and Luckmann 1966.
8. Bhaskar 1998.
9. On the relevance of this perspective, especially in the context of peacebuilding, see Roger Mac Ginty's work (e.g., Mac Ginty 2021; Mac Ginty 2014).
10. Green 2015.

11. Weber 1949.

12. Reiter 2006, 23.

13. Malejacq and Mukhopadhyay 2016.

14. Gerring 2007, 97–99.

15. Andersen 2012, 207.

16. Balancing these considerations, I decided on: (1) Herat City, Injil District, and Kushk (Robat Sangi) District in Herat Province; (2) Mazar-e-Sharif City, Dehdadi District, Kaldar District, and Chimtal District in Balkh Province; (3) Jalalabad City, Behsod District, and Surkh Rod District in Nangarhar Province; and (4) Kabul City, Farza District, and Char Asiab District in Kabul Province. In addition to the selected areas, some interviewees from other districts also participated. For example, in Nangarhar Province, some interviewees were from Khiwa (Kuz Kunar), Khogyani and Chaparhar districts.

17. We conducted research in (1) Almar District, Andkhoy, Andkhoy District, Bilcharagh District, Dawlatabad District, Garziwan District, Kohestan District, Kwajasabzposh District, Maimana City, Pashtunkot District, Qaysar District, and Shirintagab District in Faryab Province; and (2) Adraskan District, Ghoryan District, Gozara District, Gulran District, Injil District, Khushk Robat Sangi District, Khushk-e-Khona District, Pashtun Zargon District, and Shindand District in Herat Province.

18. All interviewees referenced in this book actively agreed to their statements being used. Nonetheless, I anonymized the names of most people and use pseudonyms to protect them, with exception of prominent individual authorities who can be identified on the basis of the interview data. In addition, I am referring to most interviewees by first name only. The interviewees' full, real names are known to the author.

19. The references in this book reflect this categorization. They distinguish between interviews with authorities, members of the public, and key informants.

20. Jackson and Weigand 2020; see also Jackson 2021.

21. In contrast to the interviews in 2014/2015, in 2019, more of the interviews were conducted by research assistants from the respective districts in the three provinces.

22. Yanow, 2009, 32; Stepputat and Larsen 2015, 11.

23. Andersson and Weigand 2015; Weigand and Andersson 2019; Andersson, 2019.

24. I draw primarily on the Asia Foundation's 2015 data, as this was when I conducted most of my interviews. For contextual reasons, I also use Asia Foundation data from other years at times.

　　Data collection for large-scale perception surveys was often limited in Taliban-controlled areas, making especially data from the years in which the Taliban expended control less meaningful. For a general discussion of the urban bias in research see Kalyvas 2004.

1. CONFLICT-TORN SPACES AND LEGITIMACY

1. Williams 2009; Herbert 2014; Larson and Coburn 2017.
2. Kuhn 2000.
3. Burnham 2003.
4. Miliband 1969, 265; Gramsci 1971, 52.
5. Dahl 2006, 72.
6. Weber 2009b, 77.
7. Blau 1963, 305.
8. Weber 1949.
9. Tilly 1992.
10. Elias 1982.
11. Kaldor 2006.
12. Kaldor 2006; Keen 2008.
13. Kalyvas 2001; Pinker 2011.
14. Ahmad 2017.
15. North 1981; Evans, Rueschemeyer, and Skocpol 1985.
16. Münch 2013.
17. Fukuyama 2004; Rotberg 2004.
18. Keen 2008.
19. Barfield and Nojumi 2010, 40–52.
20. Bourdieu 2020, 4; Bourdieu 1989; Bourdieu 1994.
21. Bourdieu 2020, 128.
22. Bourdieu 2020, 183.
23. Bourdieu 2020, 195–205.
24. Bourdieu 2020, 128.
25. Bourdieu 1989, 21.
26. Bourdieu 2020, 192.
27. Bourdieu 2020, 197.

28. Bourdieu 2020, 235; Bourdieu 1994, 16.
29. Bourdieu 2020, 235.
30. Bourdieu 1994. Each field is a social space or arena of competition in which power dynamics are at play. In particular, in every field, there is a permanent struggle between those who dominate and those who are dominated. Specific symbolic capital determines success in the field. In the fields of art and literature, for instance, this could be not only economic success but also exhibitions or prizes. Hence, there is also a permanent competition over what capital counts as symbolic within each field.
31. Bourdieu 2020, 311; Wacquant 1996, 11.
32. Bourdieu 1989, 22.
33. Similarly, scholars like Migdal and Schlichte (2005) and Hagmann and Péclard (2010) adopt more dynamic lenses. For example, Migdal and Schlichte define "statehood" as "a field of power marked by the use and threat of violence." This field of power is constantly changing as "the process in which power is exercised involves a constant struggle among multiple actors." However, while Migdal and Schlichte (2005, 15) set out to reconceptualize the state, I refer to the wider arrangement as political order or polity, allowing us to look at the state as one authority out of many while avoiding terminological confusion.
34. Malejacq (2019) illustrates the usefulness of a Bourdieusian approach in his analysis of "warlord survival."
35. While competition among authorities and the use of force are certainly important features of conflict-torn spaces, the authorities are also connected and may even collaborate in some essential ways, as the literature on war economies illustrates. See Kaldor 2006; Keen 2008). In Afghanistan, a number of scholars have pointed at the "network" character of the state and the wider political order (e.g., Jackson 2016; Sharan 2013; Sharan and Bose 2016). And indeed, what I call "authorities" can, figuratively speaking, also be seen as crucial knots of a network. Meanwhile, Bourdieu, who emphasizes the more structural objective relations within fields (e.g., Bourdieu 1993, 35), was not a great supporter of network analysis. Nonetheless, he acknowledged the importance of interactions, stating that it is "only by way of interactions that structures reveal themselves." Bourdieu 2020, 112.
36. For example, Hagmann and Péclard 2010; Lund 2006; Migdal and Schlichte 2005.

37. Agnew 2005, 441.

38. Kaldor 2009.

39. Weber 1980, 122.

40. Some scholars refer to "compliance" instead of "obedience." Building on Weber, I use the term "obedience" (*Gehorsam*) to define "authority" (*Herrschaft*).

41. The state consists of several branches and bodies, including the government, the police, and the army, that can be described as state authorities. In the interviews I conducted, however, many people used the term "government" to describe the entire state. Hence, when drawing on interviews, I may also refer to the "government," even when talking about what I would call the "state." What I categorized as strongmen were commonly referred to as *Qomandan* (commander) in the interviews. While these actors are often described as "warlords," I am also using the label "strongmen" frequently throughout this book, as the terminology "warlords" suggests that their authority rests on coercive means only. See Giustozzi 2005; Giustozzi 2009; Mukhopadhyay 2014; and Malejacq 2019. In addition, it allows me to consider influential individuals on the subnational level that are less known and have not gained the reputation of being warlords.

42. Delbrück 2003, 31.

43. Delbrück 2003, 31.

44. Andersen 2012; Hinsch 2008; Jackson and Bradford 2010; Schmelzle 2011.

45. Arendt 1969, 52.

46. Beetham 1991.

47. Weber 1973, 475

48. Weber 1964, 382.

49. Bourdieu 2013, 299.

50. Weber 1980, 122

51. Weber 1980; Boudon 2010.

52. Habermas 1984; Habermas 1987.

53. Building on a similar idea, the neo-institutionalists March and Olsen (1995; 1998; 2008) differentiate between a *logic of consequences* and a *logic of appropriateness* to explain actions of individuals.

54. Goodhand 2003, 2–3.

55. Weber 2009b, 78–79.

56. Weber 2009a, 222–224; Kraemer 2002, 174; Bliesemann de Guevara and Reiber 2011, 30.
57. Weber 1980, 123.
58. Scharpf 2003; Scharpf 1997.
59. Algappa 1995.
60. Tyler 2004; Tyler 2006; Jackson et al. 2013; Mzerolle et al 2013, 1.
61. Denney, Mallett, and Mazurana 2015, 5.
62. Tyler 2004; Tyler 2006.
63. Sturge et. al. 2017.
64. Denney 2015, 5.
65. In a conflict-torn setting, input, procedure, and output are not necessarily connected through institutions, and there may be a gap between the de jure "formal" institutions of what authorities claim to do and the de facto "informal" institutions of what authorities actually do that affects people's lives.
66. Scharpf 2003.
67. Tyler 2004; Tyler 2006.
68. The idea of authority has been discussed especially in relation to the state. See for example Abrams (1988), Hansen and Stepputat (2001) and Lund (2006).
69. Hoffman and Vlassenroot 2014; See also Hoffmann, Vlassenroot, and Marchais 2016.
70. Scharpf, 2003.
71. Similarly, the relationship between violence and legitimacy can also be approached through Bourdieu's conceptual lens of symbolic capital, a capital that is recognized and reflects a belief that the authority is "endowed with prestige," similar to what I describe as substantive legitimacy. In a conflict zone, violence certainly is an important form of capital. However, it is unclear under what circumstances and to what extent it is recognized and provides prestige—hence, it is symbolic capital.
72. Arendt's (1969, 56) statement is based on her understanding of power as communication, which differs from Weber's approach to power and authority. She argues that "Power corresponds to the human ability not just to act but to act in concert. Power is never the property of an individual; it belongs to a group and remains in existence only so long as the group keeps together" (1969, 44). Defining authority, Arendt (1969, 45) notes that "Its hallmark is unquestioning recognition by those who are

asked to obey; neither coercion nor persuasion is needed." For a detailed discussion of the differences between Weber's and Arendt's definitions see Habermas (1977).

73. For example, in their study of South Kivu in the Eastern DRC, Hoffmann and Vlassenroot (2014, 210) describe how an armed movement successfully constructed local support and legitimacy, challenging the influence of the Congolese army, by providing better protection against the Democratic Forces for the Liberation of Rwanda (FDLR). However, once the objective of pushing out the FDLR was achieved and when the group exerted its authority more forcefully, establishing checkpoints and imposing taxes on trade, it lost legitimacy again. Similarly, Malejacq (2019) shows how violence has helped warlords in Afghanistan to project an image of strength, enabling them to portray themselves as a security provider in order to construct legitimacy.

74. Algappa 1995, 25.

75. Khader 2011; Begon 2012; Sen 1990.

76. Beetham 2013, 23, 11. Even though Weber distinguishes the claim of legitimacy (*Legitimitätsanspruch*) from people's belief in what constitutes a legitimate authority (*Legitimitätsglauben*), his typology is grounded in the latter.

77. While it helps to distinguish these dimensions analytically, they may be identical in certain empirical settings. For instance, in the context of individual authorities, the personal narrative and claim of legitimacy may equal the official one.

78. Tyler 2004; Tyler 2006.

79. Bourdieu (2020) offers a detailed discussion of his view on "interaction" in his lecture on January 10, 1991 at the Collège de France. See also Bottero and Crossley (2011) for an extensive examination of Bourdieu's position on this concept.

2. THE STATE

1. The ANSF were also commonly referred to as the Afghan National Defence and Security Forces (ANDSF).

2. For a more comprehensive discussion of the history of Kabul and Afghanistan, see Barfield (2010); Coll (2004); Ewans (2002); Rubin (2002); and Saikal (2006), from whose work I draw on in this chapter.

3. Maley 2021, 16.
4. See Mitrokhin (2002); Bradsher (1983); Saikal (2006); and Fullerton (1984) for a detailed discussion.
5. Human Rights Watch 1991.
6. Human Rights Watch 2005.
7. Ewans 2002.
8. United Nations 2001a.
9. United Nations 2001b.
10. Islamic Republic of Afghanistan 2004; Ruttig 2014b.
11. Maley 2007.
12. For an overview of the failures of democracy promotion and the problems surrounding the elections, see Goodhand, Suhrke, and Bose (2016).
13. U.S. Department of State 2020.
14. Suebsaeng and Bixby 2021.
15. Serle and Purkiss 2017.
16. For example, Ahmad Massoud, the son of Ahmad Shah Massoud, began mobilizing support for a so-called National Resistance Front of Afghanistan in 2021.
17. Islamic Emirate of Afghanistan remains the official name of the Taliban movement.
18. Dupree 1997.
19. Barfield 2010.
20. Tarzi 2015, 88–89.
21. Barfield 2010, 221.
22. See Barfield 2010, 195–221.
23. Barfield 2010, 221.
24. Barfield 2010.
25. Yassari and Saboory 2010.
26. Barfield 2010, 262–263.
27. Goodhand 2013, 295; Goodhand and Sedra 2013, 244; Rubin 2006.
28. Maley 2021, 227.
29. NATO 2014a, 2.
30. Bowden 2021.
31. Tadjbakhsh and Schoiswohl 2008.
32. Goodhand, Suhrke, and Bohse 2016, 490.
33. Sabarre, Solomon, and Van Blarcom 2013.

34. Forugh 2015.
35. Maley 2021, 227.
36. Liebl 2007, 507.
37. Melton 2015, 4
38. Barfield and Nojumi 2010, 41–42.
39. Roy 2004, 173.
40. SIGAR 2019.
41. UNAMA 2017; In 2020, according to UNAMA (2021), the ANSF were responsible for 674 civilian deaths and 1,232 civilians injured.
42. Jalali 2016.
43. Asia Foundation 2015. The survey data used in this book has been rounded.
44. Asia Foundation 2015, 44–45; In 2019, 41 percent described the ANP as honest and fair, 36 percent thought that the ANP helped to improve security, and 32 percent perceived the ANP as protecting civilians (Asia Foundation 2019, 66). Meanwhile, 60 percent described the ANA as honest and fair (67).
45. Jalali, 2002, 72–73.
46. See Jalali (2002) and International Crisis Group (2010).
47. Karzai 2002.
48. Groll 2014.
49. Giustozzi 2012b.
50. The estimated force size of the ANA continues to fluctuate. In 2015, the size was estimated at 169,000 (Fitzgerald 2015). In 2019/2020, reported numbers fluctuated between circa 160,000 in July 2019 and 187,000 in October 2020 (SIGAR 2021, 59).
51. In order to curb the problem of ghost soldiers, the donor community initiated biometric registration of ANA soldiers to ensure that they actually existed. In 2017, the United States removed thirty thousand names of suspected ANA ghost soldiers off the payroll (see Donati and Amiri, 2017). However, the problem persisted, also due to the additional challenge of tracking whether soldiers do not only exist but also work.
52. Giustozzi and Ali 2016, 1.
53. The basic salary in 2011 was $165, excluding bouses and allowances (NATO 2011). Anecdotal evidence suggests that the basic salary had increased to around $200 by 2021.
54. Interview with a member of the public from Char Asiab, Kabul Province, May 2015.

55. Interview with a member of the public from Herat City, Herat Province, October 2014.

56. Interview with an authority from Mazar-E-Sahrif, Balkh Province, November 2014.

57. Interview with a member of the public from Khiwa, Nangarhar Province, May 2015.

58. Interview with an authority from Jalalabad, Nangarhar Province, December 2014.

59. Interview with a member of the public from Surkh Rod, December 2014.

60. Interview with an authority from Jalalabad, Nangarhar Province, December 2014.

61. Interview with an authority from Dehdadi, Balkh Province, November 2014.

62. The book uses the exchange rate of $1 = 0.015 Afghani, which was common in 2016/2017. In 2014/2015, the Afghani still had a slightly higher value ($1 = 0.018 Afghani). In late 2021, following the Taliban's capture of the state, the international withdrawal and the freezing of most of the Afghan central bank's assets the value of the Afghani decreased dramatically ($1 = 0.009 Afghani).

63. Interview with a member of the public from Mazar-e-Sharif, Balkh Province, November 2014.

64. Interview with a member of the public from Mazar-e-Sharif, Balkh Province, November 2014.

65. Interview with a member of the public from Enjil, Herat Province, October 2014.

66. Interview with a key informant from Surkh Rod, Nangarhar Province, November 2014

67. Interview with a member of the public from Surkh Rod, Nangarhar Province December 2014.

68. Interview with a member of the public from Herat city, Herat Province, October 2014.

69. Interview with an authority from Behsod, Nangarhar, May 2015.

70. Interview with a member of the public from Enjil, Herat Province, October 2014.

71. Interview with a key informant from Mazar-e-Sharif, November 2014.

72. Interview with a member of the public from Mazar-e-Sharif, Balkh Province, November 2014.

73. Interview with a member of the public from Khogyani, Nargarhar Province, November 2014.

74. Interview with an authority from Surkh Rod, Nangarhar Province, November 2014.

75. Interview with a key informant from Enjil, Herat Province, October 2014.

76. Interview with a member of the public from Surkh Rod, Nangarhar Province, November 2014.

77. Interview with an authority from Behsod, April 2015.

78. Schneider 2012.

79. Schenider 2012; Sedra 2003, 32.

80. Schenider 2012.

81. Schenider 2012; Sedra 2003, 32.

82. Schenider 2012.

83. Friesendorf and Krempel 2011, 11.

84. Friesendorf and Krempel 2011.

85. Weigand 2013.

86. SIGAR 2021.

87. NATO 2014a, 58.

88. NATO 2014a, 47.

89. Dodge 2011, 89.

90. Zucchino and Abed 2020.

91. NATO 2013.

92. Because of this, when talking about the ANP I refer to the AUP branch of it. In the interviews, I simply used the word "police," which participants took to mean the AUP.

93. NATO 2014a, 59.

94. Achakzai 2017.

95. Interview with an authority from Jalalabad, Nangarhar Province, June 2015.

96. An interview with an authority from Kabul city, Kabul Province, July 2015.

97. Interview with a member of the public from Jalalabad, Nangarhar Province, November 2014.

98. Interview with a member of the public from Surkh Rod, Nangarhar Province, November 2014.

99. Interview with a member of the public from Jalalabad, Nangarhar Province, April 2015.

100. Interview with a key informant from Jalalabad Nangarhar Province, November 2014.

101. Interview with a member of the public from Jalalabad, Nangarhar Province, November 2014.

102. Interview with a member of the public from Surkh Rod, Nangarhar Province, December 2014.

103. Interview with a member of the public from Jalalabad, Nangarhar Province, November 2014.

104. Interview with a member of the public from Jalalabad, Nangarhar Province, November 2014.

105. Interview with a member of the public from Jalalabad, Nangarhar Province, May 2015.

106. Interview with a member of the public from Surkh Rod, Nangarhar Province, November 2014.

107. Interview with an authority from Dehdadi, Balkh Province, November 2014.

108. Interview with a member of the public from Herat City, Herat Province, October 2014

109. Interview with a member of the public from Herat City, Herat Province, October 2014.

110. An interview with an authority from Kabul city, Kabul Province, July 2015.

111. Interview with a member of the public from Herat city, Herat Province, October 2014

112. Interview with a member of the public from Jalalabad, Nangarhar Province, December 2014.

113. Interview with an authority from Surkh Rod, Nangarhar Province, November 2014.

114. Interview with an authority from Behsod, Nangarhar Province, April 2015.

115. Interview with a member of the public from Behsod, Nangarhar Province, April 2015.

116. Interview with an authority from Behsod, Nangarhar Province, May 2015.

117. Interview with an authority from Behsod, Nangarhar Province, May 2015.

118. Interview with a member of the public from Behsod, Nangarhar Province, April 2015.

119. Weigand 2020.

120. An interview with a member of the pubic from Farza, Kabul Province, May 2015.

121. An interview with a member of the pubic from Farza, Kabul Province, May 2015.

122. An interview with an authority from Farza, Kabul Province, September 2014.

123. An interview with an authority from Farza, Kabul Province, September 2014.

124. An interview with an authority from Farza, Kabul Province, September 2014.

125. An interview with an authority from Farza, Kabul Province, September 2014.

126. Foschini 2020.

127. SIGAR 2015, 1.

128. Jones and Muñoz 2010.

129. Department of Defense (DoD) 2011; Department of Defense (DoD), 2012; SIGAR 2015, 2.

130. DoD 2011; DoD 2012; Felbab-Brown 2015.

131. SIGAR 2015, 2.

132. SIGAR 2015, 2; SIGAR 2015, 1.

133. NATO 2014b, 48.

134. UNAMA 2016.

135. Gaston 2021.

136. Vincent, Weigand, and Hakimi 2015, 1–26.

137. Goodhand and Hakimi 2014; International Crisis Group (ICG) 2015; UNAMA 2016.

138. Sedra 2014, 35, 7.

139. Interview with a member of the public from Jalalabad, Nangarhar Province, May 2015.

140. Interview with a member of the public from Behsod, Nangarhar Province, April 2015.

141. Interview with an authority from Behsod, Nangarhar Province, April 2015.

142. Interview with an authority from Jalalabad Nangarhar Province, December 2014.

143. Interview with an authority from Surkh Rod, Nangarhar Province, November 2014.

144. Interview with a member of the public from Khogyani, Nangarhar Province, November 2014.

145. Interview with an authority from Surkh Rod, Nangarhar Province, November 2014.

146. Interview with a member of the public from Khogyani, Nangarhar Province, November 2014.

147. Interview with a member of the public from Behsod, Nangarhar Province, April 2015.

148. Interview with an authority from Behsod, Nangarhar Province, April 2015.

149. Interview with an authority from Jalalabad, Nangarhar Province, June 2015

150. Clark et al. 2020.

151. Clark 2020.

152. Jones 2002; Andrew and Mitrokhin 2005.

153. Andrew and Mitrokhin 2005, 409.

154. Amnesty International 2007, 29.

155. Interview with a member of the public from Jalalabad, Nangahar Province, May 2015.

156. Interview with a member of the public from Kama, Nangahar Province, May 2015.

157. Interview with an authority from Guzarat, Herat Province, October 2014.

158. Interview with a member of the public from Jalalabad, Nangahar Province, April 2015.

159. Interview with a key informant from Surkh Rod, Nangahar Province, November 2014.

160. Human Rights Watch 2019.

161. Human Rights Watch 2019.

162. UNAMA 2020.

163. Quilty and Cole 2021.

164. Quilty and Cole 2021.

165. Mashal 2018.

166. Jalali 2016, 11.

167. Perito 2009.

168. After 2015, the security situation has further deteriorated in Afghanistan. With a growing number of people being exposed to the conflict, including to civilian casualties caused by the army, the ANA's legitimacy likely suffered.

169. Hoffmann and Vlassenroot 2014; see also Migdal and Schlichte 2005.

170. Barfield 2003.

171. Barfield 2003.

172. International Crisis Group 2010.

173. International Crisis Group 2010.

174. International Crisis Group 2010, 4–5.

175. Barfield 2010, 223.

176. International Crisis Group 2010, 5.

177. International Crisis Group 2010, 6.

178. Barfield 2003, 45.

179. International Crisis Group 2010, 7.

180. Barfield 2003, 35.

181. Constitution of Afghanistan, 2004 (Ratified) January 26, 2004, Article 3.

182. Constitution of Afghanistan, 2004 (Ratified) January 26, 2004, Article 6.

183. International Crisis Group 2010, 17.

184. International Crisis Group 2010, 18.

185. Barfield 2003.

186. Asia Foundation 2015, 102–104.

187. Wyler and Katzman 2010.

188. While they are formally part of the executive branch of the state, they are also part of the judicial process, as each plays a role in connecting elements the police and the courts.

189. An interview with an authority from Kabul city, Kabul Province, July 2015.

190. Interview with an authority from Jalalabad, Nangarhar Province, June 2015.

191. Interview with a member of the public from Enjil, Herat Province, October 2014.

192. Interview with an authority from Kushk Robat Sanghi, Herat Province, October 2014.

193. Interview with a member of the public from Surkh Rod, Nangarhar Province, November 2014.

194. Interview with a member of the public from Enjil, Herat Province, October 2014

195. Interview with a member of the public from Surkh Rod, Nangarhar Province, November 2014.

196. Interview with a member of the public from Surkh Rod, Nangarhar Province, November 2014.

197. Interview with a member of the public from Behsod, Nangarhar Province, April 2015.

198. Interview with an authority from Kushk Robat Sanghi, Herat Province, October 2014

199. Interview with a member of the public from Behsod, Nangarhar Province, April 2015.

200. Interview with a member of the public from Enjil, Herat Province, October 2014

201. Interview with a member of the public from Behsod, Nangarhar Province, April 2015.

202. Interview with a member of the public from Behsod, Nangarhar Province, April 2015.

203. Interview with an authority from Kushk Robat Sanghi, Herat Province, October 2014

204. Interview with an authority from Behsod, Nangarhar Province, May 2015.

205. Interview with a member of the public from Kama, Nangarhar Province, May 2015.

206. Interview with a key informant from Jalalabad Nangarhar Province, December 2014.

207. Interview with a member of the public from Enjil, Herat Province, October 2014

208. Interview with a member of the public from Enjil, Herat Province, October 2014

209. Interview with a member of the public from Surkh Rod, Nangarhar Province, December 2014.

210. Interview with a member of the public from Behsod, Nangarhar Province, April 2015.
211. Interview with a member of the public from Herat City, Herat Province, October 2014
212. Interview with a member of the public from Jalalabad, Nangarhar Province, April 2015.
213. Interview with a member of the public from Herat City, Herat Province, October 2014
214. Interview with a member of the public from Jalalabad, Nangarhar Province, April 2015.
215. Interview with a key informant from Jalalabad Nangarhar Province, November 2014.
216. Interview with a member of the public from Jalalabad, Nangarhar Province, November 2014.
217. Interview with a member of the public from Herat City, Herat Province, October 2014
218. Interview with a key informant from Herat City, Herat Province, October 2014.
219. Interview with a member of the public from Jalalabad, Nangarhar Province, December 2014.
220. Interview with a member of the public from Jalalabad, Nangarhar Province, April 2015.
221. Interview with a member of the public from Jalalabad, Nangarhar Province, May 2015.
222. Interview with a member of the public from Herat City, Herat Province, October 2014.
223. Interview with a member of the public from Herat City, Herat Province, October 2014
224. Interview with a member of the public from Jalalabad, Nangarhar Province, November 2014.
225. Interview with a member of the public from Herat City, Herat Province, October 2014
226. Barfield 2010, 223.
227. Yassari and Saboory 2010.
228. Constitution of Afghanistan 1964, Article 42.
229. Constitution of Afghanistan 1964, Article 43–45.

230. Constitution of Afghanistan 1964, Article 69–70.

231. Yassari and Saboory 2010; Amstutz 1986, 59.

232. Constitution of Afghanistan, 1987, Article 77–78.

233. Barfield 2010, 261.

234. Constitution of Afghanistan 2004, Article 84.

235. Constitution of Afghanistan 2004, Article 84.

236. Constitution of Afghanistan 2004, Article 83.

237. Constitution of Afghanistan, 2004, Article 90.

238. Constitution of Afghanistan, 2004, Article 95.

239. Constitution of Afghanistan, 2004, Article 91.

240. Larson 2015, 3.

241. Larson 2015.

242. Dodge 2011, 85.

243. Sharan and Bose 2016.

244. Schmeidl 2016, 576; Larson 2016, 607.

245. Asia Foundation 2015, 97.

246. Asia Foundation 2016, 106.

247. Naadim 2015.

248. Ahmadi and Linke 2016.

249. Barakzai 2017.

250. Johnson and Barnhart 2020.

251. Johnson and Barnhart 2020.

252. Johnson and Barnhart 2020, 60.

253. Barakzai 2017.

254. Interview with an authority from Surkh Rod, Nangarhar Province, November 2014.

255. Interview with a member of the public from Surkh Rod, Nangarhar Province, November 2014.

256. Interview with a member of the public from Jalalabad, Nangarhar Province, December 2014.

257. Interview with a member of the public from Jalalabad, Nangarhar Province, November 2014.

258. Interview with a member of the public from Jalalabad, Nangarhar Province, November 2014.

259. Interview with a member of the public from Jalalabad, Nangarhar Province, December 2014.

260. Interview with an authority from Jalalabad Nangarhar Province, December 2014.
261. Interview with an authority from Enjil, Herat Province, October 2014.
262. Interview with a member of the public from Surkh Rod, Nangarhar Province, November 2014.
263. An interview with an authority from Char Asiab, Kabul Province, May 2015.
264. Interview with a key informant from Jalalabad Nangarhar Province, November 2014.
265. Sharan and Bose 2016.
266. Liebl 2007.
267. Maley 2021.
268. Barfield and Nojumi 2010.

3. STRONGMEN AND WARLORDS

1. See Osman and Clark (2017) for a detailed discussion of the incident.
2. Irish Times 2015.
3. To identify such individuals for this chapter, I used the community-level interviews, secondary literature, and my personal observations.
4. Harding 2002.
5. Harding 2002.
6. Coll 2004.
7. Giustozzi 2009, 5.
8. Malejacq 2019.
9. Maley 2021, 244.
10. Williams 2013.
11. Harding 2002.
12. Elias 1982; Jackson 2003.
13. Reno 1995.
14. Duffield 1998.
15. For literature defining strongmen or warlords along similar lines see, for example, MacKinlay 2000; Jackson 2003; Marten 2013; Malejacq 2019.
16. While this term is sexist, in fact, almost all of these individuals in Afghanistan, and likely elsewhere, to date, have been men.

17. Jackson 2016; Sharan 2013; Sharan and Bose 2016.
18. Marten 2013.
19. Murtazashivili 2014.
20. Marten 2013.
21. Giustozzi 2005, 16.
22. Giustozzi 2005, 17.
23. Malejacq 2019.
24. Marten 2013; Giustozzi 2005.
25. Mukhopadhyay 2014.
26. Malejacq 2019, 56.
27. Murtazashivili 2014, 340.
28. Jackson 2014.
29. Hezb-e Islami was one of the biggest Mujahedin groups during the Soviet occupation, established and led by Gulbudin Hekmatyar and dominated by Pashtuns. From 2001 until 2016, Hezb-e Islami consisted of a political wing, a political party with numerous MPs in the Afghan parliament, and a military wing, which was fighting the Afghan state as an insurgency group under the leadership of Hekmatyar.
30. Hezb-e Islami Khales split from Hekmatyar's Hezb-e Islami in the late 1970s under the leadership of Maulawi Khales. He was succeeded by Din Mohammad in this position (Jackson 2014).
31. Jackson 2014, 13–14; Weaver 2005.
32. Clark and Osman 2017.
33. See Jackson (2014) for a detailed discussion of strongmen governance in Nangarhar in general and the history of the Arsala family in particular.
34. See Chayes (2006), who describes her personal experiences with Shirzai in Kandahar. Jackson (2014) and Mukhopadhyay (2014) explore his role in Nangarhar Province.
35. Jackson 2014, 20.
36. Mahaz-e Milli was another Mujahedin group established in the late 1970s under the leadership of the Gailani family. Consisting of monarchists, the group was considered to be moderate, while being called "Gucci guerillas" by hardliners, and is a political party today (see Clark 2016).
37. Jackson 2014, 20; Maass 2002.
38. Maley 2021, 244.

39. Jackson 2014, 21.

40. Mukhopadhyay 2014, 199–205.

41. Jackson 2014; Mukhopadhyay 2014.

42. Jackson 2014, 25.

43. He also kindly hosted me in his home in Nangarhar Province in May 2015.

44. See Malejacq (2019) for a detailed discussion of Ismail Khan's history and authority.

45. Interview with a member of the public from Jalalabad, Nangarhar Province, April 2015.

46. Interview with a member of the public from Jalalabad, Nangarhar Province, May 2015.

47. Interview with a member of the public from Jalalabad, Nangarhar Province, November 2014.

48. Interview with a member of the public from Jalalabad, Nangarhar Province, November 2014.

49. Interview with a member of the public from Jalalabad, Nangarhar Province, November 2014.

50. Interview with a member of the public from Jalalabad, Nangarhar Province, November 2014.

51. Interview with a member of the public from Jalalabad, Nangarhar Province, December 2014.

52. Interview with a member of the public from Jalalabad, Nangarhar Province, November 2014.

53. Interview with an authority from Behsod, Nangarhar Province, May 2015.

54. Interview with a member of the public from Jalalabad, Nangarhar Province, November 2014.

55. Interview with a member of the public from Surkh Rod, Nangarhar Province, December 2014.

56. Interview with a member of the public from Behsod, Nangarhar Province, April 2015.

57. Interview with a member of the public from Behsod, Nangarhar Province, April 2015.

58. Interview with a member of the public from Behsod, Nangarhar Province, April 2015.

59. Interview with a member of the public from Jalalabad, Nangarhar Province, November 2014.

60. Interview with a member of the public from Jalalabad, Nangarhar Province, November 2014.
61. Interview with a member of the public from Jalalabad, Nangarhar Province, December 2014.
62. Interview with a member of the public from Khiwa, Nangarhar Province, May 2015.
63. Interview with a member of the public from Kama, Nangarhar Province, May 2015.
64. Interview with a member of the public from Jalalabad, Nangarhar Province, November 2014.
65. Interview with a key informant from Jalalabad Nangarhar Province, November 2014.
66. Interview with a member of the public from Jalalabad, Nangarhar Province, November 2014.
67. Interview with a key informant from Jalalabad Nangarhar Province, November 2014.
68. Interview with a member of the public from Behsod, Nangarhar Province, April 2015.
69. Interview with a key informant from Jalalabad Nangarhar Province, November 2014.
70. Interview with a key informant from Jalalabad Nangarhar Province, December 2014.
71. Interview with a member of the public from Sherzad, Nangarhar Province, May 2015.
72. Interview with a member of the public from Jalalabad, Nangarhar Province, May 2015.
73. Interview with a key informant from Jalalabad Nangarhar Province, November 2014.
74. Interview with a member of the public from Jalalabad, Nangarhar Province, April 2015.
75. Interview with a member of the public from Jalalabad, Nangarhar Province, May 2015.
76. Interview with a member of the public from Behsod, Nangarhar Province, April 2015.
77. Interview with a member of the public from Jalalabad, Nangarhar Province, April 2015.

78. Interview with an authority from Behsod, Nangarhar Province, May 2015.

79. Interview with a member of the public from Behsod, Nangarhar Province, April 2015.

80. It is difficult though to draw conclusions about specific strongmen in Nangarhar, as the interviewees tended to mention specific strongmen more frequently when talking positively about them, while often being more general in their statements when criticizing them. So, while some people emphasize Qadir's fairness in conflict resolution, we do not know which critical views on conflict resolution are specifically about him.

81. Jackson 2014.

82. Government of the Islamic Republic of Afghanistan, 2015, 11–12.

83. Mukhopadhyay 2014,66.

84. Mukhopadhyay 2014; The political party Jamiat-e Islami evolved as a mainly Tajik Mujahedin group during the Soviet occupation of Afghanistan in the 1970s under the leadership of later president Burhanuddin Rabbani. Followers included Atta Noor, Ismail Khan, Ahmad Shah Massoud, Mohammad Fahim, and Gulbuddin Hekmatyar. The latter, a Pashtun, split off from Jamiat after a few years, establishing the Hizb-i Islami group (for details, see e.g. Rubin 1989; Ruttig 2013).

85. Mukhopadhyay 2014.

86. Mashal and Sukhanyar 2016.

87. Interview with a member of the public from Dehdadi, Balkh Province, November 2014.

88. Interview with a member of the public from Mazar-e-Sharif, Balkh Province, November 2014.

89. Interview with a member of the public from Dehdadi, Balkh Province, November 2014.

90. Interview with a member of the public from Mazar-e-Sharif, Balkh Province, November 2014.

91. Interview with a member of the public from Mazar-e-Sharif, Balkh Province, November 2014.

92. Interview with an authority from Mazar-e-Sharif, Balkh Province, November 2014.

93. Interview with a key informant from Mazar-e-Sharif, Balkh Province, November 2014.

94. See Malejacq, who, drawing on Bourdieu, argues that in Afghanistan "politics is in fact a 'competitive game' that [strongmen] . . . have the best chance of winning" (2019, 48).
95. Marten 2013.
96. Murtazashvili 2014.
97. Malejacq 2019.
98. Marten 2013.
99. Olson 1993.
100. Malejacq 2019, 21.

4. THE TALIBAN

1. Interview with a member of the public from Mazar-e-Sharif, Balkh Province, November 2014.
2. Interview with a member of the public from Mazar-e-Sharif, Balkh Province, November 2014.
3. van Linschoten and Kuehn 2012, 113–117; Rashid 2001, 21–22. See van Linschoten and Kuehn (2019) for a collection of Taliban documents over the years and Smith (2009) for a discussion of Taliban perspectives from Kandahar.
4. Rashid 2001.
5. Barfield 2010, 257.
6. Rashid 2001, 25.
7. Barfield 2010, 258–260; van Linschoten and Kuehn 2012, 144.
8. Barfield 2010, 261.
9. Nojumi 2002, 155.
10. Barfield 2010, 261.
11. Barfield 2010, 261–263.
12. Jackson and Weigand 2019.
13. UNAMA 2021.
14. Johnson (2017) shows that such claims of legitimacy include references to Islam, arguing that the foreign forces despise Islam, history, emphasizing the victory of Afghans against foreign invaders in the past and in the future, announcing an inevitable Taliban victory.
15. Johnson 2017, 16.
16. Johnson 2017, 16.

17. Jackson and Weigand April 2019.

18. Franco and Giustozzi 2016.

19. Jackson and Weigand 2019.

20. See Jackson and Amiri (2019) for a comprehensive discussion of the Taliban's command and governance structures.

21. Jackson and Amiri 2019.

22. Osman 2015.

23. Osman 2016.

24. Khaama Press 2015.

25. Marty 2016.

26. Osman and Gopal 2016, 7.

27. Amiri and Jackson 2021.

28. Giustozzi, Franco, and Baczko 2016.

29. See Jackson and Weigand (2020) for a detailed description of Taliban justice in civil cases.

30. See Alcis, Mansfield, and Smith (2021) for a nuanced analysis of taxation practices in Nirmoz Province.

31. Malkasian 2016, 110–113.

32. According to the Asia Foundation (2009, 2015, 2019), sympathy for insurgencies among Afghans in areas the researchers could access fell from 55.7 percent in 2009 to 27.5 percent in 2015 and again to 17.6 in 2018.

33. Liebl 2007.

34. Rangelov and Theros 2012.

35. Giustozzi 2012b; see also Giustozzi and Baczko, 2014.

36. Interview with authority (Taliban commander) in Herat City, Herat Province, October 2014.

37. Interview with an authority in Nangarhar Province, October 2014.

38. The NGO in question confirmed the existence of the hospital to me.

39. Interview with an authority from Kushk Robat Sanghi, Herat Province, October 2014.

40. Interview with an authority from Kushk Robat Sanghi, Herat Province, October 2014.

41. Interview with an authority from Nangarhar Province, June 2015

42. Interview with an authority from Kushk Robat Sanghi, Herat Province, October 2014

43. Interview with an authority from Nangarhar Province, June 2015

44. Jackson and Weigand 2020.

45. An interview with a member of the pubic from Kabul City, Kabul Province, May 2015.

46. An interview with a member of the public from Char Asiab, Kabul Province, May 2015.

47. An interview with a member of the pubic from Kabul City, Kabul Province, May 2015.

48. An interview with a member of the pubic from Kabul City, Kabul Province, May 2015.

49. An interview with a member of the public from Char Asiab, Kabul Province, May 2015.

50. An interview with a member of the public from Char Asiab, Kabul Province, May 2015.

51. An interview with an authority from Farza, Kabul Province, September 2014.

52. An interview with an authority from Farza, Kabul Province, September 2014.

53. See Foschini (2020) for a detailed discussion of the criminal networks in Kabul City.

54. Government of the Islamic Republic of Afghanistan 2015, The State of Afghan Cities, 12.

55. Interview with a member of the public from Jalalabad, Nangarhar Province, May 2015.

56. Interview with a member of the public from Jalalabad, Nangarhar Province, April 2015.

57. Hekmatyar subsequently signed a peace deal with the government in 2016 and even ran for president in 2019.

58. Interview with a key informant from Jalalabad Nangarhar Province, December 2014.

59. Interview with a member of the public from Jalalabad, Nangarhar Province, November 2014.

60. Interview with a member of the public from Jalalabad, Nangarhar Province, November 2014.

61. Interviews with members of the public from Surkh Rod, Nangarhar Province, December 2014 and Jalalabad, Nangarhar Province, April 2015.

62. Interview with a key informant from Jalalabad Nangarhar Province, November 2014.
63. Interview with a key informant from Jalalabad Nangarhar Province, December 2014.
64. Interview with a member of the public from Jalalabad, Nangarhar Province, November 2014.
65. Interview with a key informant from Jalalabad Nangarhar Province, December 2014.
66. Interview with an authority from Behsod, Nangarhar Province, April 2015; interviews with several members of the public from Behsod, Nangarhar Province, April 2015.
67. Interview with a member of the public from Behsod, Nangarhar Province, April 2015.
68. Interview with a member of the public from Behsod, Nangarhar Province, April 2015.
69. Interview with a member of the public from Behsod, Nangarhar Province, April 2015.
70. Interview with a member of the public from Surkh Rod, Nangarhar Province, November 2014.
71. Interview with an authority from Behsod, Nangarhar Province, April 2015.
72. Interview with a member of the public from Surkh Rod, Nangarhar Province, November 2014.
73. Interview with an authority from Surkh Rod, Nangarhar Province, November 2014.
74. Interview with a key informant from Surkh Rod, Nangarhar Province, November 2014.
75. Karwan Fidaye (suicide convoy) was likely part of the Taliban at the time, allowing leadership to influence local-level mahaz dynamics. Members of Karwan Fidaye likely operated undercover in the normal Taliban mahaz and were tasked with collecting intelligence for the leadership. As other fighters did not know who members of Karwan Fidaye were, members allegedly covered their faces when conducting operations—for instance, against commanders. Similar groups existed in other provinces, operating under other names.
76. Interview with a member of the public from Khogyani, Nangarhar Province, November 2014.

77. Interview with a member of the public from Khogyani, Nangarhar Province, November 2014.
78. Interviews with members of the public from Khogyani, Nangarhar Province, November 2014.
79. Meaning "law" or "rights."
80. Interview with a member of the public from Sherzad, Nangarhar Province, May 2015.
81. Interview with a member of the public from Sherzad, Nangarhar Province, May 2015.
82. Jackson and Weigand 2019.
83. An interview with a member of the public from Pahstunkot, Faryab Province, March 2019.
84. An interview with a member of the public from Qaysar, Faryab Province, March 2019.
85. An interview with a member of the public in Herat City, Herat Province, February 2019.
86. An interview with a key informant from Almar, Faryab Province, February 2019.
87. An interview with a member of the public from Kohistan, Faryab Province, April 2019.
88. This finding is certainly not representative of women's perspectives on the Taliban, as only thirty of the interviewees from Taliban-controlled areas in 2019 were women, compared to 197 men.
89. An interview with a member of the public from Gurziwan, Faryab Province, March 2019
90. An interview with a member of the public from Koshk-e-Kohna, Herat Province, February 2019.
91. Esser 2014.
92. An interview with a key informant from Kabul City, Kabul Province, May 2015.
93. Giustozzi 2012b.
94. Osman and Gopal 2016.
95. An interview with a key informant from Kabul City, Kabul Province, May 2015.
96. Rangelov and Theros 2012.
97. Johnson 2017.

5. COMMUNITY AUTHORITIES

1. Kakar 2003; Miakhel 2009.
2. Barfield 2010, 65.
3. Noelle-Karimi 2006, 8.
4. Nixon 2008.
5. Murtazashvili 2016.
6. Nixon 2008, 11.
7. Murtazashvili 2016, 69.
8. Murtazashvili 2016, 69.
9. Nixon 2008, 11; Murtazashvili 2016, 68.
10. Wilde and Mielke 2013, 361.
11. Barfield 2003.
12. Saltmarshe and Medhi 2011, 26.
13. Asia Foundation 2015, 96.
14. Asia Foundation 2015, 104.
15. Pain 2016, 19.
16. Nixon 2008, 11; Murtazashvili 2016, 72.
17. Nixon 2008, 11.
18. Beath, Christia, and Enikolopov 2015, 305.
19. World Bank 2013.
20. UNDP, 2014.
21. Pain 2016, 11.
22. Asia Foundation 2018, 106.
23. Qaane and Ruttig 2015.
24. National Democratic Institute 2013.
25. Larson and Coburn 2014.
26. Miakhel and Coburn 2010, 2; Wilde and Mielke 2014, 361.
27. Bhatia et al. 2018.
28. Lister 2005, 7.
29. Wardak 2003, 12.
30. Miakhel and Coburn 2010, 2; Wilde and Mielke 2013, 361.
31. For other common terms, see Murtazashvili 2016, 80.
32. Murtazashvili 2016, 78–79.
33. Murtazashvili 2016, 78–79; Nixon 2008, 31.
34. Nixon 2008, 30; Murtazashvili 2016, 79.

35. Nixon 2008, 30.

36. Wilde and Mielke 2013, 356; Murtazashvili 2016, 81.

37. Murtazashvili 2016.

38. Mielke 2013, 254.

39. Nixon 2008, 35; Murtazashvili 2016, 79.

40. Wilde and Mielke 2013, 355.

41. Nixon 2008, 35; Wilde and Mielke 2013, 360.

42. Wilde and Mielke 2013, 361.

43. Murtazashvili 2016, 74.

44. Murtazashvili 2016, 75.

45. Murtazashvili 2016, 78.

46. Murtazashvili 2016, 78.

47. Interview with an authority from Surkh Rod, Nangarhar Province, November 2014; interview with an authority from Surkh Rod, Nangarhar Province, November 2014.

48. Interview with an authority from Surkh Rod, Nangarhar Province, November 2014.

49. Interview with a member of the public from Surkh Rod, Nangarhar Province, November 2014.

50. Interview with a member of the public from Surkh Rod, Nangarhar Province, November 2014.

51. Interview with a member of the public from Surkh Rod, Nangarhar Province, November 2014.

52. Interview with a member of the public from Surkh Rod, Nangarhar Province, November 2014.

53. Interview with a member of the public from Surkh Rod, Nangarhar Province, November 2014.

54. Interview with an authority from Surkh Rod, Nangarhar Province, November 2014.

55. Interview with a member of the public from Surkh Rod, Nangarhar Province, November 2014.

56. Interview with a member of the public from Surkh Rod, Nangarhar Province, November 2014.

57. Interview with a member of the public from Surkh Rod, Nangarhar Province, November 2014.

58. Interview with a key informant from Surkh Rod, Nangarhar Province, November 2014.

59. Interview with a member of the public from Surkh Rod, Nangarhar Province, November 2014.

60. Interview with a member of the public from Surkh Rod, Nangarhar Province, November 2014.

61. Interview with a member of the public from Surkh Rod, Nangarhar Province, December 2014.

62. Interview with a member of the public from Surkh Rod, Nangarhar Province, December 2014.

63. Interview with a member of the public from Khogyani, Nangarhar Province, November 2014; interview with a member of the public from Khogyani, Nangarhar Province, November 2014.

64. Interview with a member of the public from Surkh Rod, Nangarhar Province, November 2014.

65. Interview with a key informant from Surkh Rod, Nangarhar Province, November 2014.

66. Interview with a member of the public from Surkh Rod, Nangarhar Province, November 2014.

67. Interview with a key informant from Surkh Rod, Nangarhar Province, November 2014.

68. Interview with a member of the public from Surkh Rod, Nangarhar Province, December 2014.

69. Interview with a member of the public from Surkh Rod, Nangarhar Province, November 2014.

70. Interview with a member of the public from Surkh Rod, Nangarhar Province, November 2014.

71. Interview with a member of the public from Surkh Rod, Nangarhar Province, November 2014.

72. Leslie 2015, 8.

73. To protect the interviewees, I am not disclosing the name of the village.

74. Interview with an authority from Kushk Robat Sanghi, Herat Province, October 2014.

75. Interview with an authority from Kushk Robat Sanghi, Herat Province, February 2019.

76. Interview with an authority from Kushk Robat Sanghi, Herat Province, February 2019

77. Interview with a member of the public from Kushk Robat Sanghi, Herat Province, February 2019.

78. Government of the Islamic Republic of Afghanistan, 2015, 11–12.

79. Leslie 2015, 9.

80. Interview with a key informant from Herat City, Herat Province, October 2014.

81. Interview with a member of the public from Herat City, Herat Province, October 2014

82. Interview with a member of the public from Herat City, Herat Province, October 2014

83. Interview with a member of the public from Herat City, Herat Province, October 2014

84. Interview with a member of the public from Herat City, Herat Province, October 2014

85. Interview with a member of the public from Herat City, Herat Province, October 2014

86. Interview with a member of the public from Herat City, Herat Province, October 2014

87. Interview with a member of the public from Herat City, Herat Province, October 2014; interview with a key informant from Herat City, Herat Province, October 2014.

88. Interview with a member of the public from Herat City, Herat Province, October 2014

89. Interview with a key informant from Herat City, Herat Province, October 2014.

90. Interview with a member of the public from Herat City, Herat Province, October 2014

91. Interview with a member of the public from Herat City, Herat Province, October 2014

92. Interview with an authority from Kushk Robat Sanghi, Herat Province, October 2014

93. Interview with a member of the public from Herat City, Herat Province, October 2014.

94. Interview with a key informant from Herat City, Herat Province, October 2014.

95. Interview with a member of the public from Herat City, Herat Province, October 2014.

96. Interview with a member of the public from Herat City, Herat Province, October 2014.

97. Interview with a key informant from Herat City, Herat Province, October 2014.
98. Interview with a key informant from Herat City, Herat Province, October 2014.
99. Interview with a member of the public from Herat City, Herat Province, October 2014
100. Interview with a key informant from Herat City, Herat Province, October 2014.
101. Barfield 2003; Barfield 2010.
102. Barfield 2003.
103. Algappa 1995; Nixon 2008; Noelle-Karimi 2006; Pain 2016.
104. Pain 2016.
105. Wardak 2003
106. Mielke 2013.
107. Murtazashvili 2016.
108. Larson and Coburn 2014, 2.

6. WAITING FOR DIGNITY

1. Malejacq 2019.
2. Bourdieu 1977, 192.
3. Galtung 1969.
4. While closely related, accessibility is different from an authority's ability to impact, which turns potential into actual authority. On the contrary, accessibility describes the perceived ability of *people* to access an authority. For instance, the NDS may be inaccessible but have an ability to impact.
5. Tyler 2004; Tyler 2006; Sturge et al. 2017; McCullough, Lacroix, and Hennessey 2020.
6. Arendt 1969.
7. Scharpf 1997; Scharpf 2003.
8. Tyler 2004; Tyler 2006; Mazerolle et al. 2013, 1.
9. Goodhand 2003.
10. Habermas 1984; Habermas 1987.
11. Barfield and Nojumi 2010.
12. Ruttig 2014a.
13. Arendt 1969.

BIBLIOGRAPHY

Abrams, P. "Notes on the Difficulty of Studying the State." *Journal of Historical Sociology* 1, no. 1 (1988): 58–89.

Achakzai, A. "Over 18,000 Police Officers Killed in Helmand in 15 Years." *Tolo News*, April 26, 2017. http://www.tolonews.com/afghanistan/over -18000-police-officers-killed-helmand-15-years.

Agnew, J. A. "Sovereignty Regimes: Territoriality and State Authority in Contemporary World Politics." *Annals of the Association of American Geographers* 95, no. 2 (2005): 437–461.

Ahmad, A. Jihad & Co. *Black Markets and Islamist Power.* New York: Oxford University Press, 2017.

Ahmadi, S., and L. Linke. "Struggling to Get a Quorum in Parliament: Fiddling the Figures and Suspending MPs." AAN, May 31, 2016. https:// www.afghanistan-analysts.org/en/reports/political-landscape/struggling -to-get-a-quorum-fiddling-the-figures-and-suspending-mps/.

Alcis, D. Mansfield, and G. Smith. "War Gains: How the Economic Benefits of the Conflict Are Distributed in Afghanistan and the Implications for Peace. A Case Study on Nimroz Province." *Lessons for Peace Report*, ODI, 2021.

Algappa, M. "The Anatomy of Legitimacy." In *Political Legitimacy in Southeast Asia. The Quest for Moral Authority*, ed. Muthiah Algappa, 11–30. Stanford, CA: Stanford University Press, 1995.

Amiri, R., and A. Jackson. "Taliban Attitudes and Policies Towards Education." *Centre for the Study of Armed Groups*, ODI working paper 601, 2021.

Amnesty International. *Afghanistan—Detainees Transferred to Torture: ISAF Complicity?* Melbourne: Amnesty International Publications, 2007. https://www.amnesty.ie/wp-content/uploads/2016/04/Afghanistan -Detainees-Transferred-to-Torture.pdf.

Amstutz, J. B. *Afghanistan—The First Five Years of Soviet Occupation.* Washington, DC: National Defense University Press, 1986.

Andersen, M. S. "Legitimacy in State-Building: A Review of the IR Literature." *International Political Sociology* no. 6 (2012): 205–219.

Andersson, R. *No Go World: How Fear Is Redrawing Our Maps and Infecting Our Politics.* Oakland: University of California Press, 2019.

Andersson, R., and F. Weigand. "Intervention at Risk: The Vicious Cycle of Distance and Danger in Mali and Afghanistan." *Journal of Intervention and Statebuilding* 9, no. 4 (2015): 519–541.

Andrew, C., and V. Mitrokhin. *The Mitrokhin Archive II: The KGB and the World.* London: Penguin, 2005.

Arendt, H. *On Violence.* New York: Harcourt, 1969.

Asia Foundation. *Afghanistan in 2009: A Survey of the Afghan People.* San Francisco: Asia Foundation 2009.

Asia Foundation. *Afghanistan in 2015: A Survey of the Afghan People.* San Francisco: Asia Foundation, 2015.

Asia Foundation. *Afghanistan in 2016: A Survey of the Afghan People.* San Francisco: Asia Foundation, 2016.

Asia Foundation. *Afghanistan in 2018: A Survey of the Afghan People.* San Francisco; Asia Foundation, 2018.

Asia Foundation. *Afghanistan in 2019: A Survey of the Afghan People.* San Francisco; Asia Foundation, 2019.

Barakzai, N. A. "Wolesi Jirga Sends Another Five MPs Home." *Pajhwok Afghan News,* April 22, 2017. https://pajhwok.com/2017/04/22/wolesi-jirga -sends-another-five-mps-home/.

Barfield, T. *Afghan Customary Law and Its Relationship to Formal Judicial Institutions.* Washington DC: United States Institute for Peace, 2003. http://www.usip.org/sites/default/files/file/barfield2.pdf.

Barfield, T. *Afghanistan—A Cultural and Political History.* Princeton, NJ: Princeton University Press, 2010.

Barfield, T., and N. Nojumi. "Bringing More Effective Governance to Afghanistan: 10 Pathways to Stability." *Middle East Policy* 17, no. 4 (2010): 40–52.

Bhatia, J., Jareer, N. and R. Mcintosh. "Community-Driven Development in Afghanistan: A Case Study of the National Solidarity Programme in Wardak." *Asian Survey* 58, no. 6 (2018): 1042–1065.

Beath, A., F. Christia, and R. Enikolopov. "The National Solidarity Programme: Assessing the Effects of Community-Driven Development in Afghanistan." *International Peacekeeping* 22, no. 4, (2015): 302–320.

Beetham, D. "Max Weber and the Legitimacy of the Modern State." *Analyse & Kritik* 13 (1991): 34–45.

Beetham, D. *The Legitimation of Power.* 2nd ed. Houndsmills, New York: Palgrave Macmillan, 2013.

Begon, J. "What are Adaptive Preferences? Exclusion and Disability in the Capability Approach." *Journal of Applied Philosophy* 32, no. 3, (2012): 241–257.

Berger, P. L., and T. Luckmann. *The Social Construction of Reality. A Treatise in the Sociology of Knowledge.* Garden City, NY: Doubleday, 1966.

Bhaskar, R. "Philosophy and Scientific Realism." In *Critical Realism. Essential Readings*, ed. M. Archer et. al. Oxon: Routledge, 1998.

Blau, P. M. "Critical Remarks on Weber's Theory of Authority." *American Political Science Review* 57. No. 2 (1963): 305–316.

Bliesemann de Guevara, B., and T. Reiber. "Popstars der Macht: Charisma und Politik." In *Charisma und Herrschaft: Führung und Verführung in der Politik*, ed. B. Bliesemann de Guevara and T. Reiber, 15–52. Frankfurt am Main: Campus Verlag, 2011.

Bottero, W., and N. Crossley. "Worlds, Fields and Networks: Becker, Bourdieu and the Structures of Social Relations." *Cultural Sociology* 5. No. 1 (2011): 99–119.

Boudon, R. "The Cognitive Approach to Morality." In *Handbook of the Sociology of Morality*, ed. S. Hitlin and S. Vaisey. New York: Springer, 2010.

Bourdieu, P. *Outline of a Theory of Practice.* Cambridge: Cambridge University Press, 1977.

Bourdieu, P. "Social Space and Symbolic Power." *Sociological Theory* 7, no. 1 (1989): 14–25.

Bourdieu, P. *The Field of Cultural Production.* Cambridge: Polity, 1993.

Bourdieu, P. "Rethinking the State: Genesis and Structure of the Bureaucratic Field." *Sociological Theory* 12, no. 1 (1994): 1–18.

Bourdieu, P. "Symbolic Capital and Social Class." *Journal of Classical Sociology* 13, no. 2 (2013): 299.

Bourdieu, P. *On the State: Lectures at the Collège de France 1989–1992*. Cambridge: Polity Press, 2020.

Bowden, M. "After Geneva—The New Challenges and Risks Facing NGOs and Civil Society in Afghanistan." *Lessons for Peace*, March 2021.

Bradsher, H. S. *Afghanistan and the Soviet Union*. Durham, NC: Duke University Press, 1983.

Burnham, P. "State." In *The Oxford Concise Dictionary of Politics*, ed. Ian Mclean and A. McMillan. Oxford: Oxford University Press, 2003.

Chayes, S. *The Punishment of Virtue*. London: Portobello Books, 2006.

Clark, K. "Kafka in Cuba: New AAN Report on the Afghan Experience in Guantánamo." Afghan Analyst Network, November 3, 2016. https://www
.afghanistan-analysts.org/kafka-in-cuba-new-aan-report-on-the-afghan
-experience-in-guantanamo/.

Clark, K. "Disbanding the ALP: A Dangerous Final Chapter for a Force with a Chequered History." *Afghan Analyst Network (AAN)*, October 6, 2020.
https://www.afghanistan-analysts.org/en/reports/war-and-peace/disbanding
-the-alp-a-dangerous-final-chapter-for-a-force-with-a-chequered-history/.

Clark, K., E. Gaston, F. Muzhary, and B. Osman. "Ghosts of the Past: Lessons from Local Force Mobilisation in Afghanistan and Prospects for the Future." Afghan Analyst Network (AAN) and the German Global Public Policy Institute (GPPi), July 1, 2020. https://www.afghanistan-analysts
.org/en/special-reports/new-special-report-ghosts-of-the-past-lessons-from
-local-force-mobilisation-in-afghanistan-and-prospects-for-the-future/.

Clark, K., and B. Osman. "More Militias? The Proposed Afghan Territorial Army in the Fight Against ISKP [Part 2]." *IndraStra Global* (2017):
https://nbn-resolving.org/urn:nbn:de:0168-ssoar-53877-2.

Coll, S. *Ghost Wars—The Secret History of the CIA, Afghanistan and Bin Laden, From the Soviet Invasion to September 10, 2001*. London: Penguin, 2004.

Constitution of Afghanistan, 1964. Afghanistan online. Accessed December 26, 2021. https://www.afghan-web.com/history/afghanistan-constitution
-of-1964/.

Constitution of Afghanistan, 1987. Afghanistan online. Accessed December 26, 2021. https://www.afghan-web.com/history/afghanistan-constitution
-of-1987/.

Constitution of Afghanistan, 2004. Afghanistan online, https://www.consti
-tuteproject.org/constitution/Afghanistan_2004.pdf?lang=en.

Crawford, N. C. and C. Lutz. "Human and Budgetary Costs to Date of the U.S. War in Afghanistan." Costs of War, Brown University, 2021. https://

watson.brown.edu/costsofwar/files/cow/imce/figures/2021/Human%20 and%20Budgetary%20Costs%20of%20Afghan%20War%2C%202001 -2021.pdf.

Dahl, R. A. *On Political Equality*. New Haven, CT: Yale University Press, 2006.

Delbrück, J. "Exercising Public Authority Beyond the State: Transnational Democracy and/or Alternative Legitimation Strategies?" *Indiana Journal of Global Legal Studies* 10, no. 1 (2003): 29–43.

Denney, L., R. Mallett, and D. Mazurana. *Peacebuilding and Service Delivery*. Tokyo: United Nations University Centre for Policy Research, 2015. http://i.unu.edu/media/cpr.unu.edu/attachment/1000/Peacebuilding -and-Service-Delivery.pdf.

Department of Defense (DoD). "Report on Progress Towards Security and Stability in Afghanistan (October)." 2011. https://www.globalsecurity.org /military/library/report/2011/afghanistan-security-stability_201110.htm.

Department of Defense (DoD). "Report on Progress Towards Security and Stability in Afghanistan (December)." 2012. https://dod.defense.gov /Portals/1/Documents/pubs/1230_Report_final.pdf.

Dodge, T. "Domestic Politics and State-Building." In *Afghanistan to 2015 and Beyond*, ed. T. Dodge and N. Redmann. Abdingdon, Oxon: Routledge, 2011.

Donati, J., and E. Amiri. "U.S. Military Moves to Clear 'Ghost Soldiers' from Afghan Payroll." *Wall Street Journal*, January 17, 2017.

Duffield, M. "Post-Modern Conflict: Warlords, Post-Adjustment States and Private Protection," *Civil Wars* 1, no. 1 (March 1998): 65–102.

Dupree, L. *Afghanistan*. Karachi: Oxford University Press, 1997 (1973).

Elias, N. *State Formation and Civilization*. Vol. 2 of *The Civilising Process*. Oxford: Blackwell, 1982 (1939).

Esser, D. "Security Scales: Spectacular and Endemic Violence in Post-Invasion Kabul, Afghanistan." *Environment & Urbanization* 26, no. 2, (2014): 373–388.

Evans, P. B., D. Rueschemeyer, and T. Skocpol. *Bringing the State Back In*. Cambridge: Cambridge University Press, 1985.

Ewans, M. *Afghanistan: A Short History of its People and Politics*. New York: Harper Collins, 2002.

Felbab-Brown, V. "The Dubious Joys of Standing Up Militias and Building Partner Capacity: Lessons from Afghanistan and Mexico for Prosecuting Security Policy Through Proxies." Brookings, July 21, 2015. https://www .brookings.edu/research/the-dubious-joys-of-standing-up-militias-and

-building-partner-capacity-lessons-from-afghanistan-and-mexico-for
-prosecuting-security-policy-through-proxies/.

Fitzgerald, D. "Report—Afghan National Army Numbers Inflated." *UN Tribune*, March 3, 2015. http://untribune.com/report-afghan-national-army
-numbers-inflated/.

Forugh, T. "How to Save Afghanistan's Democracy." *Foreign Policy*, February 5, 2015. http://foreignpolicy.com/2015/02/05/how-to-save-afghanistans
-democracy/.

Foschini, F. "Kabul's Expanding Crime Scene (Part 2): Criminal Activities and the Police Response." *Afghanistan Analysts Network*, February 21, 2020. https://www.afghanistan-analysts.org/en/reports/economy-development
-environment/kabuls-expanding-crime-scene-part-2-criminal-activities
-and-the-police-response/.

Franco, C., and A. Giustozzi. "Revolution in the Counter-Revolution: Efforts to Centralize the Taliban's Military Leadership." *Central Asian Affairs* 3 (2016): 249–286.

Friedrichs, J., and F. Kratochwil. "On Acting and Knowing: How Pragmatism Can Advance International Relations Research and Methodology." *International Organization* 63, no. 4 (2009): 701–731.

Friesendorf, C., and J. Krempel. "Militarized versus Civilian Policing: Problems of Reforming the Afghan National Police." PRIF Report, no. 102, 2011. https://www.hsfk.de/fileadmin/HSFK/hsfk_downloads/prif102.pdf.

Fukuyama, F. *State-Building—Governance and World Order in the 21st Century*. Ithaca, New York: Profile, 2004.

Fullerton, J. *The Soviet Occupation of Afghanistan*. London: Methuen, 1984.

Galtung, J. "Violence, Peace, and Peace Research." *Journal of Peace Research* 6, no. 3 (1969): 167–191.

Gaston, E. "Regulating Irregular Actors: Can Due Diligence Checks Mitigate the Risks of Working with Non-State and Substate Forces?" Research Report, Centre for the Study of Armed Groups, 2021.

Gerring, J. *Case Study Research—Principles and Practices*. New York: Cambridge University Press, 2007.

Giustozzi, A. "The Debate on Warlordism: The Importance of Military Legitimacy." LSE Crisis States Discussion Paper, no. 13, October 2005.

Giustozzi, A. *Empires of Mud: War and Warlords in Afghanistan*. London: Hurst & Company, 2009.

Giustozzi, A. "Hearts, Minds, and the Barrel of a Gun—The Taliban's Shadow Government." *Institute for National Strategic Studies Prism* 3 no. 2 (2012b): https://www.ciaonet.org/attachments/20157/uploads.

Giustozzi, A., and A. M. Ali. "The Afghan National Army After ISAF." Afghanistan Research and Evaluation Unit (AREU), Briefing Paper, 2016. http://www.areu.org.af/Uploads/EditionPdfs/1603E%20The%20Afghan %20National%20Army%20after%20ISAF.pdf.

Giustozzi, A. and A. Baczko. "The Politics of the Taliban's Shadow Judiciary, 2003–2013." *Central Asian Affairs* 1 (2014): 199–224.

Giustozzi, A., C. Franco, and A. Baczko, *Shadow Justice: How the Taliban Run Their Judiciary*. Kabul: Integrity Watch Afghanistan, 2016.

Goodhand, J. "From War Economy to Peace Economy?" Conference paper originally presented at State Reconstruction and International Engagement in Afghanistan, May 30–June 1, 2003. London School of Economics and Political Science and University of Bonn. http://eprints.lse.ac .uk/28364/1/Goodhand_LSERO_version.pdf.

Goodhand, J. "Contested Boundaries: NGOs and Civil–Military Relations in Afghanistan." *Central Asian Survey* 32, no. 3 (2013): 287–305.

Goodhand, J. and A. Hakimi. "Counterinsurgency, Local Militias, and State-building in Afghanistan." *United States Institute for Peace: Peaceworks*, no. 90, (2014): http://www.usip.org/sites/default/files/PW90-Counterinsurgency -Local-Militias-and-Statebuilding-in-Afghanistan.pdf.

Goodhand, J., and M. Sedra. "Rethinking Liberal Peacebuilding, Statebuilding and Transition in Afghanistan: An Introduction." *Central Asian Survey* 32, no. 3 (2013): 239–254.

Goodhand, J., A. Suhrke, and S. Bose. "Flooding the Lake? International Democracy Promotion and the Political Economy of the 2014 Presidential Election in Afghanistan." *Conflict, Security & Development* 16, no. 6 (2016): 481–500.

Government of the Islamic Republic of Afghanistan. *State of Afghan Cities 2015*. GoIRA: Kabul, 2015.

Gramsci, A. *Selection from the Prison Notebooks*. New York: International Publishers, 1971.

Green, N. "Introduction: A History of Afghan Historiography." In *Afghan History Through Afghan Eyes*. London: Hurst, 2015.

Groll, E. "The United States Has Outspent the Marshall Plan to Rebuild Afghanistan." *Foreign Policy*, July 30, 2014. http://foreignpolicy.com/2014

/07/30/the-united-states-has-outspent-the-marshall-plan-to-rebuild
-afghanistan/.

Habermas, J. "Hannah Arendt's Communications Concept of Power." *Social Research* 44, no. 1 (1977): 3–24.

Habermas, J. *Reason and the Rationalization of Society.* Vol. 1 of *The Theory of Communicative Action.* London: Heinemann, 1984.

Habermas, J. *Lifeworld and System: A Critique of Functionalist Reason.* Vol. 2 of *The Theory of Communicative Action.* Boston: Beacon, 1987.

Hagmann, T. and D. Péclard. "Negotiating Statehood: Dynamics of Power and Domination in Africa." *Development and Change* 41 (2010): 539–562.

Hansen, T. B. and F. Stepputat. "Introduction: States of Imagination." In *States of Imagination: Ethnographic Explorations of the Postcolonial State*, ed. T. B. Hansen and F. Stepputat. Durham, NC: Duke University Press, 2001.

Harding, L. "Afghan Massacre Haunts Pentagon." *The Guardian*, September 14, 2002. https://www.theguardian.com/world/2002/sep/14/afghanistan.lukeharding.

Herbert, S. "State Legitimacy in Afghanistan and the Role of the International Community." Helpdesk Research Report, October 1, 2014. http://www.gsdrc.org/docs/open/hdq1068.pdf.

Hinsch, W. (2008) "Legitimacy and Justice." In *Political Legitimation Without Morality?* Ed. J. Kuhnelt. London: Springer, 2008.

Hoffmann, K. and K. Vlassenroot. "Armed Groups and the Exercise of Public Authority: The Cases of the Mayi-Mayi and Raya Mutomboki in Kalehe, South Kivu." *Peacebuilding* 2, no. 2 (2014): 202–220.

Hoffmann, K., K. Vlassenroot, and G. Marchais. "Taxation, Stateness and Armed Groups: Public Authority and Resource Extraction in Eastern Congo." *Development and Change* 47, no. 6 (2016): 1434–1456.

Human Rights Watch. *The Forgotten War: Human Rights Abuses and Violations of the Laws of War Since the Soviet Withdrawal.* New York: Human Rights Watch, 1991. http://www.hrw.org/reports/1991/afghanistan/.

Human Rights Watch. *Blood-Stained Hands: Past Atrocities in Kabul and Afghanistan's Legacy of Impunity."* New York: Human Rights Watch, 2005. https://www.hrw.org/sites/default/files/reports/afghanistan0605.pdf.

Human Rights Watch. *They've Shot Many Like This: Abusive Night Raids by CIA-Backed Afghan Strike Forces.* New York: Human Rights Watch, 2019. https://www.hrw.org/report/2019/10/31/theyve-shot-many/abusive-night-raids-cia-backed-afghan-strike-forces.

International Crisis Group (ICG). "A Force in Fragments: Reconstituting the Afghan National Army." *Asia Report*, no. 190 (May 12, 2010). https://d2071andvipowj.cloudfront.net/190-a-force-in-fragments-reconstituting-the-afghan-national-army.pdf.

International Crisis Group (ICG). "The Future of the Afghan Local Police." *Asia Report*, no. 268 (2015): http://www.crisisgroup.org/~/media/Files/asia/south-asia/pakistan/268-the-future-of-the-afghan-local-police.pdf.

Irish Times. "Local Afghan Militia Beheads Four Islamic State Fighters." *Irish Times*, December 27, 2015. https://www.irishtimes.com/news/world/asia-pacific/local-afghan-militia-beheads-four-islamic-state-fighters-1.2477817.

Islamic Republic of Afghanistan. "Constitution of Afghanistan: Ratified January 26, 2004." Afghan Embassy, 2004. http://www.afghanembassy.com.pl/afg/images/pliki/TheConstitution.pdf.

Jackson, A. *Waiting for Dignity: Civilian-Insurgent Relations in Afghanistan.* London: C. Hurst & Co, 2021.

Jackson, A. "Politics and Governance in Afghanistan: The Case of Nangarhar Province." AREU Working Paper 16, 2014. http://www.areu.org.af/Uploads/EditionPdfs/Politics%20and%20Governance%20in%20Afghanistan%20the%20Case%20of%20Nangarhar%20Province.pdf.

Jackson, A. "Seeing like the Networked State: Subnational Governance in Afghanistan." *SLRC*, report 12, 2016. https://securelivelihoods.org/wp-content/uploads/RR12-Seeing-like-the-networked-state_Subnational-governance-in-Afghanistan.pdf.

Jackson, A., and R. Amiri. "Insurgent Bureaucracy: How the Taliban Makes Policy." *USIP, Peaceworks*, no 153 (November 2019).

Jackson, A., and F. Weigand. "The Taliban's War for Legitimacy in Afghanistan." *Current History* 118, no. 807 (April 2019) 143–148.

Jackson, A., and F. Weigand. "Rebel Rule of Law: Taliban Courts in the West and North-West of Afghanistan." Overseas Development Institute (ODI), 2020. https://cdn.odi.org/media/documents/Rebel_rule_of_law_Taliban_courts_in_the_west_and_north-west_of_Afghanistan.pdf.

Jackson, J., and B. Bradford. "Police Legitimacy: A Conceptual Review." *National Policing Improvement Agency* (September 29, 2010): http://ssrn.com/abstract=1684507.

Jackson, J., A. Z. Hug, B. Bradford, and T. R. Tyler. "Monopolizing Force? Police Legitimacy and Public Attitudes Towards the Acceptability of Violence." *Psychology, Public Policy and Law* 19, no. 4 (2013): 479–497.

Jackson, P. "Warlords as Alternative Forms of Governance Systems." *Small Wars and Insurgencies* 14, no. 2 (2003): 131–150.

Jalali, A. A. "Rebuilding Afghanistan's National Army." *Parameters*, Autumn 2002.

Jalali, A. A. *Afghanistan National Defense and Security Forces—Missions, Challenges, and Sustainability.* Washington DC: United States Institute of Peace, 2016. https://www.usip.org/sites/default/files/PW115-Afghanistan-National -Defense-and-Security-Forces-Mission-Challenges-and-Sustainability.pdf.

Johnson, T. H. *Taliban Narratives: The Use and Power of Stories in the Afghanistan Conflict.* London: Hurst, 2017.

Johnson, T. H., and R. J. Barnhart. "An Examination of Afghanistan's 2018 Wolesi Jirga Elections: Chaos, Confusion and Fraud." *Journal of Asian Security and International Affairs* 7, no. 1 (2020): 57–100.

Jones, S. C. "The KGB in Afghanistan: Defector's Documents Shed New Light on Soviet War." Woodrow Wilson International Center for Scholars, February 25, 2002. http://www.fas.org/sgp/news/2002/02/kgb-afgh.html.

Jones, S. G., and A. Muñoz. *Afghanistan's Local War: Building Local Defense Forces.* Santa Monica, CA: RAND Corporation, 2010. http://www.rand .org/content/dam/rand/pubs/monographs/2010/RAND_MG1002.pdf.

Kakar, P. "Tribal Law of Pashtunwali and Women's Legislative Authority." Harvard University Research Paper, 2003.

Kaldor, M. *New and Old Wars.* Cambridge: Polity, 2006.

Kaldor, M. "The Reconstruction of Political Authority in a Global Era." In *Persistent State Weakness in the Global Age,* ed. D. Kostovicova and V. Bojicic-Dzelilovic. Surrey: Ashgate, 2009.

Kalyvas, S. N. "'New' and 'Old' Civil Wars: A Valid Distinction?" *World Politics* 54, no. 1 (2001): 99–118.

Kalyvas, S. N. "The Urban Bias in Research on Civil Wars." *Security Studies* 13, no. 3 (2004): 160–190.

Karzai, H. *Rebuilding Afghanistan. Peace and Stability. Petersberg—2 December 2002. Annex 1.* https://unric.org/de/wp-content/uploads/sites/4/2002/12/decree.pdf.

Keen, D. *Complex Emergencies.* Cambridge: Polity, 2008.

Khaama Press. "ISIS, Taliban Announced Jihad Against Each Other." April 20, 2015. http://www.khaama.com/isis-taliban-announced-jihad-against-each -other-3206.

Khader, S. J. *Adaptive Preferences and Women's Empowerment.* Oxford: Oxford Scholarship Online, 2011.

Kraemer, K. "Charismatischer Habitus: Zur sozialen Konstruktion symbolischer Macht." *Berliner Journal für Soziologie* 12, no. 2 (2002): 173–187.

Kuhn, T. "The Natural and the Human Sciences." In *The Road Since Structure: Philosophical Essays, 1970–1993*, ed. James Conant and John Haugeland, 216–223. Chicago: University of Chicago Press, 2000 (1989).

Larson, A. "Political Parties in Afghanistan." *USIP Special Report*, 362. March 2015. https://www.usip.org/sites/default/files/SR362-Political-Parties-in-Afghanistan.pdf.

Larson, A. "House of the People? Afghanistan's Parliament in 2015." *Conflict, Security & Development* 16, no. 6 (2016): 595–612.

Larson, A., and N. Coburn. "Why Afghanistan's Provincial Council Elections Matter." United States Institute of Peace (USIP), Peacebrief 170. March 26, 2014. http://www.usip.org/sites/default/files/PB170-Why-Afghanistan%E2%80%99s-Provincial-Council-Elections-Matter.pdf.

Larson, A., and N. Coburn. "Afghan Views of Government and Elections Legitimacy Pending." United States Institute of Peace (USIP), Special Report 409, July 2017. https://www.usip.org/sites/default/files/2017-07/sr409-afghan-views-of-government-and-elections-legitimacy-pending.pdf.

Leslie, J. "Political and Economic Dynamics of Herat." *USIP Peaceworks*, no. 107, 2015. https://www.usip.org/sites/default/files/PW107-Political-and-Economic-Dynamics-of-Herat.pdf.

Liebl, V. "Pushtuns, Tribalism, Leadership, Islam and Taliban: A Short View." *Small Wars & Insurgencies* 18, no. 3 (2007): 492–510.

Lister, S. "Caught in Confusion: Local Governance Structures in Afghanistan." AREU Briefing Paper, March 2005. https://areu.org.af/wp-content/uploads/2005/03/505E-Caught-in-Confusin-BP-print.pdf.

Lund, C. "Twilight Institutions: Public Authority and Local Politics in Africa." *Development and Change* 37, no. 4 (2006): 685–705.

Maass, P. "Gul Agha Gets His Province Back." *New York Times Magazine*, January 6, 2002. http://www.nytimes.com/2002/01/06/magazine/gul-agha-gets-his-province-back.html.

Mac Ginty, R. "Everyday Peace: Bottom-Up and Local Agency in Conflict-Affected Societies." *Security Dialogue* 45, no. 6 (2014): 548–564.

Mac Ginty, R. *Everyday Peace: How So-Called Ordinary People Can Disrupt Violent Conflict.* Oxford: Oxford University Press, 2021.

MacKinlay, J. "Defining Warlords." *International Peacekeeping* 7, no. 1 (2000): 48–62.

Malejacq, R. *Warlord Survival: The Delusion of State Building in Afghanistan.* Ithaca, NY: Cornell University Press, 2019.

Malejacq, R., and D. Mukhopadhyay. "The 'Tribal Politics' of Field Research: A Reflection on Power and Partiality in 21st-Century Warzones." *Perspectives on Politics* 14, no. 4 (2016): 1011–1028.

Maley, W. "Provincial Reconstruction Teams in Afghanistan—How They Arrived and Where They Are Going." *NATO Review,* July 1, 2007. https://www.nato.int/docu/review/articles/2007/07/01/provincial-reconstruction-teams-in-afghanistan-how-they-arrived-and-where-they-are-going/index.html.

Maley, W. *The Afghanistan Wars.* 3rd ed. London: Red Globe Press, 2021.

Malkasian, C. *War Comes to Garmser: Thirty Years of Conflict on the Afghan Frontier.* Oxford: Oxford University Press, 2016.

March, J. G., and J. P. Olsen. *Democratic Governance.* New York: Free Press, 1995.

March, J. G., and J. P. Olsen. "The Institutional Dynamics of International Political Orders." *International Organization* 52, no. 4 (1998): 943–969.

March, J. G., and J. P. Olsen. "The Logic of Appropriateness." In *The Oxford Handbook of Public Policy,* ed. R. E. Goodin, M. Moran, and M. Rein. Oxford: Oxford University Press, 2008. DOI: 10.1093/oxfordhb/9780199548453.003.0034.

Marten, K. "Warlords and Governance." In *The Transnational Governance of Violence and Crime,* ed. A.P. Jakobi et al. Online edition: Palgrave Macmillan, 2013.

Marty, F. J. "On the Trail of the Islamic State in Afghanistan." *Foreign Policy,* April 5, 2016. http://foreignpolicy.com/2016/04/05/afghanistan-islamic-state-taliban/.

Mashal, M. "C.I.A.'s Afghan Forces Leave a Trail of Abuse and Anger." *New York Times,* December 31, 2018. https://www.nytimes.com/2018/12/31/world/asia/cia-afghanistan-strike-force.html.

Mashal, M., and J. Sukhanyar. "Face-Off Between Strongmen Exposes Afghanistan's Political Rifts." *New York Times,* March 23, 2016. http://www.nytimes.com/2016/03/24/world/asia/face-off-between-strongmen-exposes-afghanistans-political-rifts.html.

Mazerolle, L., Bennett, S., Davis, J., Sargeant, E., and M. Manning. "Legitimacy in Policing: A Systematic Review." Campbell Systematic Reviews, 2013: 1. https://doi.org/10.4073/csr.2013.1.

McCullough, A., A. Lacroix, and G. Hennessey. "Reconstructing Our Understanding of the Link Between Services and State Legitimacy." SLCR working paper 87, 2020.

Melton, K. "Focusing on State Legitimacy: Succeeding in Kandahar and Beyond." *USAID Study*, March 4, 2015.

Miakhel, S. "Understanding Afghanistan: The Importance of Tribal Culture and Structure in Security and Governance." *United States Institute of Peace (USIP)*, 2009. http://w.pashtoonkhwa.com/files/books/Miakhel-Importance-Of TribalStructuresInAfghanistan.pdf.

Miakhel, S., and N. Coburn. "Many Shuras Do Not a Government Make: International Community Engagement with Local Councils in Afghanistan." United States Institute of Peace (USIP), Peacebrief 50, 2010. https://www.usip.org/sites/default/files/resources/pb50.pdf.

Mielke, K. "Constructing the Image of a State: Local Realities and International Intervention in North-East Afghanista." In *Local Politics in Afghanistan: A Century of Intervention in the Social Order*, ed. K. Schetter. London: Hurst, 2013.

Migdal, J. S. and K. Schlichte. "Rethinking the State." In *The Dynamics of States—The Formation and Crises of State Domination*, ed. K. Schlichte. Aldershot/Burlington: Ashgate, 2005.

Miliband, R. *The State in Capitalist Society*. New York: Basic Books, 1969.

Mitrokhin, V. "The KGB in Afghanistan." Cold War International History Project, Working Paper, 40, 2002. https://www.wilsoncenter.org/sites/default/files/media/documents/publication/WP40-english.pdf.

Mukhopadhyay, D. *Warlords, Strongman Governors, and the State in Afghanistan*. New York: Cambridge University Press, 2014.

Münch, P. "Local Power Structures and International Military Intervention. A Review of Developments in Badakhshan and Kunduz Provinces." AAN Thematic Report, March 2013. http://www.afghanistan-analysts.org/wp-content/uploads/2013/11/20131110_PMunch_Kunduz-final.pdf.

Murtazashvili, J. B. "Informal Federalism: Self-Governance and Power Sharing in Afghanistan." *Publius: The Journal of Federalism* 44, no. 2 (2014): 324–343.

Murtazashvili, J. B. *Informal Order and the State in Afghanistan*. New York: Cambridge University Press, 2016.

Naadim, B. A. "Electoral Reform Panel Starts Recording People's Views." *Pajhwok*, August 2, 2015. https://pajhwok.com/2015/08/02/electoral-reform-panel-starts-recording-peoples-views/.

NATO. "ANA Base Pay and Incentive Pays." *NTM-A*, 2011.

NATO. "Afghan National Security Forces (ANSF)." NATO Media Back-grounder, October 2013. http://www.nato.int/nato_static/assets/pdf/pdf _2013_10/20131018_131022-MediaBackgrounder_ANSF_en.pdf.

NATO. *ISAF Security Force Assistance Guide.* Brussels: NATO, 2014a.

NATO. *RS Security Force Assistance Guide 3.1,* Brussels: NATO, 2014b.

Nixon, H. "Subnational State-Building in Afghanistan." Afghanistan Research and Evaluation Unit, Synthesis Paper Series, 2008. https://areu.org.af /wp-content/uploads/2016/01/806E-Subnational-State-Building-SP -print.pdf.pdf.

Noelle-Karimi, C. "Village Institutions in the Perception of National and International Actors in Afghanistan." ZEF Working Paper Series, no. 65. ZEF: University of Bonn, 2006. http://www.zef.de/fileadmin/webfiles /downloads/projects/amudarya/publications/ZEF_Working_Paper_Amu _Darya_Series_26.pdf.

Nojumi, N. *The Rise of the Taliban in Afghanistan—Mass Mobilization, Civil War, and the Future of the Region.* New York: Palgrave, 2002.

North, D. C. *Structure and Change in Economic History.* New York: W. W. Norton, 1981.

Olson, M. "Dictatorship, Democracy, and Development." *American Political Science Review* 87, no. 3 (1993): 567–576.

Osman, B. "Toward Fragmentation? Mapping the Post-Omar Taleban." *Afghan Analyst Network*, November 24, 2015. https://www.afghanistan -analysts.org/en/reports/war-and-peace/toward-fragmentation-mapping -the-post-omar-taleban/.

Osman, B. "The Islamic State in 'Khorasan': How It Began and Where It Stands Now in Nangarhar." Afghan Analysts Network, July 27, 2016.

Osman, B., and K. Clark. "More Militias? Part 2: The Proposed Afghan Territorial Army in the Fight Against ISK." Afghan Analysts Network, September 23, 2017. https://www.afghanistan-analysts.org/en/reports/war -and-peace/more-militias-part-2-the-proposed-afghan-territorial-army-in -the-fight-against-iskp/.

Osman, B., and A. Gopal. "Taliban Views on a Future State." NYU Center on International Cooperation, July 2016.

Pain, A. "Using Village Context Analysis in Afghanistan: Methods and Wider Implications." Secure Livelihoods Research Consortium Working Paper, 46, 2016.

Perito, R. M. "Afghanistan's Police—The Weak Link in the Security Sector." *USIP Special Report*, 227. August 2009. https://www.usip.org/sites/default /files/afghanistan_police.pdf.

Pinker, S. *The Better Angels of our Nature—Why Violence Has Declined*. New York: Viking, 2011.

Qaane, E., and T. Ruttig. "A Half-Solution: Provincial Councils Get Oversight Authority Back—for the Time Being." *Afghan Analyst Network (AAN)*, 2015. https://www.afghanistan-analysts.org/a-half-solution-provincial-councils -get-oversight-authority-back-for-the-time-being/.

Quilty, A., and M. Cole. "The CIA's Afghan Proxies, Accused of War Crimes, Will Get a Fresh Start in the U.S." *The Intercept*, October 6, 2021. https:// theintercept.com/2021/10/05/zero-units-cia-afghanistan-taliban/.

Rangelov, I., and M. Theros. "Abuse of Power and Conflict Persistence in Afghanistan." *Conflict, Security & Development* 12, no. 3 (2012): 227–248.

Rashid, A. *Taliban—Islam, Oil, and the New Great Game in Central Asia*. London: I. B. Tauris, 2001.

Reiter, B. "The Hermeneutic Foundations of Qualitative Research." *Qualitative Methods* 4, no. 2 (2006): 18–24.

Reno, W. "Reinvention of an African Patrimonial State: Charles Taylor's Liberia," *Third World Quarterly* 16, no. 1 (March 1995), 109–120.

Rotberg, R. "The Failure and Collapse of Nation-States: Breakdown, Prevention, and Repair." In *When States Fail: Causes and Consequences*, 1–50. Princeton, NJ: Princeton University Press, 2004.

Roy, O. "Development and Political Legitimacy: The Cases of Iraq and Afghanistan." *Conflict, Security & Development* 4, no. 2 (2004): 167–179.

Rubin, B. "The Fragmentation of Afghanistan." *Foreign Affairs* 68, no. 5 (1989): 150–168.

Rubin, B. *The Fragmentation of Afghanistan: State Formation and Collapse in the International System*. New Haven, CT: Yale University Press, 2002.

Rubin, B. "Peace Building and State-Building in Afghanistan: Constructing Sovereignty for Whose Security." *Third World Quarterly* 27, no. 1 (2006): 175–185.

Ruttig, T. "Still Temporary and Exclusive: A New Leadership for Jamiat." Afghan Analyst Network, July 5, 2013. https://www.afghanistan-analysts. org/still-temporary-and-exclusive-a-new-leadership-for-jamiat/.

Ruttig, T. "Elections (31): Afghanistan's Confusing Election Maths." *Afghan Analyst Network (AAN)*, June 19, 2014a. https://www.afghanistan-analysts .org/elections-31-afghanistans-confusing-election-maths/.

Ruttig, T. "Flash to the Past: Long Live Consensus—A Look Back at the 2003 Constitutional Loya Jirga." Afghan Analyst Network (AAN), January 28, 2014b. https://www.afghanistan-analysts.org/flash-to-the-past-long-live -consensus-a-look-back-at-the-2003-constitutional-loya-jirga/.

Sabarre, N., S. Solomon, and T. Van Blarcom. "Securing Legitimacy: Examining Indicators of State Legitimacy in Afghanistan." D3 Systems, May 2013. http://www.d3systems.com/wp-content/uploads/2013/11/Securing-Legitimacy _SabarreSolomonVanBlarcom-v3.pdf.

Saikal, A. *Modern Afghanistan: A History of Struggle and Survival*. London: Tauris, 2006.

Saltmarshe, D., and A. Medhi. "Local Governance in Afghanistan—A View from the Ground." Afghan Research and Evaluation Unit (AREU) Synthesis Paper, 2011. https://areu.org.af/wp-content/uploads/2016/02/1114E -Local-Governance-in-Afghanistan-SP-2011.pdf.

Scharpf, F. W. "Economic Integration, Democracy and the Welfare State." *Journal of European Public Policy* 4, no. 1 (1997): 18–36.

Scharpf, F. W. "Problem-Solving Effectiveness and Democratic Accountability in the EU." MPIfG Working Paper 03/1, February 2003. http://www .mpifg.de/pu/workpap/wp03-1/wp03-1.html.

Schmeidl, S. "The Contradictions of Democracy in Afghanistan: Elites, Elections and 'People's Rule' Post-2001." *Conflict, Security & Development* 16, no. 6 (2016): 575–594.

Schmelzle, C. "Evaluating Governance. Effectiveness and Legitimacy in Areas of Limited Statehood." SFB-Governance Working Paper Series, No. 26, Research Center (SFB) 700, Berlin, 2011.

Schneider, C. "The Afghan Police Through the Ages: 250 Years of Change." *EUPOL Afghanistan*, 2012. http://www.eupol-afg.eu/node/453.

Sedra, M. "Police Reform in Afghanistan: An Overview." In *Confronting Afghanistan's Security Dilemma*, ed. M. Sedra. *BICC brief* 28, 2003.

Sedra, M. "An Uncertain Future for Afghanistan's Security Sector." *Stability: International Journal of Security & Development* 3, no. 1 (2014): 35, 1–16.

Sen, A. "Gender and Cooperative Conflicts." In *Persistent Inequalities: Women and World Development*, ed. I. Tinker. Oxford: Oxford University Press, 1990.

Serle, J., and J. Purkiss. "Drone Wars: The Full Data." Bureau of Investigative Journalism, January 1, 2017. https://www.thebureauinvestigates.com /stories/2017-01-01/drone-wars-the-full-data.

Sharan, T. "The Dynamics of Informal Political Networks and Statehood in Post-2001 Afghanistan: A Case Study of the 2010–2011 Special Election Court Crisis." *Central Asian Survey* 32, no. 3 (2013): 336–352.

Sharan, T. and S. Bose. "Political Networks and the 2014 Afghan Presidential Election: Power Restructuring, Ethnicity and State Stability." *Conflict, Security & Development* 16, no. 6 (2016): 613–633.

SIGAR (Special Investigator General for Afghanistan Reconstruction). "Special Inspector General for Afghanistan Reconstruction, SIGAR 16–3 Audit Report, Afghan Local Police: A Critical Rural Security Initiative Lacks Adequate Logistics Support, Oversight, and Direction." Special Inspector General for Afghanistan Reconstruction, SIGAR 16–3 Audit Report, October 2015. https://www.sigar.mil/pdf/audits/SIGAR-16-3-AR.pdf.

SIGAR (Special Investigator General for Afghanistan Reconstruction). "Quarterly Report to the United States Congress." SIGAR, January 30, 2021. https://www.sigar.mil/pdf/quarterlyreports/2021-01-30qr.pdf.

Smith, G. "What Kandahar's Taliban Say." In *Decoding the New Taliban—Insights from the Afghan Field*, ed. A. Giustozzi. New York: Columbia University Press, 2009.

Stepputat, F., and J. Larsen. "Global Political Ethnography: A Methodological Approach to Studying Global Policy Regimes." DIIS Working Paper, 2015: 01.

Sturge, G., R. Mallett, J. Hagen-Zanker, and R. Slater. *Tracking Livelihoods, Services and Governance: Panel Survey Findings from the Secure Livelihoods Research Consortium* London: Secure Livelihoods Research Consortium, 2017. https://securelivelihoods.org/wp-content/uploads/Tracking-livelihoods-service-delivery-and-governance_Panel-survey-findings-from-the-Secure-Livelihoods-Research-Consortium.pdf.

Suebsaeng, A., and S. Bixby. "Team Biden: Will People 'Give a Shit' if Afghanistan Erupts?" *Daily Beast*, May 24, 2021. https://www.thedailybeast.com/team-biden-will-people-give-a-shit-if-afghanistan-erupts.

Tadjbakhsh, S., and M. Schoiswohl. "Playing with Fire? The International Community's Democratization Experiment in Afghanistan," *International Peacekeeping* 15, no. 2 (2008): 252–267.

Tarzi, A. "Tarikh-i Ahmad Shahi: The First History of 'Afghanistan.'" In *Afghan History Through Afghan Eyes*, ed. N. Green. London: Hurst, 2015.

Tilly, C. *Coercion, Capital, and European States, AD 990–1992*. Oxford: Blackwell, 1992.

Tyler, T. R. "Enhancing Police Legitimacy." *Annals of the American Academy of Political and Social Science* 593, no. 1 (2004): 84–99.

Tyler, T. R. "Psychological Perspectives on Legitimacy and Legitimation." *Annual Review of Psychology* 57 (2006): 375–400.

UNAMA. *Afghanistan. Annual Report 2015. Protection of Civilians in Armed Conflict.* Kabul: UNAMA, February 2016. https://unama.unmissions.org/sites/default/files/poc_annual_report_2015_final_14_feb_2016.pdf.

UNAMA. *Afghanistan. Annual Report 2016. Protection of Civilians in Armed Conflict.* Kabul: UNAMA, February 2017. https://unama.unmissions.org/sites/default/files/protection_of_civilians_in_armed_conflict_annual_report_8feb_2016.pdf.

UNAMA. *Afghanistan. Annual Report 2019. Protection of Civilians in Armed Conflict.* Kabul: UNAMA, February 2020. https://reliefweb.int/sites/reliefweb.int/files/resources/afghanistan_protection_of_civilians_annual_report_2019_-_22_february.pdf.

UNAMA. *Afghanistan. Protection of Civilians in Armed Conflict. Midyear Update: 1 January to 30 June 2021.* Kabul: UNAMA, July 2021. https://unama.unmissions.org/sites/default/files/unama_poc_midyear_report_2021_26_july.pdf.

United Nations. "Agreement on Provisional Arrangements in Afghanistan Pending the Re-establishment of Permanent Government Institutions." Bonn, December 2001a. https://peacemaker.un.org/sites/peacemaker.un.org/files/AF_011205_AgreementProvisionalArrangementsinAfghanistan%28en%29.pdf.

United Nations. "Security Council Resolution 1386 (2001)." Adopted by the Security Council at its 4443rd meeting, on December 20, 2001b. https://documents-dds-ny.un.org/doc/UNDOC/GEN/N01/708/55/PDF/N0170855.pdf?OpenElement.

U.S. Department of State. "Agreement for Bringing Peace to Afghanistan Between the Islamic Emirate of Afghanistan Which Is Not Recognized by the United States as a State and Is Known as the Taliban and the United States of America." February 29, 2020. https://www.state.gov/wp-content/uploads/2020/02/Agreement-For-Bringing-Peace-to-Afghanistan-02.29.20.pdf.

van Linschoten, A. S., and F. Kuehn. *An Enemy We Created—The Myth of the Taliban-Al Qaeda Merger in Afghanistan, 1970–2010.* London: C. Hurst, 2012.

van Linschoten, A. S., and F. Kuehn. *The Taliban Reader: War, Islam and Politics*. London: C. Hurst, 2019.

Vincent, S., F. Weigand, and H. Hakimi. "The Afghan Local Police—Closing the Security Gap?" *Stability: International Journal of Security & Development* 4, no. 1 (2015): Art. 45, 1–26.

Wacquant, L. J. D. Foreword to *The State Nobility* by Pierre Bourdieu, ix–xxii. Stanford, CA: Stanford University Press, 1996.

Wardak, A. "Jirga—A Traditional Mechanism of Conflict Resolution in Afghanistan." University of Glamorgan, Centre for Criminology, 2003.

Weaver, M. A. "Lost at Tora Bora." *New York Times Magazine*, September 11, 2005, http://www.nytimes.com/2005/09/11/magazine/lost-at-tora-bora.html ?_r=0.

Weber, M. " 'Objectivity' in Social Science and Social Policy." In *Max Weber on The Methodology of Social Sciences*, ed. E. A. Shils and H. A. Finch, 90–98. Glencoe, Illinois: Free Press, 1949 (1904).

Weber, M. *The Theory of Social and Economic Organization*. New York: The Free Press, 1964.

Weber, M. "Die drei reinen Typen der legitimen Herrschaft." In *Gesammelte Aufsätze zur Wissenschaftslehre*, ed. J. Wincklemann. Tübingen: J. C. B. Mohr (Paul Siebeck), 1973 (1922).

Weber, M. *Wirtschaft und Gesellschaft. Grundriss der Verstehenden Soziologie*. Tübingen: J. C. B. Mohr (Siebeck), 1980 (1921).

Weber, M. *Wirtschaft und Gesellschaft. Die Wirtschaft und die gesellschaftlichen Ordnungen und Mächte. Nachlaß. Teilband 4: Herrschaft. Studienausgabe der Max-Weber-Gesamtausgabe Band I/22-4*. Tübingen: J. C. B Mohr (Siebeck), 2009a.

Weber, M. "Politics as a Vocation." In *From Max Weber: Essays in Sociology*, ed. B. S. Turner. London: Routledge, 2009b (1948).

Weigand, F. "Human vs. State Security: How Can Security Sector Reforms Contribute to State-Building? The Case of the Afghan Police Reform." LSE International Development Working Paper Series, 13–135, 2013. http://eprints.lse.ac.uk/62690/1/WP135.pdf.

Weigand, F. "Kabul: Bridging the Gap Between the State and the People." In *Cities at War: Global Insecurity and Urban Resistance*, ed. M. Kaldor and S. Sassen. New York: Columbia University Press, 2020.

Weigand, F., and R. Andersson. "The 'Bunker Politics' of International Aid in Afghanistan." *Journal of Intervention and Statebuilding* 13, no. 4 (2019): 503–523.

Wilde, A., and K. Mielke. "Order, Stability, and Change in Afghanistan: From Top-Down to Bottom-Up State-Making." *Central Asian Survey* 32, no. 3 (2013): 353–370.

Williams, B. *The Last Warlord.* Chicago: Chicago Review Press, 2013

Williams, M. "Afghanistan's Legitimacy Crisis." *The Guardian*, October 20, 2009. https://www.theguardian.com/commentisfree/2009/oct/20/afghanistan -hamid-karzai-election.

Wyler, L. S., and K. Katzman. "Afghanistan: U.S. Rule of Law and Justice Sector Assistance." *Congressional Research Service.* November 9, 2010. https://fas.org/sgp/crs/row/R41484.pdf.

Yanow, D. "What's Political About Political Ethnography? Abducting Our Way Toward Reason and Meaning." *Qualitative & Multi-Method Research* 7, no. 2 (2009): 33–37.

Yassari, N., and M. H. Saboory. "Sharia and National Law in Afghanistan." *Jura Gentium*, 2010.

Zucchino, D., and F. Abed. "On Afghan Highways, Even the Police Fear the Taliban's Toll Collectors." *New York Times*, November 1, 2020. https:// www.nytimes.com/2020/11/01/world/asia/afghanistan-taliban-bribery .html.

INDEX

Page numbers in *italics* indicate figures or tables.

Abdullah, Abdullah: National Unity Government formation, 59; A. Noor support in 2009 and 2014 elections, 172; as Northern Alliance member, 59; Rabbani and Massoud close ties to, 59; 2014 presidential election stalemate, 59; 2019 presidential election stalemate, 60

accountability, of authority, 278

actions: assessment of Taliban, 228–229; of authority, 6, 22, 40, 276; of community authorities, 265; logic of consequences and appropriateness in, 299n52; strongmen judged by, 178–179

actual authority, 33

Afghanistan, 3–4; authority competition in, 29; Biden withdrawal from, 1, 60–61; constitution of 2004, 65, 106–107, 120; Doha Agreement and withdrawal from, 60, 189; international donors for reconstruction of, 57; IS-K growing influence concern in, 211–212; multiple authority in, 29, 31; NATO Training Mission integration, 73, 78; patronage networks in, 25, 144–146; provinces and districts of, *14*; Soviet troops 1989 removal, 56; Taliban control of, 1, 2, 17, 51, 182, 184, 185, 186, 187, 210, 213–214, 230

Afghanistan War, 1, 24, 62

Afghan Local Police (ALP), 69, 82, 135; different areas varied role of, 92–93; illegal activities of, 92; insurgent fighting role of, 89–90; interviews with public on security from, 91–92; MoI command structure for, 90; NATO on, 90; program end in 2020, 93; strongmen control of, 91, 93, 144; U.S. program design for, 90; varied views on, 102–103

Afghan National Army (ANA),
77, 303n50; Asia Foundation on,
70, 303n44; Bonn Agreement
reestablishment of, 72; civilian
casualties from, 309n168;
ghost soldiers in, 73, 303n51;
harmful interaction absence,
136; interviews with public on
lack of corruption of, 74–75,
85; interviews with public on
Taliban infiltration of, 75–76;
ITSA establishment of, 72; Kabul
support of, 100–101; legitimacy
of, 53, 70, 76, 98–99, 133–134;
military equipment lack, 73, 75;
positive view from interviews
with public, 73–74; public
perception of legitimacy, 53, 70,
76, 98–99; rural Afghanistan
insurgents fight, 71; security of,
71, 73, 82, 101; urban security
and state authority symbol of,
71, 73; U.S. financial support for,
72; visibility of, 135; as voluntary
force and strength, 69
Afghan National Army Territorial
Force, 93
Afghan National Police (ANP),
69; Asia Foundation on, 70,
303n44; AUP of, 79; conscription
authority by, 81; corruption
of, 78, 82, 83–85, 88, 101–102;
EUPOL in 2007 and, 77–78;
foreign countries impact
on, 77; Germany training of,
77–78, 81; insurgent fighting
by, 79; interviews with public

on community cooperation
with, 86–87, 89; interviews with
public on criminal violence of,
84; interviews with public on
legitimacy of, 53, 70, 99–100;
interviews with public on
positive perception of, 86–87;
Kabul police academy in
1989, 77; lack of trust for, 82;
military objectives of, 79;
public perceptions of, 82–87;
self-perceptions of, 80–82;
Turkey training of, 77; units
and departments of, 78–79; U.S.
training of, 77–78
Afghan National Security Forces
(ANSF): from Bonn Agreement,
69; civilians killed and injured
by, 70; legitimacy of, 98–104;
security and law enforcement by,
52, 59; Taliban war with, 60
Afghan state: Bonn Agreement
on construction of new, 57;
Bourdieu and, 27–28; court
corruption in, 48; fields of,
137; government to describe,
299n40; Herat City and
conflict resolution mechanisms
of, 259–261; international
community monopoly failure
in, 3; international support
decline for, 65; interviews with
public on idea of, 49–50; Islamic
Republic of Afghanistan 2001
new, 65; Kabul coercion history,
53–62; loya jirga use by, 63;
Mujahedin groups fight with,

64; national identity of, 138; network character of, 298n34; A. Noor lost support of, 180–181; official name changes for, 61–62; political order role in, 52; public perception of legitimacy in, 274–275; public security expectation in, 103; religion, tradition and participation in, 62–69; Taliban 2020 negotiations with, 60; Taliban fight with, 3; 2001 development plan for, 3; from 2001 to 2021, 6, 20, 51–52. *See also* executive branch; judicial branch; legislative branch

Afghan Uniformed Police (AUP), of ANP, 79

Agreement for Bringing Peace to Afghanistan (Doha Agreement) (2020), Taliban and, 60, 189

Agreement on Provisional Arrangements in Afghanistan Pending the Re-Establishment of Permanent Government Institutions (Bonn Agreement): ANA reestablishment by, 72; ANSF established from, 69; on *loya jirga* for transitional government, 58; on new Afghan state construction, 57; on Rabbani as interim head of state, 58

Akhundzada, Haibatullah, 189

ALP. *See* Afghan Local Police

Amanullah (king), of Barakzai dynasty (1919-1929): constitution reform by, 54; Kabul

modernization attempts, 54; *loya jirga* use by, 63, 119; secular laws institution by, 105

American Combined Security Transition Command, counterinsurgency operations support by, 73

Amin, Hazifullah: Soviet death of, 55; Taraki killed by order of, 55

Amnesty International, on NDS violence, 94–95

ANA. *See* Afghan National Army

Anglo-Afghan War, 53–54

ANP. *See* Afghan National Police

ANSF. *See* Afghan National Security Forces

arena of interaction: Bourdieu and, 29; political order as authority, 22–31, *28*; state hierarchical position in, 29

Arendt, Hannah: on authority, 277, 300n71; on power, 31, 300n71; on violence, 42, 48

armed forces, Zahir Qadir, Shirzai and A. Noor control of, 178

Arsala family, 314n33; influence of, 146–148; Zahir Qadir of, 140, 146

Asia Foundation, 67, 80; on ANA and ANP, 70, 303n44; on CDCs, 239; on insurgencies, 319n32

AUP. *See* Afghan Uniformed Police

authority: accessibility of, 276, 327n4; accountability of, 278; actions of, 276; actor visibility importance, 135, 275; actual, 33; Arendt on, 300n71; Bourdieu on prestige of, 300n70; coercion and, 21, 136;

authority (*continued*)
    competition for, 29, 31; failed
        legitimate state, 120–121; history
        of, 277; impact ability of, 33,
        136; instrumental legitimacy
        and needs response from,
        33–34; interaction modes
        and, 276; interactive dignity
        and public service by, 49,
        276–277; interconnection of,
        273; interviews with public on
        attitude of, 49, 134; legitimacy
        and actions of, 22; output
        legitimacy and actions of, 40;
        perception based on personal
        experiences, 135; physical force
        as action of, 42; political order
        as arena of interaction for, 22–31,
        28; potential, 33; self-perception
        of, 43–45; violence experience
        legitimacy of another, 48;
        voluntary obedience to, 21; Zahir
        Qadir, Shirzai and A. Noor
        individual, 177
authority for social control: actions,
    history, or idea expectations and
    perceptions, 6; command and
    obedience relationship in, 30;
    history of, 19, 40; propaganda of,
    16; right to, 40; self-perception
    compared to public perception
    of, 6, 10, 16; service delivery of, 8.
    See also instrumental legitimacy;
    substantive legitimacy

Balkh Province: A. Noor governor
    appointment, 172; strongmen in,
    170–173

Barakzai dynasty: Amanullah (king)
    of, 54, 63, 71, 105, 119; Kabul
    control through 1973, 54
Barfield, T.: on community
    governance, 263, 266; on fairness
    perceptions, 280; on judicial
    branch, 107, 117; on Taliban
    formation, 186
Beetham, D., 43–44, 301n75
Behsod district, 230; conflict
    resolution procedures in, 219;
    Taliban coercion in, 220; Taliban
    negative views, 218; Taliban
    recruitment in, 219
beliefs: Beetham legitimacy and,
    43–44, 301n75; for empirical
    legitimacy, 32; substantive and
    instrumental legitimacy needs
    and, 35, 40–41, *41*; substantive
    legitimacy rightfulness, 34;
    Weber on needs and, 39
Biden, Joseph, 1, 60–61
Bonn Agreement. *See* Agreement
    on Provisional Arrangements
    in Afghanistan Pending the
    Re-Establishment of Permanent
    Government Institutions
Bourdieu, P.: Afghan state and,
    27–28; arena of interaction
    and, 29; on authority prestige,
    300n70; on field concept of
    state, 27; on interaction, 47; on
    monopolization of symbolic
    violence, 26, 27, 48; on network
    analysis, 298n34; political order
    state understanding, 25–28, 145,
    273, 288; on power dynamics, 25;
    state definition of, 26

bribes, 78, 97; conflict resolution and paying, 217, 262, 268; in judicial branch, 111, 114, 117; in police force, 101; in state system, 48, 49, 247, 262

Bush, George W., 2, 54, 57, 59

case study approach, 12–13

CDCs. *See* community development councils

Char Asiab, Taliban insecurity concerns in, 212, 229

charisma, legitimacy and, 36

Citizens' Charter, 193, 235, 269; for food provision, 66–67; to link CDCs to state, 239

civilians: ANA casualties of, 309n168; ANSF death and injury of, 70; Taliban deaths and injury of, 188

civil society activists, 114, 132, 260, 262, 272; as key informants, 17, 74, 82, 86, 96, 112, 167

coercion, 6, 282; by authority, 21, 136; authority legitimacy and, 136; Daoud Kahn increase in, 55; involuntary obedience basis of, 32; Kabul history of, 53–62; perceptions of, 42; of police, 134; Shirzai and Zahir Qadir as threat for, 178; social pressure as, 42; strongmen use of, 141; Surkh Rod and Behsod Taliban, 220

Combined Security Transition Command-Afghanistan program, of U.S., 78

communicative action, Habermas on, 35, 280

community authority, 270–271; actions of, 265; adaptability of, 273–274; Barfield on, 263, 266; conflict resolution role, 7, 237–238, 264; councils as, 235, 237–240; elders as, 235, 241, 244; external factors impacting, 236; in Herat City, 259–263; in Herat Province, 251–263; individual actors for, 240–243; instrumental and substantive legitimacy for, 236; khans as, 241–242; in Kushk Robat Sangi district, 251–259; legitimacy of, 7–8, 243; maliks, 240–241, 244–245, 251; militarized commanders as, 242; mullahs as, 235, 242, 249; in Nangarhar Province, 243–251; Pashtunwali code and, 235; PCs and, 239; security provision and, 268–269; Shirzai and, 240–241; in Surkh Rod district, 243–251; tradition and, 266–267, 269

community development councils (CDCs), of NSP, 238, 249, 269–270; Asia Foundation on, 239; in Kushk Robat Sangi, 253

conflict: globalization impact on violent, 24; legitimacy and armed, 41–42; outside institutionalized bureaucratic systems, 21

conflict resolution, 15, 134; Behsod district procedures in, 219; community authority role in, 7, 237–238, 264; councils procedures in, 237–238, 259; elders for, 115, 247; government as body for, 109–110;

conflict resolution (*continued*)
Herat City and mechanisms of,
259–261; Herat Province judicial
system, 115–116; interviews of
public on Taliban, 185; interviews
with public on choice of, 117–118,
138–139; in Kushk Robat Sangi
district, 253–255; paying bribes
and, 217, 262, 268; from shura
councils, 110, 112, 115; Taliban
mechanisms of, 185, 210, 217–218,
231–232, 247–248, 256–258; varied
codes of law for, 104–105; Zahir
Qadir procedures of, 169

conflict-torn spaces: instrumental
legitimacy importance in,
35–36; legitimacy and, 20–50;
monopolization of force
diminished in, 20–21; physical
force in, 298n34; for political
control, 24; political order in,
28–31; substantive legitimacy in,
38; Weber state understanding
and, 23–24

conscription: after Amanullah, 71;
ANP authority on, 81

constitution: Amanullah reform of,
54; of Najibullah, 64, 119; of 1964,
1987, 1990, 119–120

constitution, of 2004, 65; judicial
branch and, 106–107; National
Assembly two houses, 120

convenience, needs-based
expectations of, 47

corruption, 1, 208, 250, 280; Afghan
state court, 48; of ANP, 78, 82,
83–85, 88, 101–102; of elders,

248; interviews with public
on ANA lack of, 74–75, 85; of
judicial branch, 48, 106, 108–109,
111, 112–118, 134; of NDS, 95; of
Shirzai, 148

councils: CDCs, of NSP, 238–239,
249, 253, 269–270; as community
authority, 235, 237–240; conflict
resolution procedures in,
237–238; Herat City conflict
resolution and, 259; Kushk
Robat Sangi district local,
254–255; mediation focus of, 237;
Mujahedin groups establishment
of, 238; Pashtunwali cultural
code hierarchical system of, 236;
PCs, 239, 249, 263, 270; rural
Afghanistan local, 110, 112, 115;
Surkh Rod district development,
244. *See also* shura

critical realism, 11

Daesh. *See* Islamic State Khorasan
Province; Tehrik-i-Taliban
Pakistan

Daoud Kahn, Mohammed:
coercion increase from,
55; PDPA power to, 54–55;
power seizure by, 54–55; Saur
Revolution killing of, 55

democratic system, input and
output legitimacy in, 37–38

Department for the Promotion of
Virtue and Prevention of Vice,
of Taliban, 77

development councils, in Surkh Rod
district, 244

Din Mohammad, 146

Doha Agreement. *See* Agreement for Bringing Peace to Afghanistan

Dostum, Abdul Rashid, 55; as Afghanistan vice president, 141; Ghani 2014 election support, 172; A. Noor rivalry with, 170–171; Qala Zaini massacre of, 141, 143; as strongman, 141; U.S. funding for, 143

Durand Line, Soviet Union military aid and, 71

Durrani, Ahmad Shah (king), 63

dynastic state, Bourdieu on, 26–27

education, Taliban policies of, 192

elders: as community authority, 235, 241, 244; for conflict resolution, 115, 247; corruption of, 248

elections: participation difficulties in, 121; public perceptions of, 67; rural Afghanistan participation inability, 122; SNTV and losing candidates vote in, 122

Electoral Reform Commission (ERC), 121

empirical legitimacy, 31, 32

ERC. *See* Electoral Reform Commission

ethnography, 17–18

EUPOL. *See* European Union Police Mission

European states: Bourdieu state understanding from, 26; monopolization of physical force legitimacy, 24; Weber on, 24

European Union Police Mission (EUPOL), 2007, 77–78

executive branch, of Afghan state: ALP, 69, 82, 89–93, 102–103, 135, 144; ANA and, 53, 69, 70–77, 82, 101; ANP, 53, 69, 70, 77–89, 99–100, 303n34; ANSF and, 52, 59, 69–70, 98–104; NDS, 69, 93–98

fairness, value-based expectations of, 47–48

Faryab Province, 13, 17; Taliban-controlled area of, 185, 230; Taliban justice system in, 224–228

Farza district, Taliban insecurity concerns in, 212–213, 229

Fazly, Fazel, 61

First Anglo-Afghan War (1839-1842), 54

fraud, in 2014 presidential election, 120–121

Germany, ANP training by, 77–78, 81

Ghani, Ashraf: Afghanistan fleeing by, 61; community level interventions by, 66; Dostum 2014 election support, 172; ERC establishment for election process, 121; National Dining Table program of, 66; National Unity Government formation, 59; A. Noor 2019 election support, 173; NSP project of, 238; Taliban 2019 peace process, 66;

Ghani, Ashraf (*continued*)
Taliban fight from, 66; 2014
presidential election stalemate,
59; 2019 presidential election
stalemate, 60
ghost soldiers, in ANA, 73, 303n51
globalization, violent conflicts
impacted by, 24
governance: Barfield on community,
263, 266; legislative branch and
king, 119; Nangarhar Province
strongmen, 146–149, 317n79; of
strongmen, 143–146; Taliban
structure of, 190
government: Afghan state described
as, 299n40; as conflict resolution
body, 109–110; Jalalabad control
by, 214–215; Kushk Robat Sangi
insecurity from, 256; Taliban
commander on corruption of, 1

Habermas, J., 35, 280
Haq, Abdul, 146–147, 155
Hekmatyar, Gulbuddin, 55, 215,
314n29; judicial immunity for
crimes of, 141; Kabul shelling by,
141; as strongman, 141; Western
funding for, 143
Herat City: council conflict
resolution and, 259; land rights
conflicts in, 260; PCs in,
263; state conflict resolution
mechanisms in, 259–261;
traditional community authority
in, 259–261, 264–265
Herat Province, 13, 17; Herat City
community authority and,

259–263; judicial system conflict
resolution in, 115–116; Kushk
Robat Sangi district community
authority, 251–259; Taliban-
controlled area of, 185, 230;
Taliban justice system in, 224–228
Herrschaft domination, Weber on, 30
Hezb-e Islami Khales, 314n30
Hezb-e Islami political party, 120,
215, 314n29
High Council of the Islamic
Emirate of Afghanistan, Rasoul
movement of, 191
House of the Elders. *See* Meshrano
Jirga
House of the People. *See* Wolesi
Jirga
human dignities, value-based
expectations of, 47–48
Human Rights Watch: on Kabul
attacks, 55–56; on KPF violence,
96–97

ideal type of state, Weber on, 23–24,
36
idea of state, 49–50, 137–138, 283–2285
impact ability, by authority, 33, 136
informal conflict mechanisms, in
rural Afghanistan, 110
input legitimacy, 40, 137; in
democratic system, 37–38
instability: Kuhn on state, 22–23;
Taliban and rural Afghanistan,
58; Weber on obedience, 34
institutionalized bureaucratic
systems: conflict outside of, 21;
political order and, 20

instrumental legitimacy, 6, 280;
authority response to needs
and, 33–34; beliefs and needs
in, 35, 40–41, *41*; for community
authority, 236; conflict-torn
spaces importance of, 35–36;
constant change of, 42–43; modes
of interaction importance, 47–48;
needs-based expectations and, 47;
of A. Noor, 175, 181; of H. Noor,
143; rational-choice theory and,
34; of Shirzai, 143; substantive
legitimacy vs., 33–35; violence
impact on, 42; of Zahir Qadir, 143
instrumental rationality, 35
insurgencies: ALP fighting role
against, 89–90; American
Combined Security Transition
Command counterinsurgency
support, 73; ANA and rural
Afghanistan fight against,
71; ANP fighting against, 79;
Asia Foundation on, 319n32; of
Taliban, 21, 184, 187, 291
interactive dignity, 4, 45–47, 50, 272;
Afghanistan political order, 273–
275; authority public service and,
49; authority self-perception
of legitimacy, 285–287; idea of
state, 283–285; interactions and,
281–283; justice and security
examples, 280–281; legitimacy
and, 8–9; limits of, 287–289;
public perceptions of legitimacy,
275–279; statebuilding failure,
289–294; violence and legitimacy
relationship, 48

international community:
Afghanistan reconstruction
funds from, 57; Afghan state
monopoly failure and, 3; Afghan
state support decline, 65;
strongmen empowered by, 143
International Security Assistance
Force (ISAF): extension of, 58;
Resolute Support Mission 2015
replacement of, 59; UN Security
Council establishment of, 57
Inter-Services Intelligence (ISI),
of Pakistan: money and
weapons channeled through,
55; strongmen connection with,
163, 167
interviews with authorities, 16; of
ANP, 80–82; on ANP legitimacy,
53, 70, 99–100; on judicial
branch, 107–109; on legitimacy
claims, 19; on NDS, 95; of
Shirzai, 149–154; Taliban judges,
10; of Zahir Qadir, 154–163
interviews with former and active
Taliban, 194–206; on Afghan
state corruption, 208; on Afghan
state illegitimacy, 209–210;
on Afghan state perceived
injustices, 208; as followers, 207;
on legitimacy claims, 208–209;
negative personal experiences
of, 208; personal motives, 207;
substantive purposes, 207
interviews with public, 10, 16;
on ALP security, 91–92; on
ANA, 73–76, 82, 85; on ANA
legitimacy, 53, 70, 76, 98–99;

interviews with public (*continued*)
on ANA military equipment
lack, 75; on ANA positive view,
73–74; on ANA security, 73,
82, 101; on ANP, 82–87, 99; on
authority action importance,
46; on authority attitude, 49,
134; on conflict resolution
choice, 117–118, 138–139; criticism
reluctance for A. Noor, 174; on
how authority gained, 46; on
idea of state, 49–50; on modes
of interaction, 46; on NDS,
96; on perceived legitimacy,
18–19; on positive view of ANA,
73–74; on services expectations,
138; on strongmen as coercive
authorities, 142–143, 164; on
Surkh Rod conflict resolution
future, 248; in Taliban controlled
areas, 17; on Taliban security
1996–2001, 210; on warlord
security interference, 86; on what
authority stands for, 46. *See also*
public perceptions
involuntary obedience, coercion as
basis of, 32
ISAF. *See* International Security
Assistance Force
*ISAF Security Force Assistance (SFA)
Guide*, 65
ISI. *See* Inter-Services Intelligence
IS-K. *See* Islamic State Khorasan
Province
Islamic Emirate of Afghanistan,
Taliban establishment of, 56, 186,
302n17

Islamic Republic of Afghanistan, as
2001 new Afghan state, 65
Islamic Sharia law: religious
authority application of, 105;
Taliban implementation of, 64,
77, 106, 107
Islamic State Khorasan Province
(IS-K), 3, 183; Afghanistan
growing influence concern,
211–212; Kabul violent attacks
from, 212; Nangarhar Province
district control, 191; Osman
on evolution of, 191; Taliban
attacks by, 62; TTP allegiance
to, 191; violence reputation,
191; Zahir Qadir on members
beheading, 140
Islamic Transitional State of
Afghanistan (ITSA), ANA
establishment and, 72

Jackson, A., 148, 190
Jalalabad: description of, 214;
government control of, 214–215;
interviews with public on
Taliban strong negative views,
216; Taliban complex threat, 213–
218; Taliban conflict resolution
procedures in, 217–218; Taliban
personal experiences in, 216–217;
Taliban presence in, 215, 229
Jamiat-e Islami party, 317n83; A.
Noor of, 171
jihadi commanders: Dostum, 55, 141,
143, 170–172; Hekmatyar, 55, 141,
143, 215, 314n29; insecurity from,
164, 167; Massoud, 55, 59, 302n16;

A. Qadir, 55, 146–147, 156–158;
Rabbani, 55, 58, 59, 186
judicial branch, of Afghan state,
137; Barfield on, 107, 117; bribes
in, 111, 114, 117; code of laws
conflict, 105; constitution of
2004 and, 106–107; corruption
of, 48, 106, 108–109, 111, 112–118,
134; government and criminal
cases, 245–246; Herat Province
conflict resolution in, 115–116;
Islamic Sharia law and, 64, 77,
105, 106, 107; legal pluralism of,
105; Pashtunwali cultural code
and urban, 114; people demand
for justice, 116–118; perceived
legitimacy of, 107–108; public
perceptions in rural Afghanistan,
109–113; public perceptions in
urban Afghanistan, 113–116; rural
Afghanistan remote, 117; secular
laws incorporation, 105; self-
perception of, 138; traditional
customary law and, 104; in urban
Afghanistan, 113–114, 117–118. See
also justice system, Taliban
justice: in normative legitimacy, 32;
people demand for, 116–118
justice system: rural Afghanistan
local council, 110, 112, 115; Taliban,
112–113, 192–193, 224–228, 264

Kabul: as Afghanistan capital, 53;
Al-Zahra Mosque attack in,
102; Amanullah modernization
attempts, 54; ANA support in,
100–101; ANP police academy
in, 77; Barakzai dynasty
control through 1973, 54; Bonn
Agreement stability in, 58; civil
deaths between 1992 and 1995,
56; fall of, 2; Hekmatyar shelling
of, 141; Human Rights Watch on
attacks in, 55–56; IS-K violent
attacks in, 212; late1980s attacks
in, 55; Mujahedin competing
groups in, 56; Najibullah control
until 1992 of, 56; A. Noor
ties with, 171–172; Parliament
building construction in, 118–119;
power struggles in, 53; suicide
attackers and criminals in, 210–
213; Taliban 1995 bombardment,
56; Taliban 1996 control of, 186;
Taliban 2021 entry into, 61–62;
Taliban control from 1996-2001,
210, 213; Taliban insecurity
in 2014-2015, 211, 213; Taliban
physical violence in, 48, 51, 211,
229; violent crime increase in, 88;
women liberal lifestyle in, 54
Kandahar: Shirzai as governor 1992-
1994, 147, 150–151; Taliban 1994
control of, 186
Karwan Fidaye (suicide convoy),
221, 321n75
Karzai, Hamid: presidential system
of, 58; A. Qadir appointment by,
157; Shirzai governor promotion
by, 150–151; Zahir Qadir
deteriorated relationship with,
158–159
key informants, civil society activists
as, 17, 74, 82, 86, 96, 112, 167

KhaD. *See*
Khedamat-e-Atlaat-e-Dawlati
Khalilzad, Zalmay, 60
Khan, Ismail, 155, 195–196
khans, as community authority,
241–242
Khedamat-e-Atlaat-e-Dawlati
(KhaD): as judicial power, 106;
NDS as successor to, 94; Soviet
Union training of, 94; Taraki
creation of, 94; violent torture
and murder reputation, 94
Khogyani district, Taliban in,
221–223, 230
Khost Protection Force (KPF):
CIA backing of, 96–97; Human
Rights Watch on violence of,
96–97
Kuhn, T., 22–23
Kushk Robat Sangi district: CDCs
in, 253; community authority
in, 251–259; community
authority security provision, 257;
conflict resolution in, 253–255;
government insecurity in, 256;
in Herat Province, 251–259; local
councils in, 254–255; Taliban
conflict resolution in, 256; Taliban
presence in, 252–253, 258–259

land-grabbing, by warlords, 165, 166
law enforcement, by ANSF, 52, 59
legal pluralism, judicial branch and,
105
legislative branch, of Afghan state,
118, 123–133; House of the Elders,
119, 120; House of the People,
119–122; king governance and,
119; Melli Jirga and, 119; MP, 121;
Najibullah National Assembly,
119; remote access to, 119; SNTV
system and, 120, 122; Taliban
Inner Shura, 119–120; Zahir
Shah Parliament houses, 119. *See
also* Parliament
legitimacy: accessible and
predictable procedures of, 8;
analytical dimensions of, 39–43,
41; of ANSF, 98–104; armed
conflict and, 41–42; of authority,
6; authority actions and, 22;
beliefs and needs divide, 35,
40–41, *41*; Bourdieu on symbolic
capital and, 26–27; charisma
and, 36; in conflict-torn spaces,
35–39; defined, 20, 31; empirical,
31, 32; European states physical
force monopolization, 24;
instrumental vs. substantive, 21,
33–35; interviews with public on
ANP, 53, 70, 99–100; of judicial
branch, 107–108; knowledge of,
31–33; normative, 31–32; official
statements on, 44; perceptions
and views on, 3, 32–33; personal
claims of, 44; rational-legal,
36–38, *37*; within rational-legal
contexts, *37*, 37–38; rightfulness
and usefulness divide in, 35; Roy
on, 68; security and justice factors
for, 15; service delivery and, 38–39,
67–68; traditional, 36, 67–68,
243; voluntary obedience basis
of, 32; Weber foundation of, 4.

See also instrumental legitimacy; substantive legitimacy

local legitimacy, 44–45; of maliks, 241; Taliban concerns, 193

logic of appropriateness, in action, 299n52

logic of consequences, in action, 299n52

loya jirga (grand assembly of elders), 178; on Afghanistan transitional government, 58; Afghan state use of, 63; Amanullah use of, 63, 119; of Ghani for 2019 Taliban peace process, 66

Machalgha practice, of conflict parties deposit, 111

Mahaz-e Milli, 147, 194, 314n36

mahaz fighting units, of Taliban, 190

Malejacq, R., 145–146; on warlords, 273–274

Maley, W.: on Shirzai, 147; on strongmen as American warlords, 143

maliks, as community authority, 240, 251; as community representative, 241; conflict resolution by, 241, 244–245; local legitimacy of, 241; Murtazashvili on, 241; state link with, 241; traditional legitimacy of, 243

Marten, K., 145

Massoud, Ahmad Shah, 55, 302n16; Abdullah close ties to, 59

mediation focus, of councils, 237

member of Parliament (MP), 135, 137; as criminals, 130; public

2015 lack of confidence in, 121; public perceptions of, 129–133; self-perceptions of, 122–129; as uncaring, 131–132

Meshrano Jirga (House of the Elders): constitution of 2004 approval of, 120; king appointment of, 119; 2004 provincial and district council election of, 120

militarized commanders, as community authority, 242

military: ANA equipment lack, 73, 75; ANP objectives of, 79; interviews with public on ANP replacement by, 84–85; Soviet Union Durand Line aid, 71; Taliban structure of, 189–190

Ministry of Interior (MoI): ALP integration into command structure of, 90; A. Noor and Dostum forced joined force, 171; A. Noor deputy minister of, 159

modes of interaction: instrumental and substantive legitimacy importance, 47–48; interviews with public on importance of, 46

Mohib, Hamdullah, 61

MoI. See Ministry of Interior

monopolization of force, 274; conflict-torn spaces diminishment of, 20–21; European states war legitimacy for, 24; of A. Noor, 172, 176, 177, 180; in political order, 20; strongmen and, 145; Weber state understanding and, 25

MP. *See* member of Parliament

Mujahedin groups: Afghan
state fight with, 64; councils
establishment by, 238; Kabul
competition from, 56; Mahaz-e
Milli as, 147, 194, 314n36;
Northern Alliance and, 57;
organized police force removal
by, 77; Soviet Union fight
against, 71, 186

Mukhopadhyay, D., 171, 172, 180

mullahs, 235, 249; Murtazashvili
on, 242; PDPA prosecution of,
242; in Surkh Rod district, 244;
Taliban and, 242

Murtazashvili, J. B.: on maliks, 241;
on mullahs, 242

Nadir Shah, Mohammed (king)
(1929-1933): *loya jirga* for election
of, 63; PDPA monarchy end of,
64; reform abolishment by, 54

Najibullah, Mohammad:
constitution of, 119; Kabul
control until 1992, 56; Kabul
police academy and, 77; as KhaD
director 1980-1985, 94; *loya jirga*
constitution ratification and,
64; National Assembly of, 119;
Taliban capture and killing of, 56

Nangarhar Province, 230; armed
groups in, 215–216; Hazrat Ali
as strongman in, 148; IS-K
2015 violent attacks in, 214;
IS-K district control in, 191;
Jackson on power struggle and

violence in, 148; Shirzai governor
appointment in 2005, 147–148,
151–152; Shirzai resignation from,
152; some positive strongmen
views in, 168–169; strongmen
governance of, 146–149, 317n79;
Taliban control form 1996-2001,
214; Zaher Qadir and, 146; M.
Zaman as strongman in, 148

National Assembly, of Najibullah,
119

National Dining Table program, of
Ghani, 66

National Directorate of Security
(NDS), 69, 93; Amnesty
International on violence of,
94; corruption of, 95; direct
presidential report by, 94;
as domestic and foreign
intelligence agency, 94–95;
human rights violations
accusations, 136; interviews
with public on, 96; interview
with authority on, 95; as KhaD
successor, 94; legitimacy of,
133–134, 282; Rasoul support
from, 191; U.S. violence support
of, 96–97; vague views on, 103;
violence of, 94–98; visibility of,
135; Zahir Qadir meeting with,
160

National Resistance Front of
Afghanistan, in 2021, 302n16

National Solidarity Programme
(NSP), 240; CDCs in, 238–239;
Ghani project of, 238

National Unity Government, Ghani and Abdullah formation of, 59

NATO. *See* North Atlantic Treaty Organization

NDS. *See* National Directorate of Security

needs-based expectations, of costs, predictability and convenience, 47

network: Afghan state character of, 298n34; Bourdieu on, 298n34

NGOs. *See* nongovernmental organizations

Nojumi, N., 280

nongovernmental organizations (NGOs), development shuras establishment, 238

Noor, Atta, 142, 156; Abdullah 2009 and 2014 elections support, 172; armed forces control by, 178; Balkh governor appointment, 172; as Deputy of MoI, 159; Dostum rivalry with, 170–171; Ghani 2019 election support, 173; individual authority of, 177; instrumental legitimacy of, 175, 181; of Jamiat-e Islami party, 171; Kabul ties with, 171–172; monopolization of force of, 172, 176, 177, 180; Mukhopadhyay on, 171, 172; public lack of trust of, 178; public perceptions of, 173–177; resignation of, 173

normative legitimacy, 31–32

North Atlantic Treaty Organization (NATO): Afghanistan

integration into Training Mission of, 73, 78; on ALP, 90

Northern Alliance. *See* United Islamic Front for the Salvation of Afghanistan

NSP. *See* National Solidarity Programme

Obama, Barack, 59

obedience: involuntary, 32; voluntary, 21, 32, 34; Weber on instability of, 34

official statements, of legitimacy, 44

Omar, Mullah, 186; death of, 189

Operation Enduring Freedom (October 2001), 57

Osman, B., 191

output legitimacy, 137; authority actions and, 40; in democratic system, 37–38; violence establishment of, 42

Parliament: House of the Elders of, 119, 120; House of the People of, 119; Melli Jirga 1977 replacement of, 119; SNTV system election of, 120; Zahir Qadir as deputy speaker of, 142; Zahir Qadir election to, 161; of Zahir Shah, 119

Pashtunwali cultural code, 64, 68, 235; elements of, 236; hierarchical system of councils in, 236; Taliban support of, 187; urban judicial system and, 114

patronage networks, in Afghanistan, 25, 145–146

PCs. *See* provincial councils

People's Democratic Party of
Afghanistan (PDPA), Soviet:
Daoud power from, 54–55;
mullahs prosecuted by, 242;
Nadir Shah monarchy end by,
64; religious vocabulary ban
from constitution, 106

perceptions, 10–12; of coercion,
42; of legitimacy, 3, 32–33, 42;
of Taliban, 7. *See also* public
perceptions

personal claims, of legitimacy, 44

personal motives, for legitimacy, 44,
207, 286–287

personal motives, self-perceptions of
authority and, 44, 207, 286–287

physical force, 41, 274; as authority
action, 42; in conflict-torn
spaces, 298n34; European states
and, 24; Taliban in Kabul, 48, 51.
See also violence

police, 7, 77; bribes for, 101;
checkpoints, 6; coercion of, 134;
distrust of, 130. *See also* Afghan
Local Police; Afghan National
Police

political control: as authority arena
of interaction, 28, *28*; conflict-
torn spaces for, 24

political order, 5, 21; Afghan state
role in, 52; authority and,
22–31, *28*; Bourdieu's state
understanding, 25–28, 145, 273,
288; distinct authority from
2001-2021, 273; institutionalized
bureaucratic systems and, 20;

interactive dignity and, 273–275;
lack of defined functions, 273;
monopolization of force in, 20;
state in conflict-torn spaces,
28–31; state role in Afghanistan,
52; Weber's state understanding,
23–25, 273, 288

political parties: Hezb-e Islami, 120,
215, 314n29; legislative branch
minor role of, 120

potential authority, 33

power: Arendt on, 31, 300n71;
Bourdieu on dynamics of, 25;
statehood as field of, 298n32;
symbolic capital and state, 27

predictability, needs-based
expectations of, 47

presidential election, Ghani and
Abdullah stalemate in 2019, 60

presidential election, of 2014: fraud
in, 120–121; Ghani and Abdullah
stalemate in, 59

presidential system, of Karzai, 58

provincial capitals, Taliban capture
of, 61

provincial councils (PCs), 239, 249,
270; in Herat City, 263

provincial reconstruction teams
(PRTs), UN Security Council
establishment of, 58–59

public perceptions: of Afghan state
legitimacy, 274–275; of ANA
legitimacy, 53, 70, 76, 98–99;
of ANP, 82–87; of authority
for social control, 6, 10, 16; of
elections, 67; of interactive
dignity legitimacy, 275–279;

of judicial branch in rural Afghanistan, 109–113; of judicial branch in urban Afghanistan, 113–116; of MP, 129–133; of A. Noor, 173–177; of state courts, 53; of strongmen, 163–170; of Taliban, 185. *See also* interviews with public

Qadir, Abdul, 55, 146–147, 156; assassination of, 157–158
Qadir, Zahir Hajji: as Afghan Parliament deputy speaker, 142, 154; armed forces control by, 178; as coercive threat, 178; conflict resolution procedures of, 169; imprisonment of, 155; individual authority of, 177; instrumental legitimacy of, 143; interview with authority of, 154–163; on IS-K beheading, 140; Karzai relationship deterioration, 158–159; legitimacy self-perception of, 161–162, 179; NDS meeting with, 160; Parliament election of, 161; on personal power of, 155; security perception of, 169; as strongman, 140, 154–163; substantive legitimacy claim, 177
Qala Zaini massacre, of Dostum, 141, 143
Quetta Shura, 190–192, 200

Rabbani, Burhanuddin, 55, 186; Abdullah close ties to, 59; Bonn Agreement on interim head of state, 58

Rasoul, Mohammad: High Council of the Islamic Emirate of Afghanistan movement of, 191; Quetta Shura 2015 war declaration by, 191–192; U.S. and NDS support of, 191
rational-choice theory, instrumental legitimacy and, 34
rational legality, of state, 49
rational-legal legitimacy, 36–38, 37, 40
rational-legal sources, of substantive legitimacy, 36–38, 37, 40
Relief Effort for Afghan Communities and Households (REACH) program, 66–67
religion: in Afghan state, 62–69; Taliban legitimacy on basis of, 64
research study: authorities and population interviews, 10, 16; case study approach, 12–13; data analysis, 18–20; data collection methods, 15–18, 297n24; ethnography and, 17–18; methodology, 9–10; on perceptions, 10–12
Resolute Support Mission, ISAF 2015 replacement by, 59
respect, value-based expectations of, 47–48
Roy, O., 68
rural Afghanistan: conflict resolution mechanisms in, 110; election participation inability, 122; informal conflict mechanisms in, 110; local council justice system, 110, 112, 115; *Machalgha* practice in, 111;

rural Afghanistan (*continued*)
Pashtunwali cultural code in,
64; remote judicial system in,
117; symbolic violence and, 104;
Taliban and instability in, 58;
Taliban control of, 184, 187;
Taliban justice system, 112–113;
wealthy strongmen as authorities
in, 64

Sadozai Durrani dynasty, 54
Saur Revolution (1978), 119; Daoud
Khan death in, 55; government
community authority violence
after, 242
Second Anglo-Afghan War, 71
secular laws, Zahir Shah and,
105–106
security, 309n168; ANA urban
symbol of, 71, 73; by ANSF,
52, 59; interviews with public
on NDS, 96; interviews with
public on state responsibility
for, 118; Kushk Robat Sangi
district community authority
for, 257; in normative
legitimacy, 32; restrained use of
violence and, 49; substantive
legitimacy expectation of
coordinated, 281; Taliban
provision of, 195; warlords
as provider of, 301n72; Zahir
Qadir perception of, 169
Security Force Assistance (SFA), 65
self-perceptions of authority, 43;
of ANP, 80–82; interactive
dignity and legitimacy, 285–287;

in judicial branch, 138; local
legitimacy and, 44–45; of MP,
122–129; official statements of,
44; personal motives and, 44,
207, 286–287; public perception
compared to, 6, 10, 16; of Shirzai,
154, 179; of Taliban, 185; of Zahir
Qadir, 161–162, 179
service delivery, legitimacy and,
38–39, 67–68
SFA. *See* Security Force Assistance
Sherzad district, Taliban in, 221–223,
230
Shirzai, Gul Agha, 142; armed
forces control by, 178; as
coercive threat, 178; confidence
of, 153–154; corruption of, 148;
development projects of, 148,
151; individual authority of, 177;
instrumental legitimacy of,
143; interview with authority
of, 149–154; Karzai governor
promotion of, 150–151; legitimacy
self-perception of, 154, 179;
Maley on, 147; Nangarhar
reconstruction program of,
151–153; provincial governor in
2005, 147; resignation of, 149; on
Soviet Union war, 149–150; as
strongman, 149–154; substantive
legitimacy claim, 177
shura (councils), 237; conflict
resolution from, 110, 112,
115; NGOs establishment
of development, 238; urban
Afghanistan judicial cases to,
115–116

single, nontransferable vote (SNTV) system: losing candidates vote from, 122; for Parliament election, 120

SNTV. *See* single, nontransferable vote

social action, Weber on, 35

social constructivism, 11

social control: perceptions of, 15; voluntary obedience to, 32; Weber on, 39. *See also* authority for social control

social pressure, as coercion, 42

Soviet Union: Afghanistan 1989 troop removal, 56; Amin death by, 55; Durand Line military aid, 71; KhaD training by, 94; Mujahedin groups fight with, 71, 186; PDPA of, 54–55, 64, 106, 242; Shirzai and war with, 149–150

state, 51–139; arena of interaction hierarchical position, 29; Bourdieu as one player of authority, 29; Bourdieu on dynastic, 26–27; Bourdieu on field concept of, 27; Bourdieu understanding of, 25–28; bureaucracy for services, 6; in conflict-torn spaces, 28–31; definitions of, 23; Kuhn on instability of, 22–23; rational legality of, 49; strongmen lack of incentive for formation of, 145; symbolic capital and power of, 27; Weber and fragility of, 25; Weber on ideal type of, 23–24, 36; Weber understanding of,

23–25, 273, 288. *See also* Afghan state

statebuilding, failure of, 289–294

statehood: as field of power, 298n32; possible legitimate, 292

strongmen, 21, 140–181; 299n40; ALP control by, 91, 93, 144; ANP and security involvement with, 82–83; in Balkh Province, 170–173; community level influences by, 167; corrupt conflict resolution procedures, 165; criminal activities and, 166; governance of, 143–146; Hazrat Ali as, 148; international community empowering of, 143; interviews with public on coercive authority of, 142–143; ISI connections speculation, 163, 167; judged by actions, 178–179; legitimacy of, 7; Malejacq on, 145–146; Nangarhar Province governance, 146–149, 317n79; Northern Alliance establishment of, 69; patronage networks of, 25, 144–146; power from militias and security forces command, 144; public perceptions of, 163–170; public perceptions of A. Noor, 173–177; Shirzai as, 149–154; state formation lack of incentive by, 145; substantive legitimacy and, 146; Taliban 2021 forced exile, 181; use of force and coercion by, 141; Western funding impact on, 7; Zahir Qadir as, 140, 154–163; M. Zaman as, 148. *See also* warlords

substantive legitimacy, 6, 139, 279;
belief in rightfulness in, 34;
beliefs and needs in, 35, 40–41,
41; for community authority,
236; in conflict-torn spaces,
38; constant change of, 42–43;
construction of, 293; coordinated
security expectation, 281;
instrumental vs., 21, 33–35; modes
of interaction importance, 47–48;
rational-legal sources of, 36–38,
37, 40; Shirzai and Zahir Qadir
claim for, 177; strongmen and,
146; as symbolic capital, 34; of
Taliban, 185, 207; value-based
expectations and, 47–48; violence
impact on, 42; Weber on, 21
Sufism, Taliban rejection of, 187
Surkh Rod district, 230; conflict
resolution in, 244–246,
249–251; customary law in,
247; development councils in,
244; interviews with public on
corruption, 250; local elders
and councils conflict resolution
preference, 247; local level code
of law missing in, 246; maliks
and state relationship, 251; maliks
as community authority in, 244;
mullahs in, 244; Pashtunwali
cultural code in, 243–244; Taliban
coercion in, 220; Taliban conflict
resolution in, 247–248, 257–258;
Taliban negative views in, 218;
Taliban recruitment in, 219
symbolic capital, 134, 298n29,
300n70; Bourdieu on

interactions and, 47; Bourdieu
on legitimacy and, 26–27;
substantive legitimacy as, 34
symbolic violence: Bourdieu on
monopolization of, 26, 27, 48;
rural Afghanistan and, 104

Taliban, 21, 182–234, 290, 292;
actions assessment for, 228–229;
Afghanistan control by, 1, 2, 51,
182, 184–187, 210, 213–214, 230;
Afghan state 2020 negotiations
with, 60; Afghan state fight
with, 3; ANSF war with,
60; background on, 186–194;
Barfield on, 186; Behsod and
Surkh Rod districts on, 218–220;
Char Asiab insecurity concerns
from, 212; civilian deaths and
injuries by, 188; commander
on government corruption, 1;
conflict resolution procedures,
185, 210, 217–218, 231–232, 247–248,
256–258; court influence from,
105; December 2001 defeat
of, 57; Doha Agreement and,
60, 189; education policies,
192; Farza district insecurity
concerns from, 212–213; fight
for justice of, 196–198; Ghani
fight against, 66; governance
structure, 190; groups labeled
as, 183; growing influence of, 7;
Haq killed by, 147; independent
groups of, 190–191; insiders
on legitimacy of, 207–210;
insurgency fighting, 21, 59, 184,

187, 291; interaction procedures, 232–233; interviews in controlled areas of, 17; interviews with public on ANA infiltration by, 75–76; interviews with public on conflict resolution of, 185; IS-K attacks on, 62; Islamic Emirate of Afghanistan establishment by, 56, 186, 302n17; Islamic Sharia law implementation by, 64, 77, 106, 107; Jalalabad complex threat, 213–218; Jalalabad conflict resolution procedures by, 217–218; Jalalabad strong negative views of, 216; judges interviews with, 10; justice in Herat and Faryab Provinces, 224–228; justice system of, 112–113, 192–193, 224–228, 264; Kabul 2014-2015 insecurity from, 211; Kabul control from 1996-2001, 210, 213; Kabul physical force by, 48, 51; Kabul suicide attackers and criminals, 210–213; Khogyani and Sherzad districts on, 221–223; Kushk Robat Sangi and presence of, 252–253, 258–259; Kushk Robat Sangi conflict resolution by, 256; leadership structure of, 189; local legitimacy concerns, 193; mahaz fighting units, 190; military structure of, 189–190; mullahs and, 242; A. Noor and Dostum fighting against, 171; Obama on insurgency of, 59; perceived source of injustice fight by, 49; perceptions of, 7,

234; perspectives on joining and deserting, 194–207, 232; presidential palace 2021 entered by, 182; provincial capitals capture, 61; public perception of, 185; Qala Zaini massacre deaths of, 141; rural Afghanistan instability and, 58; as security threat, 184; self-perception of, 185; service delivery of, 194; state opposition as reason to join, 7, 194–207; strongmen 2021 forced exile by, 181; substantive legitimacy of, 185, 207; Sufism and local customs rejection by, 187; suicide convoy of, 221, 321n75; Surkh Rod and Behsod coercion by, 220; Surkh Rod and Behsod recruitment by, 219; taxation practices of, 193; threats and legitimacy claims of, 188–189; 2001 Afghanistan liberation, 2–3. *See also* interviews with former and active Taliban

Taraki, Nur Muhammad: Amin order to kill, 55; KhaD creation by, 94

taxation practices, of Taliban, 193

Tehrik-i-Taliban Pakistan (TTP) insurgency group, IS-K allegiance of, 191

tradition: in Afghan state, 62–69; community authority and, 266–267, 269

traditional authority, of Zahir Shah, 65

traditional customary law, 104, 105; Herat City community authority and, 259–261, 264–265 traditional legitimacy, 36, 67–68, 243

Training Mission, NATO, 73, 78

Trump, Donald, 60

TTP. *See* Tehrik-i-Taliban Pakistan

Turkey, ANP training by, 77

United Islamic Front for the
Salvation of Afghanistan
(Northern Alliance), 56;
Abdullah member of, 59;
Mujahedin groups and, 57;
strongmen establishment in, 69

United States (U.S.): Afghanistan
War cost, 1; Afghanistan
withdrawal, 1, 60–61; ALP
program design by, 90; ANA
financial support, 72; ANP
training by, 77–78; Combined
Security Transition Command-
Afghanistan program of, 78;
Dostum funding from, 143; NDS
violence support from, 96–97;
Rasoul support from, 191; Taliban
and Doha Agreement with, 60

UN Security Council: ISAF and,
57–59, 65; PRTs establishment
by, 58–59

urban Afghanistan: on judicial
system corruption, 114; judicial
system lack of alternatives in,
117–118; official judicial system
use, 113–114; public perceptions
on judicial branch, 113–116; shura
judicial cases in, 115–116; Taliban
attacks in, 184; violent crime
increase in, 88

U.S. *See* United States

value-based expectations: of human
dignities, fairness and respect,
47–48; substantive legitimacy
and, 47–48

violence: Amnesty International on
NDS, 94–95; Arendt on, 42, 48;
Bourdieu on monopolization
of symbolic, 26, 27, 48; Human
Rights Watch on KPF, 96–97;
instrumental and substantive
legitimacy impacted by, 42; IS-K,
62, 191, 212, 214; in Nangarhar
Province, 148; of NDS, 94–98;
output legitimacy established by,
42; security and restrained use
of, 49; symbolic, 26, 27, 48, 104;
Taliban in Kabul, 48, 51, 211, 229;
Weber on monopolization of
legitimate, 26

visibility of actor, 136; of ANA and
NDS, 135; authority importance,
135, 275

voluntary obedience: to authority,
21; legitimacy as basis of, 32; to
social control, 32; Weber on, 34

war: economies of, 24; European
states and monopolization of
force legitimacy, 24; Taliban and
ANSF, 60; Weber on European
states and, 24. *See also specific war*

warlords, 7, 142; ANP and security
involvement with, 82–83;
interviews with public on
security interference from,
86; lack of support for, 123;
land-grabbing by, 165, 166;

Malejacq on, 273–274; Maley on strongmen as American, 143; as security provider, 301n72

war on terror, of Bush, 2, 54, 57, 59

Weber, Max, 301n75; on beliefs and needs, 39; conflict-torn spaces and, 23–24; on European states and wars, 24; on *Herrschaft* domination, 30; on ideal type of state, 23–24, 36; on interaction, 47; legitimacy foundation of, 4; monopolization of force and, 25; on monopolization of legitimate violence, 26; on obedience instability, 34; political order state understanding, 23–25, 273, 288; on social action, 35; state fragility and, 25; on substantive legitimacy, 21; on voluntary obedience, 34

Western funding: for Hekmatyar, 143; strongmen impacted by, 7

Westernization, Zahir Shah reinstatement of, 54, 119

Wolesi Jirga (House of the People): constitution of 2004 approval of, 120; election of, 119; inauguration of, 121–122; 2004 election of, 120

women: rights, 64, 106, 222–223, 244, 246, 254, 292; Taliban justice system and, 226–227

World Bank: Citizens' Charter of, 66–67, 193, 239, 246, 269; REACH initiatives of, 66–67

Zahir Shah (king) (1933-1973), 58; Parliament of, 119; secular laws and, 105–106; traditional authority in 2001, 65; Westernization reinstatement, 54, 119

Al-Zahra Mosque attack, in Kabul, 102

Zaman, Jawed, 148

Zaman, Mohammed, 148, 158

GPSR Authorized Representative: Easy Access System Europe, Mustamäe tee
50, 10621 Tallinn, Estonia, gpsr.requests@easproject.com

www.ingramcontent.com/pod-product-compliance
Lightning Source LLC
Chambersburg PA
CBHW022132020426
42334CB00015B/867